19

JACKIE ROBINSON

MAURY ALLEN

Jackie Robinson

A LIFE REMEMBERED

Franklin Watts 1987 *New York / Toronto*

Photographs following page 84: courtesy
of the Robinson family: pp. 1, 2, 7, 9, 11;
Pasadena City College: p. 3; UCLA: pp. 4, 5;
Los Angeles Dodgers, Inc.: pp. 6, 8, 10, 12,
14 (top); Detroit Tigers: p. 13 (bottom); UPI:
p. 14 (bottom); St. Louis Cardinals: p. 15;
National Baseball Library: p. 16.

Photographs following page 180; courtesy
of Los Angeles Dodgers, Inc.: pp. 1, 6; United
Press Photo: p. 2; New York Yankees: p. 3;
Atlanta Braves: p. 4; Lou Requena: pp. 5, 10, 11;
the Robinson family: pp. 7, 12, 13; National
Baseball Library: pp. 8, 9; Associated Press:
p. 14; the author: p. 15; Mack Robinson: p. 16.

Library of Congress Cataloging-in-Publication Data

Allen, Maury, 1932–
Jackie Robinson: a life remembered.

Includes index.
1. Robinson, Jackie, 1919–1972. 2. Baseball players—
United States—Biography. I. Title.
GV865.R6A44   1987   796.357'092'4   [B]   86-34016
ISBN 0-531-15042-9

By Maury Allen

Roger Maris: A Man for All Seasons
Sweet Lou
(with Lou Piniella)
Mr. October: The Reggie Jackson Story
Damn Yankee: The Billy Martin Story
You Could Look It Up
Where Have You Gone, Joe DiMaggio?
Big-Time Baseball
Bo: Pitching and Wooing
Voices of Sport
Now Wait a Minute, Casey
The Record Breakers
The Incredible Mets
Joe Namath's Sportin' Life
Reprieve from Hell
Ten Great Moments in Sports
Reggie Jackson: The Three Million Dollar Man
Ron Guidry: Louisiana Lightning
Baseball's 100

For Janet, Jennifer, and Ted,
with all my love for all my life

and

For all the kids in Brooklyn
who we played stickball, punchball,
and three–man basketball with,
and for all those
who wept with us in the school yard
when Bobby Thomson hit the home run

CONTENTS

ACKNOWLEDGMENTS

CASEY STENGEL ONCE SAID, "THERE COMES A TIME IN EVERY man's life, and I've had plenty of them." There comes a time in every writer's life when he sits down and writes the book he must. For me, that book is *Jackie Robinson: A Life Remembered*. My idea for the book was really born on that day in 1947 when Robinson played his first game at Ebbets Field, and it was destined to become an almost-constant goal of my writing career. It was still just an idea in 1972, when Jackie Robinson died, and the idea, I thought, went with him.

But in the 1980s, as the fortieth anniversary of Robinson's arrival in Brooklyn approached, the idea revived and matured. It came to fruition as middle-aged and elderly men across the country volunteered to me their remembrances of their days with Jackie Robinson. Those famed players and others—some 200 interviewees in all—contributed from their hearts what they remembered best about a man who brought a great change to the sports scene in the United States, and this book is the result.

To all those who donated from their memory banks, who were so generous with their time and thoughts—from Pee Wee Reese to the Reverend Jesse Jackson, Stan Musial to Arthur Ashe, Duke Snider to Floyd Patterson, Roy Campanella to Cool Papa Bell, Don Newcombe to Don Drysdale, Ralph Kiner to Terry Moore—I offer my deepest thanks. You are all heroes of mine, special men talking about a very special man, a man of history, Jack Roosevelt Robinson.

This book is based on people's memories, but it was framed by the record that went before. I am especially grateful to my newspaper colleagues who recorded Jackie's career so accurately and colorfully, and to the authors of books that have made Jackie Robinson live again in our minds and hearts. I relied on many of those books for source material and depth, including the brilliant work by Jules Tygiel called *Jackie Robinson and His Legacy,* a "must read" for all Robinson fans; Harvey Frommer's *Rickey and Robinson;* Jackie's autobiography, with Carl Rowan, *Wait Till Next Year;* Jackie's later autobiography, with Alfred Duckett, *I Never Had It Made;* Robert W. Peterson's breakthrough book on black baseball, *Only the Ball Was White;* Arthur Mann's *Branch Rickey* and *The Jackie Robinson Story;* Murray Polner's *Branch Rickey;* Leo Durocher's autobiography, with Ed Lynn, *Nice Guys Finish Last;* and dozens of baseball record books, the most helpful being Macmillan's *Baseball Encyclopedia* and Seymour Siwoff's *Book of Baseball Records.*

No book is the effort of a writer alone. It's a team project from the start. The key players on this team included my Hall of Fame agent, Julian Bach, who never lost faith in the project from day one, my editor at Franklin Watts, Ed Breslin, who worked on this manuscript with enthusiasm and skill, and all the people who put their various talents together to produce this work.

CHAPTER

One

"I DON'T KNOW NOTHING ABOUT NO JACKIE ROBINSON"

THE BROOKLYN DODGERS TODAY PURCHASED THE
CONTRACT OF JACK ROOSEVELT ROBINSON FROM THE
MONTREAL ROYALS. HE WILL REPORT IMMEDIATELY.

(ANNOUNCEMENT FROM THE
BROOKLYN DODGERS' FRONT OFFICE
APRIL 10, 1947)

JACK ROOSEVELT ROBINSON

BROOKLYN N.L. 1947 TO 1956
LEADING N.L. BATTER IN 1949.
HOLDS FIELDING MARK FOR SECOND BASEMAN PLAYING
IN 150 OR MORE GAMES WITH .992.

LED N.L. IN STOLEN BASES IN 1947 AND 1949.
MOST VALUABLE PLAYER IN 1949.
LIFETIME BATTING AVERAGE .311.
JOINT RECORD HOLDER FOR MOST DOUBLE PLAYS
BY SECOND BASEMAN, 137 IN 1951.
LED SECOND BASEMEN IN DOUBLE PLAYS 1949–50–51–52.

(DEDICATION ON HALL OF FAME PLAQUE
COOPERSTOWN, NEW YORK,
JULY 23, 1962)

$\mathcal{T}$HE ESSENCE OF HIS LIFE WAS missed on those two announcements, the most important announcements of his professional career: he was a black man.

"I was on a ship in the South Pacific coming back from Navy service in Guam," recalls Brooklyn Dodger captain Pee Wee Reese. "It was late in October of 1945. They had dropped the big one at Hiroshima, and I was finally on my way home after two years. I hadn't seen my daughter, Barbara, since I left home when she was eleven days old. I was thinking about that when a sailor came up to me on the ship. He was all excited. He had heard something on the radio he thought might be of interest to me. 'Hey, Pee Wee, the Dodgers just signed a nigger ball player.' I didn't think too much about it. I knew my father, who was a railroad detective back in Louisville, wouldn't be overly fond of the idea. The Dodgers were signing a lot of players, and all I was interested in was getting back home, seeing my family again, and resuming my career. A few minutes later the same guy came back. He had heard more about it on the radio. 'The guy's name is Jackie Robinson, and they say he had played at UCLA.' It didn't mean a thing to me. I had never heard of him. Then the sailor said, 'Not only is he a nigger, but he's a shortstop.' Now *that* was different. 'No kidding,' I said. That was the first time I thought of Jackie Robinson. I'll never stop thinking about him."

"I remember when Jackie came through with the Brooklyn Dodgers to my hometown of Daytona, Florida," says Ed Charles, the black third baseman of the 1969 World Champion New York Mets. "Everybody in our part of town wanted to see him. Old people and small children, invalids and town drunks all walked through the streets. Some people were on crutches, and some blind people clutched the arms of friends, walking slowly on parade to that ball park to sit in the segregated section. We watched him play that day and finally believed what we had read in the papers, that one of us was out there on that ball field. When the game was over, we kids followed Jackie as he walked with his teammates to the train station, and when the train pulled out, we ran down the tracks listening for the sounds as far as we could. And when we finally couldn't hear it any longer, we ran some more and finally stopped and put our ears to the tracks so we could feel the vibrations of that train carrying Jackie Robinson. We wanted to be part of him as long as we could."

On April 6, 1972, almost a quarter of a century after his Brooklyn arrival, Jackie Robinson, bent now from diabetes, tired, white-haired, suffering with heart problems, walked slowly into the unscheduled reunion of the old Brooklyn Dodger players. There were hundreds of people in Brooklyn's Our Lady Help of Christians church, but all eyes were on Jackie and Pee Wee, Carl Furillo and Sandy Koufax, Don Newcombe, Ralph Branca, and Joe Black, reunited at the funeral of one of their fallen leaders, Gil Hodges, their big first baseman. Author Roger Kahn had locked them together in *The Boys of Summer*, and on this gray, raw early spring afternoon they seemed never to have been young and athletic. There were audible gasps and silent homage as Robinson, looking so much older than the rest, walked slowly down the center aisle to a waiting seat in a front-row pew. Reese was sitting a row in front of Robinson. Robinson showed no signs of recognition as he stared straight ahead at the glistening casket of Hodges. At the age of forty-seven, the manager of the Mets had suffered a massive heart attack as he walked from a golf course to his motel room in West Palm Beach, Florida. "What time are we meeting for dinner?" he asked Met coach Joe

Pignatano. Before Pignatano could answer, Hodges fell over backwards on the concrete walk, striking his head. "He was dead before he hit the ground," a doctor reported.

Reese turned full to Robinson and nudged him.

"Jack," he said, quietly. "It's me, Pee Wee."

"Oh, I'm sorry," Robinson replied with some embarrassment. "I just can't see."

The two old friends and former teammates chatted in that Brooklyn church for a few minutes in quiet tones. Jackie looked at Pee Wee with those intense eyes the captain remembered so well.

"I didn't expect it to be Gilly," he said. "I thought it would be me."

Reese remembers the conversation with unhappiness. He recalls, with emotion: "Jack just looked older than I had remembered him. He seemed to have trouble walking, and he absolutely couldn't see. It was so sad. You just forget how the years go on, and all of a sudden we are all grandfathers. Jackie just seemed to get older faster than the rest of us. It had to be what he went through. I don't think Jack ever stopped carrying that burden. I'm no doctor but I'm sure it cut his life short. Jackie Robinson never could stop fighting."

Early that summer of 1972, Robinson traveled the country. He spoke often at college campuses. He pressed his theme that baseball was dragging its feet on awarding high-level jobs to qualified black players. Bill Lucas, Hank Aaron's brother-in-law, was the only black who held a responsible executive position in baseball's hierarchy. He was Atlanta's farm director.

There were black players on every big league team that year, the cycle being completed in 1959 when Pumpsie Green broke in with the Boston Red Sox a dozen years after Robinson became the first of his race to play a big league game in modern organized baseball. But other than Lucas, there were no black officials in the game, no managers, no general managers, no scouting directors, no ticket managers, no public relations directors, no presidents of teams, no assistants to the presidents, no farm directors. In the previous quarter of a century there had been eleven black players elected by the Baseball Writers Association of America as Rookie of the Year in the National League and four more in the American League. Fifteen of the previous National League Most Valuable Players were black. Three American League MVPs were black. After their playing careers were over, black stars went back to Mobile and Omaha and San Francisco and New York and Denver. Once out of uniform, they became invisible.

Robinson addressed this problem everywhere he went. He called for an end to baseball's bigotry in hiring practices. He rallied young people at college campuses. He discussed the problem at NAACP meetings. He pinpricked the game everywhere he went, challenging the smug complacence of the baseball establishments. But he seemed to be ignored. For many baseball people, Jackie Robinson was passé, he was of another time.

The main symbolic issue, the breakthrough Robinson really urged, was that of hiring a black manager for a major league team.

"We're looking into it," said American League president Joe Cronin.

"The clubs are waiting for the right man," said National League president Chub Feeney.

Some of the black players seethed. "We've heard it all before," said Bill White of the Cardinals when he had first been mentioned as a potential first black manager several years earlier.

Bowie Kuhn, the commissioner of baseball, carefully read all of Robinson's comments. He was a man of goodwill. He didn't quite know what to do about it. Kuhn discussed the matter with his aide, Joe Reichler, a former Associated Press sports columnist who knew Robinson well, and asked him to set up a meeting with the former star.

On a splendid June afternoon, Robinson met Kuhn for lunch at New York's famed 21 Club on West Fifty-second Street. It was a comfortable, if not confrontational, luncheon. Kuhn and Robinson discussed the matter with civility. Kuhn could make no promises on the selection of a black manager, but he did suggest that baseball would like to honor Robinson on the silver anniversary of his arrival in Brooklyn. The commissioner felt that reminder might help generate attention for the problem. Robinson made no commitments.

"About the only thing they completely agreed on," says Marty Appel, Kuhn's biographer, "was their shoe size. Somewhere in the conversation they discovered each wore a size thirteen and a half shoe."

There was no further communication until late September. Kuhn decided to invite Robinson to the World Series in Cincinnati. He asked Reichler to contact Robinson, invite him to be an honored guest at the second game of the 1972 Series and throw out the first ball. Baseball would thus mark Robinson's twenty-fifth anniversary in that style. Robinson would also be given an award on the field for his work in drug rehabilitation, an area of social welfare he had become immersed in the previous year, with the death of his son, Jack, Jr. Without conditions, Robinson agreed.

On Saturday morning, October 14, 1972, I walked through the American Airlines lounge at New York's LaGuardia Airport. I sat in the waiting area marked for flight 271 to Cincinnati. I casually read the morning papers and studied stories about the starting lineups for the first Series game between Cincinnati and Oakland. There was a murmur in the lounge, and I looked up to see Jackie Robinson walking slowly to an empty seat. His wife, Rachel, was with him, as were his son, David, and a friend of David's. I had seen him less than seven months earlier at Gil Hodges's funeral, and now he seemed even older. His hair was so incredibly white, and his famed pigeon-toed walk seemed so labored. He seemed to be in pain as he shuffled from side to side to get comfortable in the plastic and metal airport lounge seat. He was a big man, and these seats all seemed constructed for children.

I walked over to say hello. He started to get up as we shook hands, but I sat down quickly in the seat next to him. His words seem labored in that familiar, eloquent, high-pitched tone.

"How do you feel?" I asked.

"About the same," he said. "Some days good, some days bad."

He introduced me to his family, and we all chatted for a few moments about the relative merits of the two teams in the Series. Jack seemed so tired. I got up to leave. Jack had once worked for my newspaper, the *New York Post*, and asked me to send regards to our sports editor, Ike Gellis, and to several other people he knew there from his days as a *Post* columnist.

"Have a good flight, Jack. I'll see you in Cincinnati."

"Thanks. Good luck." Then he paused for an instant. "I'm OK. I just keep going on as best I can."

The following afternoon, October 15, Red Barber stood in front of the microphone at Cincinnati's Riverfront Stadium. He had begun his big league broadcasting career in Cincinnati in 1934. He had been the first person outside the official Brooklyn Dodger organization told about the impending arrival of Jackie Robinson in Brooklyn. Branch Rickey and Barber had lunch together one afternoon late in March 1945. They had been together at Brooklyn Borough President John Cashmore's office at a lengthy morning meeting involving the Red Cross. Both Rickey and Barber participated in the volunteer program for the organization. Now they sat at a table at Joe's Restaurant in downtown Brooklyn. Rickey, the operating head of the Dodgers, told his popular Brooklyn announcer in that nearly empty restaurant, late that afternoon, "I'm going to bring a Negro to the Brooklyn Dodgers." Barber, a southerner, born in Mississippi, raised in central Florida, was speechless. His first thought was to quit the Brooklyn broadcasting job. His wife later reminded him of some economic realities and he stayed and had a fine working relationship with Robinson.

"We were never buddy-buddy," Barber says. "I had the same relationship with Jackie I had with every other ballplayer in Brooklyn. I reported what they did. I never had a close relationship with any ballplayer. I never had a ballplayer in my home in all the years I was in Brooklyn, not Jackie, not Pee Wee, not any of them. I didn't think I could be a fair reporter if I did."

Now he stood on the field at Cincinnati and introduced Robinson. Barber, one of the most loved men in Brooklyn baseball history, the fellow most Brooklyn fans called the Old Redhead, extolled the brilliance of Robinson's playing career. There were 53,224 fans in the stands that day, some still shuffling to their seats as Robinson approached the microphone. Polite applause rolled through the ball park. Robinson began speaking, and his voice seemed full of energy.

"I want to thank my wife, my family, and Captain Pee Wee Reese," he said of his teammate standing nearby, "and I want to thank all of you fans here today."

He spoke of how much he enjoyed playing baseball, how much the game meant to him, and how much he hoped young people across America would involve themselves in this great game. He had fulfilled his obligations to baseball, and now he spoke from the heart.

"Someday," he said, "I'd like to be able to look over at third base and see a black man managing the ball club."

Reporters sitting in the press box, listening to his talk, shook their heads. "Same old Jackie," one said. The huge crowd in this Ohio border town across the river from Kentucky, seemed not to hear his remarks. He finished talking and walked quietly away from the microphone.

Robinson walked slowly to the stands and joined Bowie Kuhn in a front-row box. One of the Oakland players, Reggie Jackson, walking on crutches and wearing street clothes after severely pulling a hamstring muscle in the final playoff game against Detroit for the pennant, hobbled over to introduce himself.

"You've always been my hero," Jackson said.

"Thank you," Robinson said. "Sorry you're injured. I'm sure you'll play in a lot more Series before you're through."

Robinson had been estranged from baseball for many years. He had attended an occasional old-timers game at Shea when his Brooklyn teams were there and had even visited Los Angeles the year before for a Brooklyn reunion. Mostly, he was outside the game, almost never watching it on television, very rarely attending a game in person, clearly not conversant with the current crop of players.

He sat next to Kuhn for the entire contest. He seemed to enjoy it. He made comments about the game to Kuhn, a serious, dedicated baseball fan, unlike his predecessor, General William D. Eckert, labeled the Unknown Soldier, who had been selected by baseball owners as a mistaken figure for another general with a similar name. Robinson did not see all the plays clearly with his failing eyesight, and saw many of the players as shadows. He did notice one player, outfielder Bobby Tolan of the Reds, having trouble at the plate with his swing.

"He's holding his bat too high," he told Kuhn.

"Why don't you talk to him after the game."

When the game had ended, and the Oakland team beat the Reds 2–1 with Tolan hitless in four tries, Robinson asked Kuhn if he could enter the clubhouse.

"Certainly," replied Kuhn.

The commissioner asked Reichler, longtime AP reporter, to escort Robinson into the Cincinnati clubhouse. He was introduced to Tolan by Reichler and soon began a technical discussion with the young black player about the way he was guarding the plate. Tolan got six base hits in the next three games.

In the clubhouse several players rushed to Robinson with baseballs and asked him to sign his autograph. He gently refused. Pete Rose, who would wind up with more base hits than any player in the history of baseball and played with the same aggressive style as Robinson, offered a ball and a pen.

"I'm sorry," Robinson said, "I can't see it. I'd be sure to mess up the other names on it. I'm blind in this right eye and barely can see out of the other eye. It's difficult for me to watch a game. I can hardly see where the ball is. I'm sorry."

Rose said, "My father used to take me to Crosley Field to watch you play. I really enjoyed that. I loved the way you ran the bases."

Several other Cincinnati players, Johnny Bench, Joe Morgan, Tony Perez, Denis Menke, all came over to chat. Robinson was amused when they described how their fathers had all watched him. Perez, a Cuban, said, "The Brooklyn Dodgers trained in Havana. They are the favorite team in Cuba."

Robinson smiled. That was in the spring of 1947. Rickey had arranged for the Dodgers to train in Havana to avoid segregation problems in Florida. The memories were vivid.

Robinson had dinner with his family in Cincinnati that night and flew home early Monday morning. He attended to some business in New York. He worked on a speech he would deliver at a symposium in race relations in Washington, D.C., scheduled for the next Monday evening. Robinson had always been an exceptionally poignant writer. "Unless we are able to prove blacks and whites can work together as we did in baseball, the breach that's here now will get wider," he said in the heat of the late 1960s. "In baseball we didn't live together but we played together. After the game we went our separate ways. But on the field there was understanding, and no one will ever convince me that the things that happened there did not affect people."

Robinson was committed to an Albany speech for New York governor Nelson Rockefeller and returned home over the next weekend. He was bleeding from behind his eyes. Rachel Robinson called the sponsors of the Washington symposium, told them Jackie was ill, and canceled his appearance.

At 6:26 in the morning, Tuesday, October 24, 1972, the phone rang at the office of the police dispatcher in Stamford, Connecticut, some ten minutes from the home of Jackie Robinson. "Send an ambulance, quickly, please," the dispatcher heard a distraught female voice ask.

A fire department ambulance arrived at the Robinson home in less than twelve minutes. He was carried into the ambulance. He was unconscious. An oxygen mask was placed over his face, and an ambulance service volunteer massaged his heart as the vehicle sped toward Stamford Hospital. Jack Roosevelt Robinson died at 7:10 A.M.

"When he arrived at the hospital he was not breathing," said his personal physician, Dr. John Borowy. "Despite all our attempts to revive him he did not respond."

The news was soon on the wires to newspapers across the country. My office called me at home, and I began calling teammates of Jackie's on the Brooklyn Dodgers for comment. Pee Wee Reese was the first player called.

"This is getting to be a terrible habit," Pee Wee said, in reference to the death of teammates Hodges and Robinson. "I can't say I'm shocked. I hadn't seen Jackie since Gil's funeral, but he had a premonition. I'm sure of that."

The "Boys of Summer" would be gathering again at a funeral.

On Friday, October 27, a young black minister by the name of Jesse Jackson delivered the eulogy.

"What an honor that was when I was asked to deliver that eulogy," remembers Jackson. "To give a young black minister a chance to be seen and heard in front of such a distinguished throng—that was special. That was typical of Jackie Robinson."

For Jackson, later to force his personna on the nation, it was a premier performance. He was effusive and dramatic as he spoke of Robinson.

"He turned a stumbling block into a stepping stone," Jackson said with rising enthusiasm in his voice. "When Jackie took the field, something reminded us of our birthright to be free. Jackie began playing a chess game; he was the black knight. He was checking the king's bigotry and the queen's indifference. His body, his mind, his mission can not be held down by a grave."

In the late summer of 1986, as the fortieth anniversary of the arrival of Jackie Robinson in Brooklyn approached, teammate Don Newcombe said that too many people, especially young blacks, didn't even know who Jackie Robinson was.

"I remember Martin Luther King sitting in my house at my dinner table," the former Dodger pitcher was saying, "and he was talking about Jackie. 'You will never know how easy it was for me because of Jackie Robinson.' I never forgot those words. It's a shame today when I ask a young ballplayer or a young black kid I am counseling on drug and alcohol abuse who Jackie Robinson was and he can't tell me. It was Jackie and then it was me and Campy, and I'm the only one of the three of us left who can get around, and I make sure I talk about Jackie wherever I go. He was my idol, my mentor, my hero. As long as I'm alive, as long as I have a breath to breathe, I won't let anybody forget Jackie Robinson."

Early in the spring of 1986 a reporter interviewed Vince Coleman, the black base-stealing star of the St. Louis Cardinals. He asked him what he knew of Jackie Robinson.

"I don't know nothing about no Jackie Robinson," Coleman said.

In his office in Phoenix, former Dodger teammate Joe Black,

once a burly pitcher, now one of the most successful black businessmen in the country, wept as he read that. He soon wrote Coleman a letter:

As one of the better players in Major League baseball, you probably receive a great deal of fan mail. However, my reason for writing is not to bestow accolades upon you for your athletic exploits, but rather I want to discuss respect and responsibility.

I have experienced the joys of seeing my name in headlines as a Major League player and I live a good life now. Yes, I have a college degree (two earned and six honorary doctorates) so educational preparation, discipline, desire and dedication are the primary reasons that I am numbered among those who earn big salaries. But a modicum of success is due to the sacrifices and exploits of Jackie Robinson.

It hurt me to read that Vince Coleman says he "don't know nothing about no Jackie Robinson." Are black athletes so blinded by greed for dollars and ego trips that they fail to remember that someone had to "open the doors"? We, as blacks, are doomed to second-class status as long as we refuse to research our heritage and gain increased pride from those who have gone before us. Do you admit knowing athletic heroes such as Joe Louis, Jesse Owens, Ray Robinson, Roy Campanella, Satchel Paige or Bob Gibson?

Vince, Jackie Robinson was more than an athlete. He was a man. Jackie Robinson stood alone as he challenged and integrated modern-day Major League baseball. His task was not easy nor quick. He suffered many mental and physical hurts. He accepted and overcame the slings, slams and insults so that young black youths, such as you, could dream of playing Major League baseball.

When you have time, go into the Cardinal office and ask Stan Musial, Who was Jackie Robinson? Or ask your coach, Red Schoendienst. Best wishes for a year of good health.

Jack Roosevelt Robinson was born in Cairo, Georgia, on January 31, 1919. He was raised in Pasadena, California. He was a big league ballplayer over ten years and 1,382 games for the Brooklyn

Dodgers. He died October 24, 1972, and was buried in Cypress Hills Cemetery in Brooklyn.

He engendered more emotion, more hatred, more passion than anybody who ever played the game. He was twenty-eight years old when he played his first game for the Brooklyn Dodgers in 1947. He played first base, second base, third base, one game of shortstop and the outfield for the Dodgers. He batted .311 and stole 197 bases in his career. He was the National League Rookie of the Year in 1947 and the Most Valuable Player in the National League in 1949. He achieved in 1962 the highest honor anyone in his profession could obtain, when he was elected to the Baseball Hall of Fame in Cooperstown, New York. He played on six pennant winners, and one world's championship team and never played on a team finishing worse than third place. He won one batting title and batted over .300 six times in his career. He stole home twenty times. He scored over 100 runs six times in his career. Throughout his career, through his entire fifty-three years of life, those numbers were always second to one word. It took on different forms at different times, colored, Negro, black. For millions of white Americans, in rural towns in Georgia and cotton fields in Mississippi, in coal mines in Pennsylvania and factories in New York, in big cities and small villages, Jackie Robinson meant only one thing: nigger.

CHAPTER

Two

PEPPER STREET,
PASADENA

$\mathcal{J}$HE LATE AFTERNOON SUN glistened above the hills of Mount Wilson in the bucolic quiet of Pasadena, California. It was a soft summer day in 1986, and as Willa Mae Robinson Walker, Jackie Robinson's only sister, crossed the street from Jackie Robinson Park to the Jackie Robinson Community Center at 1020 North Fair Oaks, she smiled gently and remembered a time some sixty years ago.

"This very street, North Fair Oaks, that was the dividing line between blacks and whites. We lived over there on the black side in that big house at 121 Pepper Street, and we couldn't even cross to this side, the white side," she said.

Pasadena is some fifteen miles north and east of downtown Los Angeles, a bedroom community for Hollywood stars in the old days, a setting for many movies, an area of fine stores, expensive homes, and much movie history. Its most famous buildings are probably the Pasadena Playhouse and the Rose Bowl. Jackie Robinson starred in the Rose Bowl. He was not allowed to enter the Playhouse.

Jackie Robinson was born in the early evening of January 31, 1919, in a small sharecropper's farmhouse outside Cairo, Georgia. He was the fifth child of Jerry and Mallie Robinson. The other children were Edgar, Frank, Mack, and Willa Mae, three years older than Jackie, the baby of the Robinson clan.

"Jack was a mama's boy," says Willa Mae. "Always was. When he finished Pasadena Junior College, he had scholarship offers from dozens of schools. He chose to stay home and go to UCLA. Why? Because he didn't want to leave his mama."

Jack Roosevelt Robinson. Why Roosevelt?

"I don't really know about that," says Willa Mae. "I didn't even know about that Roosevelt part until years later. One day when Jack was seventeen, eighteen years old, he got in trouble with the cops over some traffic speeding problem. They made him go to court, and he sat there all day. They never called his name. He was really angry at that and finally went up and asked when they were going to call him.

" 'What's your name?' the court officer asked.

" 'Jack Robinson,' he said.

" 'We don't have a Jack Robinson. We have a Roosevelt Robinson.'

" 'I guess that's me,' Jack said."

In the spring of 1919, Jerry Robinson announced that he was through being a farmer. He wanted to move into town and get a job there. Mallie was concerned that her brood would grow hungry without being able to grow their own turnips, raise their own chickens, and eat their own eggs. They argued. Mallie also heard rumors around that Jerry Robinson was eyeing another man's wife and planned to take up with her. Tensions increased in the small farmhouse. Mallie, a deeply religious woman, prayed for guidance. When Jerry announced that he was taking off to look for a job, maybe as far away as Texas, Mallie did not plead for him to stay. He ran away to Florida, rumor had it, with the other woman.

"We never saw him again," says Willa Mae, "but after Jack became famous he did show up one time. Jack didn't have anything to do with him and that was it."

Mallie Robinson had a brother Frank who had served in the Army in World War I and was stationed in California. He returned late in 1919 for a visit, extolled the conditions in California, and told his sister she would do better there with her family than she ever could in Georgia.

Promised housing by the brother, Mallie Robinson collected

her family in the spring of 1920, scraped together the necessary fare by selling some of her furniture and clothes to neighbors, and boarded a train headed west to California.

"I was six or seven when we got there," says Mack Robinson, a silver medalist at the 1936 Berlin Olympics and a second-place finisher to Jesse Owens in the 200 meters. Mack Robinson, retired now, worked as a construction laborer a good part of his adult life.

"What my mother didn't know when she brought us here, what none of us knew, was that Pasadena was as prejudiced as any town in the South. They let us in all right, but they wouldn't let us live. It isn't much better today.

"When we first came here we lived at 45 Glorietta Street. It wasn't much of a place and we were all squeezed in there, but we managed."

Mallie worked as a domestic, and as the children grew up they contributed financially to the family. The Robinson family was on and off welfare several times but finally saved enough money to purchase the house on Pepper Street. It had been owned by a black who had a niece who looked white. The niece had made the original purchase. There would eventually be three Robinson-family houses on the Pepper Street site as the children grew and married, sort of a Pasadena version of the Kennedy compound at Hyannis.

"It was an all white neighborhood, and this lady across the street, this Mrs. Carey, was actually afraid of black people," says Willa Mae. "She complained to police and would slam her door when one of us appeared on the street to play. My mother got us to walking in the other direction when we needed to go to a store to avoid trouble."

There were also, as there almost always are, decent people willing to help the Robinsons.

"There was a bakery down the block, and at the end of the day one of us would be sent there to collect the old bread for free. They used to say 'Leave it for the Robinson Crusoe family.' Then there was the milkman who would stop by at the end of his day's route and drop off a few containers of milk without charge. People did help."

While many of the neighbors, including the Careys, gave the Robinsons a hard time, Mack Robinson explains why peace finally settled on the area.

"We just kicked some white ass," Mack says. "Kids aren't so tough when you can knock them down with a punch."

Mack is angered that Pasadena has never seen fit to properly honor Jackie or himself for their athletic deeds. The only official city money spent on a Jackie Robinson memorial is the plaque on the ground in front of where the Pepper Street house once stood. The house was torn down years ago as part of a redevelopment. The sign reads: "JACKIE ROBINSON resided on this Site with his Family From 1922 to 1946."

"I went to a Fiftieth reunion in Columbus, Ohio, of the 1936 Olympic team," Mack says. "It was quite an event. In Pasadena it meant nothing."

Mallie soon had regular jobs as a domestic, and the children worked after school. The biggest problem in the early years was baby Jackie, too small to leave at home alone and too young for school.

"My mother figured I could take him to school with me and he would play in the sandbox all day. There was a little fuss about that, but after a while they let us do it and it worked out fine," Willa Mae says.

Finally young Jack was old enough to enter Grover Cleveland School. He was well behaved in school and did his work but was not an exceptional student.

"In those days he would come home from school, gulp down a glass of milk, put his books on that old dresser, and be out the door playing ball with the kids. How that boy loved playing ball," Willa Mae says.

With three older brothers, Jack often played in street games and in the neighborhood lots as the youngest player on the teams. His brother thinks it helped his professional career.

"When he was playing with older boys, he had to learn how to make up for his lack of size and strength," says Mack. "I have to think the quickness did it."

All of the Robinson kids, including Willa Mae, were terrific athletes. "I used to pitch in the baseball games and played soccer and field hockey and ran track. I really enjoyed sports,'' she says.

Bill Brown, a retired cement mason, remembers something else the boys did but the girls were not allowed to participate in.

''We used to play cards in the alleyways behind the houses,'' says Brown. ''Jack was a little young for it, but he wanted to play so I taught him cards. We played all kinds of card games for a penny out there. I also taught him how to play bridge when he was about ten or twelve. He got real good at it.''

Following in the footsteps of his brothers, young Jack soon became a recognized athlete around Pepper Street and at the Grover Cleveland School, the George Washington Junior High, and Muir High School. Jack got his first taste of professional sports at the age of seven or eight when kids in school bribed the talented Robinson to play on their teams by offering him part of their lunches or even a dollar. He would rush home from school with that dollar and quickly offer it to Mallie for the family funding.

''There were a lot of days we were hungry,'' says Mack. ''We all worked after school to make a few dollars, cutting lawns, shining shoes, delivering groceries, running errands.''

''I guess that you would call Jack hyper,'' says Willa Mae. ''I could never remember him walking when he could run. He just seemed on the go all the time.''

With Mallie working as a cleaning woman for neighborhood women, with all of the children pitching in financially as best they could, with an occasional gift from the neighborhood bakery or milk wagon, and with a rare gift from the welfare department, Mallie kept the family together.

''I think it was her religion that did it,'' says Willa Mae. ''Not a day passed that Mamma didn't pray to God for help.''

In some few years Pepper Street began changing in ethnic makeup. Several more black families moved into the area. Mexicans moved in, Orientals moved in, poor whites moved in. All of these groups were bound together—by their poverty rather than by their race.

''They called it the Pepper Street gang,'' says Willa Mae, ''but it isn't what they call a gang today. They weren't out to do trouble or rob anybody. They just were a bunch of kids who enjoyed being together and mostly playing ball games."

"I think it was 1933 when he was in junior high school that we began to notice what an athlete Jack was," says Mack. "He was uncanny. He just took up a sport and he was the best in the neighborhood before anybody knew it. I think the first time he played Ping-Pong he won the city championship. I think that was the first time he got his name in the papers."

Mack Robinson is a handsome man with a brush mustache and white hair. He is a broad-shouldered, husky gentleman who has a little trouble moving around these days because of a recent knee operation, the result of years of running track and working on his feet. He lives with his second wife, Del, in a small house on McDonald Street in Pasadena, a few blocks away from the original house on Pepper Street. Del is busy in the backyard feeding the chickens and rabbits. There are photographs everywhere of the children, ten in all, and the dozen grandchildren, many of whom live nearby and march through the house to attack the cookie jar. He orders a few of the smaller ones to deliver a hug and a kiss before they can get that cookie and props his leg up on a recliner and talks of a time half a century ago. There is, leaning against a side wall, a huge blowup of a 1936 photograph of Mack as an Olympian teammate of Jesse Owens and another photograph of brother Jackie in his rookie season in Brooklyn.

MACK ROBINSON: "Kids today have too much of a good time. They don't know how to work. Everything is given to them. We had a rough time in my day. Sometimes I feel like we are in a lost world. When we were young we had to fight for everything we got. Now they are handed it. Then they get mad when they don't have more. These kids today have money for drugs. We didn't have money for bread.

"What hasn't changed is the prejudice in the world. That's still the same. The white man doesn't recognize what he is doing to the world. If he doesn't recognize it soon there might not be any world. I'm not a politician but I know enough to see what's going on. Blacks are better off in some ways today than they were when we were kids, but in a lot of ways we aren't. There's no adequate housing, there are no good jobs, there is still prejudice in a lot of ways. When I was a kid they wouldn't let us in the swimming pool but one day a week. Now, at least, we have our own swimming pools.

"I went to Pasadena Junior College and then I went to the Olympics in 1936. I finished second to Jesse and when I got back I could only get a job as a street sweeper. I lost that when they had a fuss over the pools. Then I got into construction labor. I worked on building the Rose Bowl. Jack played there later, and I always took pride in that.

"My life always seemed to be one step ahead or one step behind the times. I never was able to make full use of my athletic skills. We didn't think of making money in sports then. We just thought of enjoying ourselves and competing for the fun of it. I think we were better people for it. I'm not sure these kids today getting big money in track and field will ever learn to enjoy their lives. It is nice to be comfortable but I think when you have too much you get awfully spoiled.

"The reason Jackie made it was the strength he got from our mother. She instilled that pride in him. She wouldn't take anything from anybody. She was a real strong woman. It took a lot of guts to come out to California with five small kids. Her grandfather had been a slave and now she was setting out on her own to build a new life. Jackie inherited a lot from her; we all did.

"My life was tough. I never made much money. I had a lot of kids to support. I had a lot of trouble. One of them died. One of them was murdered by a girlfriend. Through it all I kept working, kept everybody eating. I accomplished all this without help.

"Jack was the baby of the family and things got better when he was growing up. We even had a car by the middle 1930s, and he used to borrow my car to take out his girlfriends. We had this 1936 Ford and that's the car we still had in 1947 when Jack played for Brooklyn and five of us drove cross-country to see him play.

"People asked me through the years why he made it with the Dodgers. Was he better than anybody else? I can't say that.

Maybe he was just the right man at the right time. Sometimes that is more important than who is best.

"I remember when Branch Rickey first signed Jack and we all said, 'What's this all about?' We didn't really think it was for the big leagues. There had been all that talk about a black team in Brooklyn. Jack said, 'No sir, this is a chance to make the big league Brooklyn Dodgers.' That was exciting. Why did Rickey sign him? That was business, clear and simple. He wanted a black player because he thought it would help the Brooklyn club win and he thought it would bring people into the ballpark. I don't criticize him for that. Everybody can understand business. I think what was more important, why I admire Rickey, is that he had the guts to do it. A lot of them were talking about having a black in the game but only Rickey did it. He stuck his neck out. He could have had it chopped off like one of those chickens we have out in the backyard. But he did it. Jack was the right man and did the job. Jack wasn't all that certain he could make it. He used to call out here on the phone, and he would say it was awful rough and people were writing him nasty letters and he was scared for his life a good part of the time. But he was a strong fellow, very determined, and if anybody could make it, Jack was the one.

"We followed his career and Jack always stayed close to the family. He was my mother's baby, the favorite, and when he would come home after he went to Brooklyn, she would always put out a big spread and all the relatives would come over and we would have a big party. Jack never changed after he went to Brooklyn. He was the same, just a hardworking fellow who wanted to make something out of his life—and he certainly did.

"The only thing upsets me now is that the city of Pasadena never really recognized Jack for what he did, being the first and all, and being a great player, a Hall of Famer, with the Brooklyn Dodgers. You would think they would mark that somehow, but they never did. They built a nice statue to Jack out at UCLA but that had nothing to do with Pasadena. They just don't care out here. Nothing has really changed, like I say.

"We still go out to the ballpark once in a while, maybe twenty-five times in all the years the Dodgers have been out here, but we pay our way in. We don't ask for any special privileges. We did have a free ticket the day they retired Jackie's uniform number 42, and that was a wonderful day. We all enjoyed that. I'm old now and the past doesn't matter much. I just wish that the young kids knew more of what we went through and had an appreciation of what it was like. It's just too easy for them; they don't have to work on anything, and they waste time taking drugs and killing themselves now.

"I watch the game on television once in a while now, and they have some good ballplayers, but they don't have a Jackie Robinson. He was something. I loved watching him out there. I really enjoyed when he played in New York, and I enjoyed going back there once or twice every year then to see him play.

"Jack was sick a good part of the time at the end of his life, and we didn't see him very much. Then he died in 1972 and I drove across country to New York for his funeral. All we did on the way was talk about all the good days when we used to take that same trip to see Jackie play. I don't get around very good anymore, but I still have those memories. Maybe that's all you have when you get my age."

A few blocks away, in a small house on Worcester Street, Willa Mae Robinson Walker lives with her daughter and grandson. She is a widow. Her husband, James, a school custodian, died several years ago of a heart attack. She is a thin woman with gray hair. She has a warm smile and an outgoing personality. She welcomes a visitor warmly and is proud to talk about her baby brother.

WILLA MAE: "I moved out of the Pepper Street house in the early 1940s into this house. Jack had his bachelor party right here the night before he married Rachel in 1946. He had all his old friends from the Pepper Street gang and they had a great time. Jack didn't drink or smoke, but he didn't stop other people from doing it and they drank a lot that night.

"When we first moved to Pepper Street we had a bad time. Nobody wanted us out there since the neighborhood was all white. [It is now a neighborhood of mixed heritage, blacks, poor whites, Latins, Asians—all living peacefully in these small, neat houses.] They did everything they could to get us out of there. One night we even had a cross-burning. We didn't know who did it, but there was one family, the Careys, we always suspected. They were just mean. They used to call the cops all the time on us for the silliest things, mostly for being out on the street. Jack was the one who was out the most. He just didn't enjoy playing indoors. He wanted to be outside.

"He would come out, bounce a ball on the street, and they would yell, 'Get off the street, nigger.' He would yell back at them, 'Shut up, cracker.' That kept up for a long while but finally they saw that we wouldn't move, we wouldn't give in and they would have to live with us or move themselves. They decided to live with us. I can't say we became friends, but they stopped bothering us. That was all we ever wanted.

"A neighbor woman, Mrs. Eva Armstrong, would come in once in a while to help us out while my mother was at work cleaning houses, but most of the time I was in charge of the house. I did the cooking and the cleaning, looked after Jackie, ran the errands for shopping, and kept us all clean and neat.

"Jack was only interested in sports. He wasn't a great student, but that was only because somewhere along the line he decided sports would be his life. He always talked of coaching teams in football and baseball, and I think that's what he would have done if he didn't become a baseball player.

"People used to ask me how Jack got so good throwing a baseball and a football, and I said it was from throwing rocks at the other kids who threw rocks at him. That was something we all did. It was more of a game than anything else. I don't think anybody was trying to hurt anybody else. We went through plenty with our neighbors after we moved to the house on Pepper Street, but it ended after a few years for two reasons. We all got older, and they all got tired of it.

"A lot of that changed, of course, after Mack became a famous athlete around here, and then Jack. Then they all started bragging how they knew the famous player from Pasadena Junior College, Jackie Robinson, and you would think they were great buddies. That's how people are, I guess.

"Jack played at Pasadena and then went to UCLA because he didn't want to be away from his mama. After that, he played some professional football in Hawaii, came back to get a coaching job, and went in the Army. When he came back from the Army, I acted as his secretary and he wrote letters to a lot of colleges looking for jobs. He was hired by three or four until they found out he was a Negro. Some never had asked on the application. Then he did get a coaching job. He also had sent a letter to the Kansas City Monarchs about playing for them, and one day a letter arrived while he was out. I opened it and it offered a job, and I talked to Mack and he called Jack and Jack asked what we thought. 'Take it,' Mack said, and he wrote them back he would take the job if they offered more money.

"Jack went to Brooklyn, and I used to go there every year for a visit. I went to every World Series he was in except the 1955 World Series, and that's the one they finally won. In those early days in Brooklyn I don't think we ever stopped worrying about him. He got so much hate mail and so many threats on his life and he talked about quitting, and we worried all the time about him. We used to read some things in the paper about the hate mail and the people trying to get him out of baseball, and the phone would ring and we would be afraid to pick it up. We used to think it would be a call from somebody saying Jackie was dead. Jackie's mamma was scared all the time, but she wouldn't really ever let on. She just prayed he would be all right and she trusted in God. One time in spring training he had to be snuck out of the ballpark with two Negro sportswriters, and when he called later he told us if they didn't get him out of there in time a gang was coming after him. 'I might have been lynched,' he said, and we just sat down and cried. Was it worth it? There were lots of times we just thought he should come home and coach at a black school and be done with it. But that wasn't Jack. He was determined to do it so he did it.

"We always worried about him because he was so quick to anger if somebody said something that was insulting. I don't think Jack ever looked for a fight, but I don't think he ever walked away from one, neither.

"He would come home in the winter and play tennis and golf with friends around here and be really relaxed. After the first year or two, he just never talked much about what went on with the bigotry back there. It just wasn't something we wanted to spend a lot of time worrying about if we didn't have to.

"Jack never did stop fighting for the black players though, and a lot of them forgot about that. He would talk about housing all the time and he would talk about better conditions in spring training, and he was always after that Casey Stengel about not having a black player with the Yankees, and I think he was very happy when they finally got Elston Howard. Jack had known him from some barnstorming games, and he was a real fine young man.

"Jack was always intense about everything he did and he worried a lot about his family and about the situation with blacks in this country, and that wore him down. Then Mamma died in 1968 and I had to call Jack on the phone to tell him, and he couldn't talk and Rachel took the phone. Later on, I heard that Jack had suffered a heart attack after that, and it was only a few years later before he passed.

"I'm around town and I get to different events, and some of the young people know I'm Jackie Robinson's sister and a lot of them don't. They don't seem to care very much, and a lot of them don't want to hear what it was like years ago. They are just interested in what they are doing now, and I can't really blame them. We probably are all that way. When I was growing up I didn't think about how tough it was for my mother, raising us. You can't spend all your time thinking about what went before. You just have to spend your time enjoying yourself and making the best life you can for yourself and your family.

"I miss Jack and I think about him often. We don't talk to Rachel much because she is busy back there in New York. I guess that's the way things are."

On one side of Fair Oaks is the Jackie Robinson Park, and on the other side is the Jackie Robinson Community Center and a post office called the Jack Robinson branch. In the post office letters and essays were hung marking Jackie Robinson's fortieth anniversary as a professional baseball player. The winning essay was entitled "Jackie Robinson Was More than Just a Baseball Player."

The Jackie Robinson Community Center is an impressive

low-slung building with a variety of community facilities ranging from prenatal care and substance-abuse centers to aid to senior citizens and baby care. Gene Stevenson is the director, and Toni Stuart is the public relations spokesperson. He is black and she is white. The racial makeup of the center is mixed.

"I grew up in Shreveport, Louisiana," says Stevenson. "I was in the seventh grade when Jackie broke in with Brooklyn. I took strength from his accomplishments."

Mrs. Eva Armstrong, the woman who helped the Robinson family, participates in the senior-citizen programs at the center.

"I'm an old lady now, she says. "I can't remember back in those days what I did with the Robinson family. I helped care for them. I cared for my own family and helped them. We were neighbors. I didn't know much about baseball. Still don't. All I know was Jackie Robinson was a wonderful boy. He grew up to be a wonderful man. I had six children of my own, and when Mallie asked me to help her out and look after hers a bit I didn't worry about it. Two or three more wouldn't matter none."

Willa Mae knew a few of the seniors and did not know others. She was introduced to them as Jackie Robinson's sister. A few looked up from their card game to say hello. Some concentrated on the game. She was introduced to some of the young people who worked in the center. They seemed not to recognize the name of Jackie Robinson even though they worked in a center bearing his name.

"Somebody told me he was a football player who died in the war," one young man said.

Across the street at Robinson Park, the sound of a basketball hitting against the backboard filled the afternoon air. Behind the courts a large swimming pool was filled with howling and laughing youngsters. Black bodies splashed in the pool with glee. Less than a quarter of a mile from the site where Jackie Robinson was refused access to a swimming pool because of the color of his skin, youngsters escaped from the summer heat in a pool and playground area named in his honor.

"I know Jackie Robinson was a baseball player," said Michael Gray, sixteen, a young volunteer aide at the park. He was working in a crafts room with small children, and he seemed puzzled when asked if he knew who Jackie Robinson was. "I never really learned much about him."

Willa Mae told the young man gently that her brother Jackie Robinson was the first black to play baseball in the big leagues. The boy seemed stunned.

"When did you say that was?" he asked.

"Back in 1947," she said.

"That was some long time ago," the boy said. "I never knew about that."

The boy shook his head and walked off. How could he know that dark-skinned Americans such as Jackie Robinson were not in baseball in the big leagues forever?

"Sometimes I worry that the kids don't know a lot about Jackie," says Willa Mae. "Then sometimes I think maybe it's better. Why relive all that anguish?"

CHAPTER

Three

THE DUSKY FLASH

*P*ASADENA CITY COLLEGE IS A
sprawling community college of some 19,000 students located at
1570 East Colorado Boulevard in Pasadena. Its graduates include
baseball stars Irv Noren, Darryl Evans, and Dick Williams, tennis stars Stan Smith and Ellsworth Vines, basketball star Michael
Cooper, track Olympian Mack Robinson, actors William Holden
and Nick Nolte, police chief Robert McGowen of Pasadena,
many successful businessmen, and several nationally known government officials. Its most famous graduate is Jackie Robinson.
When he attended the school in 1937 through 1939 it was known
as Pasadena Junior College.

The main building of the college was completed in 1936,
with a cornerstone reading "Knowledge and Character." Jackie
Robinson transferred to PJC after two years at Muir Technical
High School. He was a recognizable student on campus almost
from the beginning because he was the younger brother of Mack
Robinson, who had joined the United States Olympic team in
1936 out of PJC.

For two years Jackie Robinson was an outstanding football,
baseball, basketball, and track star at Pasadena. He would continue his athletic exploits at UCLA with impressive performances
again in all four sports. He was the first UCLA winner of four
varsity letters for sports in one year.

[33]

In the school newspaper, the *Pasadena Chronicle*, it was reported in the spring of 1937 that, "Coach Jack Thurman's baseball team saw shortstop Jack Robinson, a Muir Tech transfer, handle the situation ably in a game against the Cal frosh. Robinson and George Bodenschot led the hitting with two hits in four times at bat."

A photo accompanying the article showed a picture of the eighteen-year-old Robinson in the pinstriped PJC uniform with a serious face and a bony body. "First baseman Neil Reese, Robinson, and Bodenschot, a trio of sluggers, all connected with doubles but this was not sufficient to win. Chapman College beat PJC 5–2."

Later on that spring, Robinson earned a varsity letter in track as he ran the 100 yards and 200 yards and broad-jumped for PJC.

The paper reported that fall that the 1937 undefeated team opened in the Rose Bowl with PJC playing Loyola. "As the first half drew to a close, Jackie Robinson intercepted a desperate Loyola pass on his own 25 and eluded the entire Loyola team to chalk up the Pasadena TD in a 25–7 win."

The school yearbook summed up Robinson's exploits on the basketball court with a picture of Robinson, this time with a wispy mustache growing on his upper lip. "Robinson and Bill Busik were the outstanding players on the hoop squad just as they had been on the football field. Robinson came close to capturing the title of no. 1 scoring man in the league, but teamwork rather than individual stellar play was chiefly responsible for Pasadena's excellent showing in a league of exceptionally good teams."

By 1938 Robinson had reached star status on the baseball team with an article reporting that "The star of the team might be said to be Jackie Robinson, who besides leading the team with an average of .417, was chosen as the all–Southern California shortstop and the California Junior College shortstop. Robinson's speed gave him all base stealing honors. *The dusky flash was credited with 25 thefts in 24 games.*"

In track he became the national junior college record holder in the broad jump in a meet against Compton with a leap of 25 feet, 6½ inches, breaking his brother Mack's record.

In a notes column in the *Chronicle* it read, "Jackie Robinson, kid brother of Mack, Pasadena's World Reknowned Olympic star, has been cutting up capers in night softball games at Brookside Park. Jack, regular shortstop on John Thurman's varsity nine, has been showing as much speed on the bases as his more famous brother has shown on the cinder path.''

In a column called "Down in Front," writer Shavenau Glick wrote on November 12, 1937, that, "Jackie Robinson and Bill Busik turned in their usual 4-star performances. Robinson turned the game into a complete rout as he sprayed the field with footballs. Not only did he pass to Tom Collins for a sure six, but he also turned in one of the most beautiful runs of the year when he ran an intercepted pass back 92 yards for a touchdown.''

In his last basketball game for PJC, Robinson was reported as leading his team "in a riot and in victory. He engaged in a successful fight after the game with Long Beach star Sam Babich.''

The accolades were beginning to come up regularly with Hank Shatford writing in the May 20, 1938, *Chronicle* that Jackie Robinson was "the greatest base runner ever to play on a junior college team.'' Shatford outdid himself when he announced in print, "I consider Jackie Robinson the greatest all-around athlete ever to attend PJC.'' He was named the *Chronicle*'s Outstanding Athlete and, despite a broken foot in his final year at PJC, the outstanding football and basketball player in the school's history.

It was often suggested in later years by Robinson observers that baseball was really a minor sport at PJC for Jackie and that he was more known as a football and basketball player. In his final year at the school a summary of his career reported, "His record in the sport of baseball is more brilliant than in any other.''

Tom Mallory, Robinson's football coach at Pasadena Junior College, said that Robinson was such a good athlete in any sport he tried it would be impossible to suggest he was better in any one. Mallory, a retired physics teacher, is seventy-seven and still lives in Pasadena.

MALLORY: "He excelled at every sport, not only the team sports, the individual sports, too. He was a great Ping-Pong player. He was a wonderful handball player. He played badminton. He was just so damn quick in every sport that he could play every game with ease.

"He was a great dribbler in basketball and could fake guys right out of the play. I remember when I had him in football, and we were playing Compton Junior College and he was coming down the field toward our side and there were four Compton guys converging on him. He rolled one way, faked another, and the four Compton guys crashed out of bounds onto our bench as Jackie ran in untouched for a score.

"He was touchy about the racial issue. We didn't have too many black players on the team in those days. Some people would say they didn't want to play against 'the nigger.' I saw what an athlete he was and I wanted him.

"He was a lousy practice player. He laid low in practice and he looked chicken. He didn't like to get hit in practice, and he didn't run very hard. You probably wouldn't use him if you just judged him on what he did in practice. Once the game began, he was some competitor. He knew how to win. Despite all that individual talent, he was quite a team player. He would block for the other guys, and he was a terrific tackler on defense.

"I was born in Missouri and came to Pasadena in a Model T Ford in 1937 to teach physics and coach football. I was the physics department chairman for forty years. I really enjoyed coaching football. Jackie was not only a great player for me, he was a tremendous person. I treated him the same as I treated any other boy on the team I had. That was all he wanted. The only racial thing I can remember was one time we were playing a team that was really giving it to him, calling him nigger this and nigger that and our guys went into a huddle and made sure the other side saw they had their arms around the black kid and treated him the same as anybody else.

"We started a Hall of Fame around Pasadena a few years ago, and the only three blacks that got in it were all kids I had coached, Kenny Washington, the great UCLA back, Jackie Robinson, and Ray Bartlett, another great athlete at Pasadena and UCLA. He was a close friend of Jackie's.

"I followed Jackie's career in baseball, of course, and I wasn't surprised by any of it. He was a very fine athlete and a fine man, and it was a privilege to coach him in school. I can't say that I expected he would turn out as he did, but I wasn't terribly surprised either. Jackie Robinson was the kind of athlete who comes along once in a lifetime. You get a kid like that who can do so many things on a football field and you are getting a kid who will make you look like a real smart football coach."

Ray Bartlett is a retired police detective who lives in nearby Altadena, California. He was active in local politics for many years and retired last year.

BARTLETT: "I didn't live on Pepper Street, but I lived in the same area as Jackie. I went to Washington Junior High School and Muir Tech with him. Muir was predominantly a black school in those days, and then we moved over to Pasadena Junior College, which was almost all white.

"I played all four sports, football, basketball, baseball, and track, the same as Jackie, and I recently was named to the Pasadena Hall of Fame, and that was a great honor. I did a lot of blocking for Jackie, and we were the only two players from Pasadena to make the junior college All-America teams.

"Jack was an extremely competitive person and a very determined athlete. He hated to lose. I think he saw sports as an avenue out of poverty, and that is why it was so important to him. He fought the racism in the community very bitterly. Pasadena was an extremely conservative town, and we took a lot of name-calling in those days. There wasn't much you could do about it. You couldn't fight everybody. Jack was dedicated to being the best athlete he could possibly be because he saw that as an escape. I think he expected to coach and teach after college. There certainly wasn't any thought of professional sports because it just wasn't out there for us then.

"After we finished at Pasadena we went on to UCLA together and continued our schooling. Neither of us thought about sports as a living because it wasn't happening. Actually we probably didn't talk much about the future because we weren't sure what it would be.

"The last year we were in school I dated a girl by the name

of Rachel Isum. The black students used to hang out in this one building after school. I was there talking to Rachel one day, and Jackie walked in. Everybody in school knew he was a star athlete. I introduced Rachel to Jack, and they began going out after that.

"Jack left school before graduation in 1941, and later we played with the Honolulu Bears professional football team in Hawaii. Jackie left after the season ended on December 5, 1941. I stayed on for a few more days, and then on December 7, 1941, I was riding on one of those electric buses going out to the beach from my duplex. I didn't hear any sirens, but all of a sudden we saw puffs of smoke in the sky. The bus driver stopped the bus and let everybody off, and we saw all these Army Air Corps people running around. I didn't see any Japanese fighters in the sky, but I did get back home soon. I turned on the radio and heard that it was the real McCoy and we should all stay in our homes. Jackie was on a ship home by that time.

"I got back to the states about a month later and got a job in the shipyards during the war. I saw him once or twice after that, but I heard soon thereafter that he was in the Army, and I didn't see him again until after the war. He was with the Brooklyn club, but I was already in the police department and we didn't get together often.

"We always felt as if we were friends, and I followed his career and we met a couple of times through the years at civic occasions out here. I had a tremendous feeling of pride when Jack accomplished what he did, and it was something I have always considered an important part of my own life.

"We went our separate ways, and I didn't know much about Jack's life after he left baseball. I guess the first thing I heard about him was when his son was killed in that accident. Then a year or so later I heard he had passed away. It was very sad. The funeral was a few days later, and it so happened it was on my birthday. That was a terribly sad day for me.

"Jackie Robinson was a great athlete, the best I have ever seen, a fine man, and a very intelligent fellow. I think he would have succeeded in anything he did. I'm honored to have been a friend of his."

In the spring of 1942 Robinson received a letter at his Pasadena home. It began, "Greetings." The United States had decided to induct Robinson into the service despite the fact that he was supporting his mother and that football injuries had given him some foot trouble.

"Jack had been working with a youth job upstate when the letter from the Army came. I called him," says Willa Mae, "and told him he had been inducted."

"I'm not surprised," he said.

Robinson was soon inducted and sent to Fort Riley, Kansas, for basic training. The Army, in 1942, was as segregated an institution as existed in American life. Robinson, subject to military segregation and to local segregation off the post, was restless and unhappy in the Army. He thought conditions might be slightly better if he could become an officer. He applied for officer candidate training. There was no action on his request. Robinson was assigned to a cavalry unit.

Robinson soon got a lucky break. Joe Louis, the heavyweight boxing champion of the world, was assigned to Fort Riley. Louis was in a special services unit. His major Army job was to teach boxing to young soldiers, talk boxing, and entertain the troops with exhibitions. He would also box several times for Army relief and generate millions of dollars in income for that charity. It did not prevent the government from dunning Louis for back taxes many years later, a situation many believed exacerbated his weakened physical condition and caused his early death.

When Louis arrived at the base he found out that Robinson, a fellow athlete he had met in California, was in the camp. He located his unit, and they arranged a golf date on a segregated course.

Robinson was pleased to be with the champion. He happened to complain to Louis about the raw deal blacks were getting in service and especially about the runaround blacks were getting as they tried to enter Officer Candidate School. There were black officers in the Army, but most of them had been trained at OC schools on northern posts. The champion responded by making some phone calls. He reached Truman Gibson, a black civic leader and civilian adviser to the secretary of war. Gibson investigated the discrimination, learned that no blacks were being accepted at the Fort Riley OCS, and brought some pressure to bear on the leaders of the post. Soon, Robinson and several other blacks at Fort Riley were receiving letters that they had been accepted into the OCS training program effective immediately.

Robinson received his commission the following January and was named morale officer for a black unit at the post. It was a vital job, for morale was lowest with black soldiers who were suffering from Jim Crow laws while being asked to train for their chance to fight and die in Europe or the Pacific.

Robinson was soon embroiled in a post exchange situation as he attempted to open up the PX to more black soldiers. It was one of the many incidents Branch Rickey would hear about when he began scouting Robinson more thoroughly. It was this incident and others in the military that would suggest Robinson was a "troublemaker." It would only be through the dedicated efforts of Rickey and his associates that the truth about these Army cases would come to light. Robinson was clearly a man who fought for his rights. In some eyes, that constituted a troublemaker. In Rickey's eyes, it stood for the kind of fighter he wanted to handle the pressure he knew Robinson would have to withstand.

Jackie Robinson's Army career took a final, fatal turn after he was transferred to Fort Hood, Texas. One afternoon at Fort Hood he found himself on a bus riding to a post hospital where he was being treated for a bad ankle, an old football injury. Robinson, now a lieutenant, was sitting in the middle of the bus with the light-skinned wife of a black fellow officer. Robinson soon heard the driver yelling for him to move to the back of the bus.

Texas, in 1943, was as deeply prejudiced and segregated as any other part of the South. Robinson, however, wearing his uniform, knew that racial segregation of facilities had been outlawed on military bases, though the Army units had not yet been integrated. It would be under President Harry Truman's executive order in 1948 that the Army was to be truly integrated, breaking up a tradition that had lasted for many years.

Robinson's complexion was quite dark, and the driver assumed the woman was white. Companionship between a black man and a white woman represented the ultimate fear for bigots. It violated every value of ethics and morality that the bus driver knew.

"Listen you," the driver shouted, "I said get to the back of the bus where colored people belong."

"Now you listen to me," Robinson responded, "you just drive the bus and I'll sit where I please."

At the final stop on the post before Robinson would switch to a city bus to continue the ride, the driver went for help. He told two military policemen at the post gate about the incident. They approached the lieutenant and asked him to follow them to the office of the duty officer, Captain Gerald M. Bear.

Robinson and Bear exchanged some heated words over the incident. Tempers flared. Bear said Robinson would be court-martialed.

He had heard the expression so many times in his life, along the play areas on Pepper Street, at Pasadena Junior College, at UCLA, where he was one of the school's greatest stars, in the Army at Fort Riley, and again now at Fort Hood in Texas: uppity nigger. For talking back, for fighting for his rights, for defending his dignity, Jackie Robinson, looked on as a troublemaker by some and a hero by many, was to find himself on trial for insubordination.

He was acquitted of the charges at the court-martial and transferred out of Texas to Fort Breckinridge, Kentucky. He soon applied for discharge. He requested separation from service based on his ailing ankle but knew the problems at Fort Hood and the court-martial would hasten the termination of his military career. The Army was too busy fighting a war in 1944 to spend too much time fighting one of its own soldiers. Robinson was granted a separation from service on medical grounds that November.

Before leaving Breckinridge for California, Robinson was walking across a recreational field. In storybook fashion, in the pattern of a Frank Merriwell adventure, a long, batting-practice fly ball bounced near Robinson. He picked it up and fired a strike to the outfielder chasing it.

Robinson, who had not played ball in the military because all teams were segregated, soon was talking to some of the players.

One soldier, Hilton Smith, had pitched for a famed black team, the Kansas City Monarchs. Robinson and Smith exchanged some banter about the lightness of the ball compared to the standard baseballs Robinson had used at UCLA.

"You seem to know a bit about baseball. Are you a ballplayer?" Smith asked.

Robinson said that he had played some baseball at Pasadena Junior College and at UCLA.

"Are you interested in professional baseball?" Smith asked.

"I don't know. I might be."

For a black American in 1944 professional baseball meant only one thing: the Negro leagues. Robinson, while awaiting his discharge, considered professional ball an impossible dream. He was going to be a college coach, and his career was clearly defined. He had already begun writing letters to several colleges.

Smith suggested that if Robinson was interested in professional ball he should write to J. L. Wilkinson, the white owner of the black Kansas City Monarchs.

"I'll talk you up to him and get you a tryout," Smith said.

Robinson sent off the letter and thought nothing further about it. He arrived home in Pasadena before Thanksgiving and soon received and accepted a job offer from Sam Houston College in Houston, Texas. It was a small Negro college with an enrollment of under 300 students, most of whom were girls. Robinson was hired as the basketball coach of the tiny school. He went to Houston and developed a hustling, aggressive team that recorded several impressive victories.

"I was his secretary, like I said," said Willa Mae. "We knew Jack was looking for a job, and I was writing out all those letters of application for him. This letter came and I saw that it was a job offer from the Kansas City Monarchs. They wanted him to report to their spring training the next spring. I called Jack and told him. He was excited, not because it was a job in baseball but because it was a job that paid a lot more than he was receiving as a coach at that small college."

The Monarchs were a famed team. They were probably the outstanding team in the Negro leagues for many years and had drawn remarkably large crowds. They had sent many of their players against big leaguers in barnstorming tours on many fall afternoons. The Negro leagues were loosely organized and players appeared on several teams over several seasons. One of the more reliable and financially successful teams had been the Monarchs. One of their superior drawing cards was Leroy (Satchel) Paige, the skinny, flame-throwing right-hander with the hesitation pitch and a world of showmanship.

J. L. Wilkinson had been a father figure to his black players for many years. He was a totally unprejudiced man, loved the game of baseball, enjoyed leading his team, paid his players fairly, and was loved and admired by most of them. He was also shrewd and knew that a famed athlete such as Jackie Robinson would bring a lot of people to the Kansas City games.

Robinson's athletic career had begun in earnest in Pasadena JC in 1937, and he was very well known by California sports fans. The fame had spread across the country when Robinson had starred in the annual all-star game in Chicago against the professional Chicago Bears, the National Football League champions known as the Monsters of the Midway. Robinson, with teammates Tommy Harmon of Michigan, Norm Standlee of Stanford, and George Franck of Minnesota, had excelled in the 1941 game. He scored one of the all-stars' two touchdowns on a long pass from Boston College's Charlie O'Rourke.

None of this fame had been lost on Wilkinson. He saw Robinson as a possible KC star, a definite drawing card, and a man who would help his team win.

Black sports fans were excited when it was announced that Robinson had signed with the Monarchs. Black newspapers had long been reporting the exploits of the UCLA star they identified as Jitterbug Jackie Robinson, for his speed and explosiveness in four college sports. Robinson signed a contract in March of 1945 with the Monarchs, and the black newspaper the *Chicago Defender* reported, "The Kansas City Monarchs slipped one over on the other owners when they signed Jackie Robinson." KC player Newt Allen, who had seen Robinson play college baseball at UCLA, told Wilkinson, "He's a very smart ballplayer, but he can't play shortstop. He can't throw from the hole. Try him at second base." But the team's regular shortstop, Jesse Williams, injured his arm, and by the time spring training ended in Houston and the Kansas City Monarchs began playing their league schedule, Robinson was the shortstop.

In Brooklyn, Branch Rickey was receiving scouting reports on many black players. He was already looking for the right one for his Great Experiment, and he was also looking for other talented black baseball players to strengthen his Dodger organization. Two of Rickey's scouting assistants, Clyde Sukeforth and Tom Greenwade, had already been watching black players. Greenwade knew a great deal about Robinson. He had sources all over the country and had talked to several of his scouting pals about this young Robinson. He fooled with his schedule and told Rickey he would be in the Kansas City area early in April to look at a few black players. One of the kids he liked was a youngster by the name of Robinson.

CHAPTER

Four

BASEBALL'S
SHADOWY MEN

*B*ASEBALL MIRRORED AMERICA. America mirrored baseball. Blacks were shadowy figures in the country's life. In their own society they were born, lived, and died. In white America they remained invisible. Newspapers seemed not to notice them. Magazines never reported on them. Movies never starred them. There would be the cinematic appearance of a Hattie McDaniel as a slave maid or the beautiful face of Lena Horne singing "Stormy Weather" or the dancing feet of Bill (Bojangles) Robinson—never anything serious. There were no black Clark Gable roles, no adventurous black Randolph Scott, no tough guy Jimmy Cagney with dark skin. In a country so heavily influenced in morals and mores by movies, blacks simply did not seriously exist.

Baseball had gained its most significant emotional hold on the country in the 1920s. A gregarious former Baltimore waif named George Herman (Babe) Ruth hit home runs at an incredible pace. His power and grace on the field, his humanity and childishness off the field, his overblown body and hedonist lifestyle had all contributed to his appeal. He had charisma before anybody had ever heard the word.

Sportswriters embellished his character and exaggerated his legends and lore with his outrageous comments, only some of which he actually made. He was a hero to most, even if some saw him as a lovable oaf. There were, of course, jealousies and detractors. The big fellow who called everybody "keed" because he simply couldn't remember names, had a large, bulbous nose and thick lips. Some of his adversaries actually spread the then-scandalous notion that Ruth had "nigger blood." The rumors enraged him.

There were so many other great stars through the 1930s and 1940s, including Lou Gehrig, Hank Greenberg, Joe DiMaggio, Ted Williams, Joe Medwick, Stan Musial, Dizzy Dean, and Lefty Grove. America was in love with these men, imitated their every action on city street corners and rural roads. The national pastime. The *white* national pastime.

Blacks admired Greenberg and DiMaggio and Dean and Williams and the rest. Most of them knew little of the black men riding nine to a car over dusty Southern roads and into big cities for a Negro National League or Negro American League game. Radio had exploded in the 1930s, bringing baseball into every home. It brought white baseball.

Organized baseball, as it is known today, is dated from 1869. Baseball, in some form, had probably been played in this country for a hundred years by then, but contracts, schedules, salaries began with the founding of the Cincinnati Red Stockings. This was only four years after the bitter, emotional end of the Civil War. Blacks were filtering through the South in search of work, and many wandered North. Some played ball. A few even entered this new professional league. Racism was part of the soft underbelly of America. A man named Adrian Constantine (Pop) Anson, generally known as Cap Anson, born in Marshalltown, Iowa, on April 17, 1852, was clearly the designated hitter for banning blacks in 1884. Anson, the husky first baseman and manager of the Chicago White Stockings (he had fifteen seasons of .300 average or better), refused to play a team from Newark with a black pitcher named George Stovey. He had been involved in a similar incident in 1881, involving a Toledo team with a black player named Moses Fleetwood Walker. That game was played. This game was not. In effect, blacks were banned, not only because Anson, a strong figure in the game, wanted it so, but because most other whites did also.

The banning of blacks in big league baseball, without any written evidence, was a cabal of ownership, players, fans, and press. No one cared enough to fight it. Baseball, by inertia, soon became a white man's sport. That is, organized, professional, major-league baseball. It prospered in a less organized, but no less skilled or enjoyable, form among some talented black players.

Was Babe Ruth the best baseball player ever? Who knows? He was never challenged by some seventeen or eighteen percent of the population. Maybe there would have been some Bob Gibsons, some Dwight Goodens, some Don Newcombes, some Oil Can Boyds among his pitching opponents if the game had been opened to blacks.

Young black players, accepting their lots and knowing the unwritten rules, began excelling in the 1920s and 1930s in their own "colored" leagues. There were hundreds of players of note, many of whom could have been big league stars but for the Cap Ansons of the world. Josh Gibson hit long home runs. Cool Papa Bell was the fastest player around, so fast, the legend goes, "he could turn off a light in his hotel room and be asleep before it got dark." Martin Dihigo was a brilliant pitcher. Buck Leonard was a slugging first baseman. Ray Dandridge was a stylish infielder. Bill Yancey was a graceful shortstop. Turkey Stearns was a slugging outfielder. Judy Johnson was a marvelous infielder. Satchel Paige, before he entered the mainstream with the Cleveland Indians, was the fastest pitcher around. In 1945, in this loose, disorganized, mostly unreported collection of American outsiders, entered one Jack Roosevelt Robinson, shortstop of the Kansas City Monarchs.

After Branch Rickey's 1945 decision to sign a black, as announced to his wife, Jane, the Brooklyn board of directors, and Red Barber, scouts were dispatched to size up the array of black baseball talent. Scouts named Wid Matthews, Tom Greenwade, George Sisler, and Clyde Sukeforth were ordered to search the Negro leagues. Middle-aged white men—clean-cut, often wearing brimmed felt hats, and furiously scribbling on pads—stood out in the scroungy ballparks through the East, South, and Midwest, where most Negro league games were played. Even in those occasional games played in Comiskey Park, Briggs Stadium, or Yankee Stadium, they were highly visible.

Cool Papa Bell, born James Bell in Starkville, Mississippi, on May 17, 1903, lives in quiet retirement in St. Louis. He gained his fame with the Negro league St. Louis Stars. He gained his nickname for his coolness under fire as a young pitcher. He was named to the baseball Hall of Fame in 1974.

BELL: "We never thought the door would open. We just played because we loved the game. I think some of the guys were hurt when Jackie was picked to go up. He was a good player, but he wasn't the best in our league. The best hitter I ever played with was Turkey Stearns. He was a little old by then, but he could really drive that baseball. I remember one time he hit five home runs in Wrigley Field. He nearly blew that fence down.

"I would have liked to get a chance to see how good I could do. I did pretty good when I played against them in barnstorming games. I played twenty-nine summer seasons of baseball and twenty-one winter seasons. I played about nine, ten months a year. The best I ever made was four-fifty a month.

"We talked once in a while about baseball letting us in but not much. It just wasn't going to happen. See, Judge Landis was in charge in those days and didn't want no black folks in the game nohow. I don't know what was behind it, but he was the man we knew kept us out. There were also a lot of bad owners against us, a lotta cranks you know, and we didn't fuss much with playing in the big leagues. It wasn't part of our idea.

"We played a lot of games against the big leaguers and did pretty good most of the time. I remember once, in the middle 1920s sometime, we had a game scheduled against some big league all-star team. Then it got canceled because three of their players wouldn't play us. One was Ty Cobb. The other two was Harry Heilmann and Howard Ehmke, the big pitcher. But some of the big-leaguers supported us. Bill Terry and Pepper Martin played against us, and both of them said in the paper the next day they thought I could play in the big leagues.

"We had a good level of ball, a lotta good players. We even had lights before the big leagues did. In 1929, I played night ball in St. Louis with the St. Louis Stars. I think it was six, seven years later before they played any night ball in the big leagues.

"As far as Jackie Robinson was concerned, he was good enough to play in our all-star game in 1945, I remember that. He played shortstop for the West team. He was an outstanding runner. As far as being the one to break the color line, maybe there were some better players but as things turned out he was the right man for the job. Maybe they weren't just looking for the best player, they were looking for an intelligent young man who could handle what had to be handled. He certainly proved he could do it, didn't he?"

William J. (Judy) Johnson was called the Negro league Pie Traynor in the 1920s and 1930s for his excellence at third base. He was thin and wiry and could slap line drives all over the field. He was born in Snow Hill, Maryland, on October 26, 1899. He lives now in Marshallton, Delaware. He was elected to baseball's Hall of Fame in 1975.

JOHNSON: "I was with the Pittsburgh Crawfords and the Homestead Grays, and I never got to see Jackie Robinson play with Kansas City. I used to play around Philadelphia a lot, in Darby, and one time we played against a team led by Mr. [Connie] Mack. He came up to me after the game and told me how much he enjoyed my play and thought I was a very fine third baseman. I said, 'Why don't you keep some Negroes on your team?' He said Judge Landis didn't want that and nobody could go against him. I remember once I beat him a ball game, and when it was over he told the papers, 'If Johnson was a white boy, he could name his price.' That was nice to hear, but it didn't put no money in my pocket.

"I never talk about salaries. I didn't then and I don't now. That just stays with me. Just say I made a living and let it go at that. I used to play a lot in Cuba in the wintertime. I played for Adolph Luque, and he didn't like to lose. He carried this pistol around with him, and when we lost a tough ball game down there he would shoot off the pistol in the clubhouse. Just about frighten everybody to death. The guys would just see him getting angrier and angrier as he screamed at us, and finally you just dove under the bench because, sure as anything, here comes that pistol, bang, bang, bang, with big holes in those clubhouse walls.

"The Negro leagues were tough. We'd drive everywhere in those old cars because we couldn't afford trains, and there wouldn't be much sleeping. We went from Pittsburgh once to Hot Springs, Arkansas, in two cars without a stop all the way down. Sometimes I would go three, four days without seeing a bed or getting in a hot shower. I was young. I didn't mind it all that much. Once in a while you'd play for a generous promoter and if you drew a crowd and maybe had a good game, he'd give you a big bonus, treat the whole club to ice cream after the game.

"I actually got to baseball late because when I was growing up around Wilmington I wanted to be a prizefighter like Jack Johnson. A lot of people said I looked like him. I used to spar with my younger sister. She was pretty good, too. I got my nickname because I looked like another player in the Negro leagues by the name of Jude Gans. They used to say I was a young Jude. It became Judy and that's what they all called me. Make sure you don't say it was because I was a Punch and Judy hitter, like they call those weak batters today.

"I was through playing by the time Jackie came along, and I don't have any regrets that I didn't get the chance. I was just glad somebody got it. When I was a kid, I played on integrated teams around Pennsylvania, Maryland, and Delaware and I always did pretty good. I'm sure I could have played in the big leagues but some things you just can't change. I never thought about it when I was playing myself because it was just the way it was. I must admit I was real surprised when I heard about Jackie Robinson, because I didn't know much about him and there didn't seen to be any talk in our league that anything like this was going to happen. Actually I'm glad there wasn't, because a lot of guys would have tried to impress the scouts watching them instead of just playing good baseball. Sometimes I think that's what is missing from the game today—good, solid baseball with bunting and stealing and good fundamentals. Now they make so much money they won't bother to learn how to bunt or move a runner. I was glad for Jackie when it happened, but I'll tell you this: he wasn't the only one who could have played up there."

Agitation to admit blacks into organized baseball had abated somewhat during the early years of World War II, but with the war winding down early in 1945, newsmen, politicians, union activists, and radicals among the general population clamored for baseball to give black players a chance. "If they are good enough to fight and die for this country," the cry became, "they are good enough to play ball." Blacks certainly did fight and die for the United States in World War II. What was striking was that they did it in segregated units, from the famed black bomber pilots of the Army Air Corps to the black troops in Europe, who suffered heavy casualties in the Italian campaigns.

A black reporter named Joe Bostic showed up one day without permission at the Dodger training camp at the Bear Mountain Inn, in New York state. The Dodgers were using the fields at Bear Mountain or the facilities at nearby West Point, because of wartime restrictions on baseball spring training travel. Rickey had become enamored of a white Army cadet at the West Point academy by the name of Glenn Davis. He was an all-American football player, the famed Mr. Outside to Doc Blanchard's Mr. Inside, but, he also excelled at baseball and the Dodger boss saw his speed, batting power, and outfield skills as a possible source of success for the Dodgers. Rickey loved young, fast ballplayers. With the war soon to be over, he was more eager than ever to bring the Dodgers back to the top with fleet feet. Davis could not be approached until his West Point eligibility ended. By that time, Rickey had moved in another direction for his talent.

On this early April day in 1945, some two weeks after Rickey had revealed his plans for signing a black player to his select group in secrecy, Bostic arrived with pitcher Terris McDuffie and first baseman Dave (Showboat) Thomas. Both were veteran stars of the Negro leagues, well past their primes.

Rickey was livid when he learned that Bostic was pushing his team into trying out these two players. Nobody pushed Branch Rickey. He had a master plan, a set timetable for everything, including the signing of a black player. This was not part of the plan. Reluctantly, Rickey allowed the two players to work out for some forty-five minutes. Manager Leo Durocher seemed uninterested. Rickey, his face fixed in an unbreakable stare, watched quietly. Then he got up and left. The workout was over. No contracts were offered.

Some ten days later, under political pressure from Isadore Muchnick, a white Boston politician who represented a black district, the Boston Red Sox allowed three black players to work out. Neither General Manager Eddie Collins nor Manager Joe Cronin were on hand. The three players were Marvin Williams, a hard-hitting second baseman; Sam Jethroe, a flashy outfielder; and an outstanding college football and basketball player with some baseball credentials named Jackie Robinson.

Sam Jethroe was born January 20, 1922, in East St. Louis, Illinois. After playing in the Negro leagues, the dynamic center fielder played four years in the big leagues with Boston and Pittsburgh. His lifetime average was only .261 but he stole ninety-eight bases in those four seasons includng a league-leading thirty-five in both 1950 and 1951. He lives now in Erie, Pennsylvania, and runs Sam's Bar in the downtown area.

JETHROE: "I remember when we tried out in Boston. There weren't many people there, a couple of coaches maybe, no players, and a handful of sportswriters. We shagged some fungoes in the outfield, hit maybe ten or fifteen balls apiece, ran the last one hard to first so they could time us, and that was it. I don't even think I broke a sweat. It was a cold, raw day, I remember that. I played in Boston later. It was always cold and raw up there in April. I didn't know Jackie hardly at all. I was playing with the Cleveland Buckeyes and he was with Kansas City. We probably played a few games against each other down South that spring. He hit the ball good that day. He had that line drive stroke. I hit it pretty good myself. They just didn't sign us, that's all. Later I heard something about the manager, Joe Cronin, being afraid of sending us to their Louisville farm club. I didn't believe that. There were other places to send us, like Boston.

"Jackie was a little older than me; he had been an officer in the Army, and he had gone to college. You could see he was a good player, and he would be a big leaguer for sure if they would let him. The war was still on then, and we figured maybe things would change after all the guys came back. Jackie said he thought there might be other clubs for us if Boston didn't want us. I went back to the Negro leagues and had a couple of good years. Then Cleveland called me up, and I tried out with them. The same thing happened, nothing. Then Jackie went to Brooklyn and that opened the door, and the Braves bought my contract, and I went to Boston. I told the sportswriters I thought if I wound up in Boston it would be with the Red Sox, but it didn't work that way.

"The thing that helped Jackie was that college education. He knew how to talk to people. He was a great player, everybody knows that, but he had to do more than play when he broke in. He had to take care of himself and do what they said and mind his own business. We got to be good friends later on when I played in Boston.

"I had this apartment down by the ballpark and he would come over and spend some time with me, and we just enjoyed talking together and remembering how it was when we first started out playing and how much better it was in the big leagues. I played in the Negro league for three or four years and never got much out of it, except for a little glory, never made much money. But I didn't make much money in the big leagues either, maybe $14,000 when they let me go in Pittsburgh. Then I came back here to Erie, opened up a bar, and I've been at it ever since. I've done all right. I guess I wouldn't have this if it wasn't for Jackie Robinson. If he didn't make it maybe they never would have taken me up there."

These occasional tryouts, the political pressures, the increased agitation by some groups for a chance were not heavily publicized. The average reader of sports pages across America in 1945 could not be aware how close the color line was to being crossed. Baseball fans rooted for their home teams, still filled with men classified 4-F by the draft, older players, and finally a few returning servicemen. The bottom was reached in 1944 when the St. Louis Browns played the crosstown St. Louis Cardinals in the World Series. The Browns' roster was further depleted by military losses in the spring of 1945, and a one-armed player named Pete Gray would make the team. He hit a .218 in seventy-seven games. Baseball fans remember the 1945 season well for another reason. It was the last time the Chicago Cubs won a pennant. They would lose the World Series on a big hit by a returning serviceman named Hank Greenberg, later to meet up with Jackie Robinson in far different circumstances.

In the Negro leagues there was not much serious talk about playing the big leagues. When the Germans surrendered in May of 1945, and the Japanese capitulated unconditionally in September, everything changed.

Monte Irvin finally had his hopes raised. Irvin was born February 25, 1919, in Columbia, Alabama, and soon settled with his family in Orange, New Jersey. He played for the Newark Eagles until his signing by the New York Giants in 1949. He had previously been scouted by the Dodgers who considered him too old. After hitting .293 in eight big-league seasons with the Giants and the Cubs, Irvin worked for a beer company, did some public relations, and then became a liason in the office of the commissioner of baseball. The only black executive in the baseball ruling office, he dealt mostly with the problems of black players. He retired in 1985 and now lives in Homosassa, Florida. He continues on special assignment for the commissioner's office. He was named to baseball's Hall of Fame in 1973.

IRVIN: "When I signed out of high school to play for the Eagles in 1937, there was no hope of playing in the big leagues. The feeling at the time was that it simply wouldn't happen. The big leagues were for the whites and the colored leagues were the only place we could play. I think some of that thinking changed during the war and shortly after the war. Blacks had jobs in factories, in defense plants, in the military, in all aspects of American life.

"I was about eight or nine years old when we moved from Alabama. It was completely segregated. Blacks couldn't even go to a movie because the local movie house didn't have a balcony and the balcony would be the only place we could sit. My grandfather had been a slave, and my father was a sharecropper, and we were dirt poor. I was one of ten children and sports was just a great relief.

"I really plunged into sports when we moved to Orange. I was able to win sixteen varsity letters in baseball, football, basketball, and track. After high school I was offered a scholarship to the University of Michigan, but I couldn't raise the money to get out there. I went for a year to a small black school in Pennsylvania called Lincoln University.

"I played summer baseball with the Newark Eagles until 1942. Then I entered the service and saw combat in France and Belgium. When I got back I still had some war nerves and really couldn't play up to my potential.

"In 1945 I heard the Dodgers were looking at me, but I wasn't very sharp in my game yet. One day this man came up to me and introduced himself. His name was Clyde Sukeforth, and he said he was a scout for the Dodgers. He said Mr. Rickey was interested in starting a team in Brooklyn with black players called the Brown Dodgers or the Brown Bombers or something like that. He never gave us any hint that he was looking at us for the big club. He said the Brown Dodgers would play in Ebbets Field when the white Dodgers were on the road. As I said, I was still suffering some from war nerves and wasn't playing very good baseball. Sukeforth told me he had seen me play five or six games by then, and he would watch me again over the next few weeks. And he just wanted me to know that he thought highly of my skills and had also been checking around about my character, and he was pleased to tell me he found out I was a fine young man. I guess I should have thought more of it since they bothered to check around the neighborhood and the schools. But for Negro league players then the idea of playing in the big leagues was so foreign it simply made no impression at all on me.

"I think Sukeforth told me he had looked at Campanella, myself, and Satchel Paige, though he knew Paige was a little old by then. There was no mention that I can recall of Josh Gibson, who used to hit those massive home runs, or Buck Leonard, or Ray Dandridge. They were probably the best three players in our league. Sukeforth seemed to be concentrating on the younger guys, and that should have been more of a hint but it wasn't. Then later that year I read about Jackie being signed by the

Dodgers, the Brooklyn Dodgers of the National League, and I was disappointed it wasn't me. I felt happy for him and immediately began thinking there would be more of us. Actually we weren't sure it would be just one guy or whether it was now open to all of us if we had the ability. In a way the signing of Campanella and Newcombe later was even more important. That told the rest of us that Jackie was not just going to be an isolated case.

"After another couple of years in the Negro league I was signed by the Giants in 1948 and made it to the big club the next year. I was over thirty years of age. In later years I often wondered just how good I could have been if they had signed me when I was twenty. Jackie and I never became real close. He was sort of a loner. We had this intense rivalry between Brooklyn and New York, of course, and we would be together at a banquet in the winter once in a while and kid each other about some game, but I wouldn't describe our relationship as warm. Actually, about the closest we ever got was in 1954 and 1955 when Jackie was working real hard to break down the barriers for blacks staying in the spring training hotel. We would talk on the phone about that and got together a couple of times over the winter to discuss how we might best go about this. He was always very cordial and very concerned. I think he looked at that as one of his more serious problems, and when the hotels down in Florida and the hotels in the big leagues began accepting all the players on equal terms, I think he looked at that as one of his more notable achievements.

"We had some pretty bitter games in later years between the Dodgers and Giants, and everybody knows how much Leo [Durocher] hated Jackie. He just wanted to beat him so badly. I don't think it was based on race. I think it was based on the fact that Jackie and Leo were two of the most fierce competitors I ever saw, and neither would give an inch, they wanted to win so badly.

"Black players today don't understand what Jackie and the rest of us went through in those early days. It's pretty easy for these guys now. I remember going into Philadelphia and getting called every racial name under the sun. The hatred was as plain as the nose on your face. It was like a black traveling in the white part of South Africa these days. We all took a lot to play in the big leagues, Jackie the most of course because he was the first. Nobody, black or white, should ever forget what Jackie did.''

A husky fifteen-year-old from Philadelphia by the name of Roy Campanella played with the Baltimore Elite Giants in 1937. By 1945 he was one of the best players in black baseball, a hard-hitting, strong-armed catcher with an explosive bat. It was his personality—upbeat, gregarious, chatty—that was as much a part of Roy Campanella's reputation as the line drives he slugged. Campanella, the son of an Italian father and a black mother, was extremely likable. In the Negro leagues, later with Brooklyn, and in the aftermath of a horrendous tragedy in 1957 when his car skidded on an icy Long Island road and left him paralyzed, Campanella always had a sunny disposition. In ten seasons he won three National League MVP awards, hit over .300 four times, anchored the great Dodger pitching staff, and never wavered from his belief that he should always be grateful for the opportunity of playing professional baseball.

He lives in Los Angeles now and works for the Los Angeles Dodgers in the community relations department. He speaks to kids and fans, visits spring training at Vero Beach each year, and clearly is an inspiration to people everywhere. Roy Campanella simply does not allow one to be sorry for oneself.

CAMPANELLA: "I met Jackie for the first time at the Negro league all-star game in 1945. I was with the Baltimore Elite Giants, and he played for the Kansas City Monarchs. He had a big reputation as a college athlete, so everybody knew who he was. He was a good shortstop, ran well, and had a good, tight contact swing. He was clearly a fine player.

"We talked a little that day and then we met again later that year at the Woodside Hotel in Harlem. We were scheduled to play on a team in Venezuela together, and we were there waiting to leave. We had dinner one night, and he just told me in the middle of the conversation that he would be signing soon with the Dodgers. I didn't think much of it because we all heard talk of this Brown Dodger team they were supposed to be starting. 'The Brooklyn Dodgers. The big-league club,' he said. I was shocked.

Jackie didn't go into any further details, and I didn't press him. We just knew that this sounded awful big.

"A day or so later the Brooklyn Dodgers contacted me and asked if I had a contract for the next season. I told them the only deal I had now was to play winter ball for a couple of months in Venezuela. They asked me not to sign anything else, and they would be in touch. They contacted me when I returned, and I signed to play in the Brooklyn organization in 1946.

"Jackie and I had a very good relationship. He respected me, and I respected him. We may have had some different ways of doing things, but no two people are exactly alike. He was a tremendous athlete with great pride and desire. He knew he had to walk a very tough chalk line off the field, and that was something we all had to deal with. We knew we couldn't pop off with umpires or say ridiculous things to the press. We had to be constantly on guard. I never considered any of that pressure. I just considered it the course we chose to take if we wanted to play big-league baseball. I was grateful I could play, and if I had to wear a shirt and a tie and jacket all the time off the field, that's the way I dressed anyway. I enjoyed looking neat and knew I was representing the ball club all the time.

"Maybe there were some things we had to do that white players didn't have to do. I knew if I didn't like a certain pitch when I was catching and disagreed with the umpire's call I wouldn't turn around. I would just say what I had to say facing the pitcher. Maybe I got a lot more to say that way, too.

"In the early days we couldn't stay in the same hotels with the rest of the club, and when we did we couldn't eat in the dining rooms. Jackie was always annoyed by that. I didn't care that much. But he fought that hard, and one day he just sat down in the dining room, and that was that. He was served and nobody made a fuss over it.

"Jackie changed a little in his later years. He got a little more outspoken, and that was something that may have caused him trouble. He went after things his way, and I went after them my way. That's just the way things were. Would it have been different if he followed me into the big leagues? Who knows? I admired, respected, and liked Jackie Robinson. Everybody knows that."

There was no flood of black players into the big leagues after the signing of Jackie Robinson with the Montreal club in October of 1945. The Dodgers moved aggressively to sign Campanella and Don Newcombe. There were a couple of other insignificant signings of blacks. Robinson played in Montreal for the Dodgers' farm club in 1946 and moved to Brooklyn in 1947. The American League was silent on the matter until July 3, 1947, when the flamboyant Cleveland Indians owner, Bill Veeck, purchased the contract of Larry Doby from the Newark Eagles. Doby made his Cleveland debut as a pinch hitter two days later. He struck out. He went on to become a tremendous player for the Indians, leading the league in home runs twice and RBIs once. He batted .283 in a fine thirteen-year career with the Indians, White Sox, and Tigers. Doby later scouted and coached in the big leagues, and even served Veeck as a manager for a short period in 1978— one of only three black managers in the forty years since Jackie Robinson broke in with the Dodgers. (Frank Robinson managed for a little more than two seasons with Cleveland, and Maury Wills managed in Seattle for less than one season.) Doby is now with the New Jersey Nets of the National Basketball Association as director of community relations.

DOBY: "Things were just as bad for me when I broke in. People tend to forget that. I was called every name you could imagine, from nigger to everything else. The first time I played in St. Louis, somebody tormented me from the stands by yelling I didn't belong in the American League. 'Get in the National League with all the other niggers and nigger lovers,' he screamed. You felt like blowing up, but you couldn't. Things were rough. I would arrive in a town with the team, and I had to carry my own bag and look for a cab and go to some seedy, old black-run hotel while my teammates were taken to the best hotel in town. It was grating on me, but I did it because I wanted to play. It was a heavy burden, but the Bible says certain people are given a burden like that by God because they can handle it. I guess I handled it.

"When Jackie was first signed late in 1945, I was in the Navy in the South Pacific. I had played for the Newark Eagles and at the Great Lakes Naval Training Station before I went to the Pacific. Mickey Vernon and Billy Goodman were on my team and Vernon thought I was such a good player I should be in the big leagues. He said he would write Calvin Griffith, the Washington Senators owner, a letter and see if he could get me a tryout. I had grown up in Paterson, New Jersey, and had played on integrated teams there. The Great Lakes teams were segregated, but the teams in the Pacific were not. There just weren't enough of us to segregate.

"When I got back after the war I didn't hear from the Washington Senators or anybody else and rejoined the Eagles. One day Campanella told me the Brooklyn Dodgers were scouting guys for a new team of black players they were supposed to be starting. He said some players actually thought it was a cover-up for a possible big league chance. Nobody knew. There were lots of rumors, just like in the Navy.

"I barnstormed that winter with a team that Jackie played on and got to know him. Later on, after he joined the Dodgers, we played again on a couple of barnstorming teams. I had a friendly feeling toward him, but Jackie was not an easy man to know. I think he always felt he was part of history. Jackie had a large ego and I was rather shy. I just played ball and didn't see it as more than a chance to enjoy what I did and make a living. Jackie appreciated and discussed his place in history and thought of himself in the same light as Paul Robeson and Joe Louis. He used to say baseball was the all-American game unless you were black, and that he was out to change that. It would be the all-American game for everybody.

"Then I got my chance with the Indians, and I was able to do the job. I still felt a lot of prejudice. They had allowed me in, but it hadn't changed people very much. It was as if they had taken down the sign No Blacks Allowed, but they hadn't taken down that sign in your heart.

"I think of all that now, and I think there isn't enough understanding of the past. Not only by the fans and the press, also by the players. A guy like Dave Winfield makes twenty million dollars, and he can buy a house anywhere he wants and do anything he wants, but I don't think people understand why

Winfield has this opportunity, what went before, just how hard things really were. I don't think kids are conscious of the past. I think they should stop and think about it more and pause to consider what has changed, and how it was changed, and how severe that price was in those days thirty-five and forty years ago.

"I remember how hard it was on me, how angry people were when I came into the big leagues. People know about Jackie because he was the first, but it was rough for me and for the guys who came after me and for black players for a long, long time.

"In 1954 we had the greatest team in the history of the American League with 111 wins at Cleveland. I had 32 homers and 126 RBIs and led the league, and Yogi [Berra] won the MVP award. That was a crime. You don't think my skin color had something to do with me not winning? I do. I'm not bitter. I'm just stating facts. I think we have made a great deal of progress in this country. But there is still a long way to go. Black players have to be better than white players. Black managers have to be better than white managers. That is just the way it is. Young blacks don't know the history. They don't know a lot about Jackie Robinson and Larry Doby and all the others who went before them. All they see is Winfield and the big money, and they want that. They are not interested in how anybody got here, what the conditions were, how hard we had to fight, how much abuse we had to take.

"Jackie Robinson went through a lot. We all went through a lot. It wasn't easy being a black man in America in 1947. It's a little easier today, sure, but not a whole lot."

Even as blacks moved into the big leagues, there was still a separate and unequal system for signing them. Whites were signed out of high school and sent to the minors. Blacks, for the most part, were still being signed out of the Negro leagues. They would enter the big leagues at a later age and therefore lost many years of earning capacity. A big, hulking pitcher by the name of Joe Black was signed by Brooklyn after starring for the Baltimore Elite Giants.

BLACK: "The Negro league was where black players had to earn their credentials. We weren't being signed out of high school.

I had been a star at Plainfield High in New Jersey and then went on to Morgan State. Finally the Dodgers signed me, and I was sent to Montreal. Jackie had played there and a lot of people thought I looked like Jackie. Then I was brought up to Brooklyn, and I roomed with Jackie for a while. The first night we were together he said, 'Hey, you're a big guy, wanna fight?' I laughed. He said we can't fight in this league. He was still feeling a lot of the pain six or seven years later. I remember one time we walked on the field and some loudmouth started yelling at him from the stands, 'Hey, Jackie, king of the niggers, hey Jackie.' Then he began singing "Old Black Joe" and calling Jackie a coon and screaming all kinds of vile things at him. Jackie just stared straight ahead, but you knew he was burning inside. He was a combative person by nature and that restraint went against his personality. He had to hold a lot in, and it angered him terribly. Holding that much anger can really hurt a man, and I think all that name-calling in those years killed him. I really do think that.

"All kinds of things were still happening when I joined the Dodgers in 1952. On a close pitch to the plate, if Jackie got the call the fans would scream, 'nigger lover, nigger lover' at the umpire. There would be a lot of things coming from the bench. I think most of the animosity came from fringe players. There were economic reasons to all this. They were afraid they would lose their jobs. A lot of them felt if they couldn't beat you on the athletic field, they could beat you down with ugly comments.

"Some players were very kind. I once got Stan Musial out in a big spot, and some guy yelled at him, 'Hey Stan, you have trouble seeing that white ball coming out of that big black body?' Musial came up to me later and said, 'Don't let those guys bother you. Just do your job.' Those things helped.

"Jackie had more confidence in his ability than any player I ever saw. He helped me a great deal that way. He just told me I was better than the hitter. Pretty soon I began believing it. He also helped me in other ways. He used to get a lot of requests for appearances in Brooklyn. In those days they were fifty dollars a shot and a chicken dinner. He would ask me if I wanted to go. I could always use the fifty. He would call the promoter up and get me the job, and I would make a few extra bucks that way.

"I guess the thing I noticed most when I joined Brooklyn was the difference in personality between Jackie and Campy. Jackie had built up this internal defense system. He had been hurt so much for so long that he had grown immune to all of it. At least publicly. Campy never seemed to get any abuse. Everybody liked him. He was just grateful for the chance to play, and there were not a lot of angry letters directed at him. Jackie was still getting vicious hate mail by the time I got there, and Campy was getting letters requesting his autograph. Campy did the best he could and that was it. Jackie demanded respect as an athlete, and everything he did on the field seemed aimed in that direction. He wanted to play hard, gain that respect, win, and go home to Rachel and the children. He spent his meal money making phone calls to Rachel. I spent mine eating sweets. Everybody is different in this world.

"I was always influenced by Jackie, and when my career ended after the 1957 season I went back to school, finished up my education, and got into business. I am a vice-president for marketing for the Greyhound Corporation, and I suppose I am considered one of the most successful black businessmen in America. A lot of that success comes from playing with Jackie Robinson. He helped develop my own pride.

"Jackie was a tremendous person, and I think every black player is a direct descendent of Jackie Robinson. For a black kid not to know Jackie Robinson and what he did is very disturbing to me. Jackie was a major influence in the lives of many blacks in this country, on and off the ball field. Not know Jackie Robinson? That's almost like not knowing your own family."

CHAPTER

Five

MONTREAL,
MON AMI

*B*RANCH RICKEY FIRST LAID eyes on Jackie Robinson on August 28, 1945, in the business offices of the Brooklyn Dodgers at 215 Montague Street, an address every Dodger fan had well memorized from Red Barber's gentle suggestions that ticket requests for the next series against the Giants or Cards or Cubs could be addressed there.

That was the day scout Clyde Sukeforth, returned from a scouting mission to Chicago, was instructed to bring Robinson in for a personal interview with the man the press called the Mahatma in recognition of his status as the exalted leader of the Brooklyn club. Branch Rickey was revered and respected by most reporters. He was ravished by some. Jimmy Powers, the vitriolic sports editor of the *New York Daily News*, labeled him El Cheapo for his constant public battles over contracts with so many of his players.

Rickey was a complex personality. He was born December 20, 1881, in Stockdale, Ohio. He was a college man from Ohio Wesleyan—a player, a coach, a spiritual leader, a significant figure in the history of that institution. He was a big-league catcher of little note with the St. Louis Browns and the Yankees in parts of four seasons in the early part of this century. He was a manager of both the St. Louis Browns and Cardinals. He developed the St. Louis Cardinal farm system. He encouraged the use of baseball scouts on a national basis. He built the Cardinals into a pennant-winning team. He took over the Brooklyn Dodgers in 1942 and would develop a farm system second to none, which would result in the Brooklyn club being the dominant National League baseball team through the late 1940s and 1950s.

Rickey was a flamboyant figure: a religious mystic and loquacious, sometimes convoluted, speaker— an orator, if the occasion moved him, of overwhelming skills. He sometimes seemed far too intellectual for so mundane a challenge as professional sports. He was a moral man who made some clearly immoral maneuvers to get ahead in the game. He would take on the chore of rebuilding a new team and a new league in the twilight of his life when he structured the New York Mets of the fledgling Continental League. His most noted act was the signing of Jackie Robinson to a professional contract with the Brooklyn organization on October 23, 1945.

Why did he sign a Negro?

Morality? Perhaps. To make money? Perhaps. To corner the market on black players and produce a long line of winners for Brooklyn? Perhaps. To show up his fellow owners? Perhaps. All of the above, most certainly.

Rickey would not have signed Robinson for morality alone. He had been in professional baseball as a player and executive for forty years by then. He said St. Louis was the wrong place, but he had been in Brooklyn for four years by then. All the evidence indicates Rickey thought it was the right time, the right place, and Jackie Robinson the right man. Circumstances coming together are far more significant in history than a single action, no matter how moral the cause. Jackie Robinson was signed for a myriad of reasons, some of which Rickey himself may not have totally understood.

When he coached the baseball team at Ohio Wesleyan, Rickey had a black player by the name of Charley Thomas. Rickey never tired of telling the story of how he was chagrined when Thomas could not get a hotel room in South Bend, Indiana, when they played there. Rickey allowed Thomas, who would later become a successful dentist, to sleep on the floor in his room. Rickey often told the tale of Thomas rubbing his hands as if to peel off his black skin. "Oh, I wish I could make the skin white," Thomas would say. Rickey claimed the scene never left him. He was so moved, the reasoning goes, he felt compelled to make a place for a black in baseball.

If he was so moved by this, why, then, were there no black executives in the Dodger organization where the integration of the front office would have been far less traumatic than the integration of the playing field? And there is no evidence that Rickey was active in the integration of housing in St. Louis or New York, where he lived, or in the integration of the military during World War II where he might have had some influence as a well-known leader of a famous baseball team. There was some moral significance to the Robinson signing by Rickey. There is no doubt of that. He had the courage, the confidence, and the passion to go against the common tide. But Rickey, from all evidence, was a pragmatic man. He was extremely bright, and he understood human nature. He knew the move would work. He knew he would financially benefit as would Robinson and all blacks to follow. He also knew history would forever link Branch Rickey to this revolutionary social action, no small consideration to a man of Rickey's massive self-importance.

He planned carefully. He had his scouts examine nearly one hundred black players, more than three dozen in great detail. They were scouted more thoroughly than Pee Wee Reese, Carl Erskine, Duke Snider, or Dixie Walker ever were. It was far more than the question of whether they could hit or throw. Josh Gibson was quickly eliminated because he was a hopeless drunk. He would be dead at the age of thirty-six before Jackie Robinson played his first big league game in 1947. Dodger reports said Satchel Paige would be difficult to handle. Buck Leonard, Cool Papa Bell, and Ray Dandridge were considered too old. As more and more names were eliminated, the name of Jack Roosevelt Robinson came more significantly to the fore. He was a well-known California college athlete from a fine family. His brother, Mack, was a recognized Olympian. He was intelligent. He was competitive. He was a marvelous all-around athlete, something Rickey admired in all his players. He liked athletes who could run, and he especially liked those who participated in basketball and football as well as in baseball. He felt that such participation increased their athletic poise and skills. There was one other factor in the Robinson case. He was an extremely dark-skinned man. His bloodlines indicated no white skeletons in the woodshed. This appealed strongly to the moralistic side of Rickey. It would also eliminate the reverse discrimination of some people suggesting that a lighter-skinned black had mixed ancestry and was trying to pass for white.

Rickey's dossier was now filled. All signs pointed to Robinson as the man he wanted to break the color line. There were so many complications to this signing that Rickey wanted no foul-ups. He assigned the task of bringing Robinson in for that famed face-to-face session to his favorite scout, Clyde Sukeforth. Rickey knew the laconic former catcher from Maine would not be corralled by newsmen on his way out to Chicago to see Robinson and spill the beans. Sukeforth spoke only when spoken to. Rickey gave Sukeforth his instructions: "Go out to see Robinson and check out his throwing arm. If you like him, bring him in for a meeting with me. If he can't come in, tell him I'll come out to see him."

Sukeforth had been in professional baseball for more than twenty years by then. He knew how the game was played, on and off the field. Rickey had said that he was scouting players for the Brown Dodgers, a supposed exhibition team he would put in Ebbets Field. When Rickey told him he would go to see Robinson if Robinson couldn't come in to see him, Sukeforth knew his boss meant business. This was no ballplayer who would play when the Dodgers were on the road. This was a guy Rickey felt strongly about. Sukeforth, like most of his fellows from Maine, kept his thoughts to himself. He did what his boss asked him to do.

Clyde Sukeforth is eighty-five years old now and lives in the small town of Waldoboro, Maine, near where he was born in Washington on November 30, 1901. He had ten seasons in the big leagues as a light-hitting but smart-fielding catcher. He was a thin man, never weighing more than 155 pounds, now or in his playing days, standing 5 feet, 10 inches, learning a lot about the game through the years, and working faithfully in the Dodger organization after he came back to the big leagues during the depths of the player shortage in 1945 to catch eighteen games at the age of forty-four. He scouted for the Atlanta Braves after leaving the Dodger organization over a minor salary dispute and retired to his Maine home in 1975.

SUKEFORTH: "I never had any racial feelings at all. I never thought about it, and it never bothered me. When Mr. Rickey told me to scout the colored players I looked at them the way I looked at the white players. Could they run, field, throw, hit, hit with power? That's all I was interested in. If there was anything else involved in the signing of Jackie Robinson, that would be Mr. Rickey's responsibility, not mine.

"I went out to Chicago on the overnight train and got there early Friday. His team, the Monarchs, was scheduled for three games there, and that would certainly give me a line on him. When I got there I found out he had injured his right shoulder in a fall in a game earlier that week. I looked at a couple of other players Friday night, and I decided to talk to Robinson before the Sunday game. I was in the stands. I gave an usher a couple of bucks and asked him to bring Robinson over. He walked to the stands, and I identified myself as a scout for the Brooklyn Dodgers. I told him Mr. Rickey wanted to look at his throwing arm, but I heard he was injured. 'That's right,' he said. I told him I was staying downtown and asked if he would come over after the game and meet me in my room at the Stevens Hotel. He looked me over for a while and then said he would. I watched a few innings of the game and then went back to my room at the hotel to do some paper work on my reports.

"Before I went up to my room I told the doorman a colored man would be coming by later to see me and to let him up to my room. I gave him a few bucks, and he said he would. I can't remember what time it was but I think it was about midnight when Robinson knocked on the door of my room. I opened it up and let him in. He was a wonderful-looking athlete, a very good-looking man, with those big, broad shoulders and large hands. I think he was wearing a gray sports jacket and gray slacks.

"We sat down to talk about his baseball ability and the fact that Mr. Rickey wanted to meet with him personally. He had a very distinct voice, very cultured, and chose his words carefully.

There was something about the fellow that impressed me as his being somebody special. Determination was written all over his face. This wasn't a young man who would be pushed around. It wasn't hard to tell he was a highly intelligent man. I was very impressed.

"Maybe we talked an hour and a half or so and then I had to leave for Toledo, Ohio, early the next morning. I asked him if he could arrange to take a few days off since his arm was injured, catch a train for Toledo, meet me in the ballpark late the next afternoon, and we would ride the train in together to New York. He said he would; we shook hands and he left.

"The next morning I caught the first train to Toledo. I was sitting in the ballpark thinking about him when he suddenly arrived. I saw him in the stands. I told him we could leave together from the ballpark as soon as I checked the train schedule. I saw there was a train that left Toledo that night and got into Brooklyn early the next morning. We had dinner in the hotel that evening and took a cab together to the train station. I had arranged for a reservation for each of us in the sleeper car. We talked some more and then I said I would retire. I don't know how late he stayed up that night, but when I got up and got out that morning he was already up and dressed. I asked him to join me in the diner for breakfast. He said, 'No, that's all right, I'll eat with the boys.' I think he went in the back with the colored porters and had breakfast with them. I don't think the trains were integrated in those days, and I think he just didn't want to start off his Brooklyn association by making a scene. I had breakfast quickly and came back to the sleeper car, and he was ready. We pulled into Grand Central Station very early that morning, and I told him we would make a reservation in a Brooklyn hotel so he could clean up and get some rest before he met with Mr. Rickey. 'That's not necessary. I have connections here in New York.' We got off the train together and I took a cab to Brooklyn. He went his way and I went mine.

"A few hours later I was sitting in Mr. Rickey's office. The secretary knocked on the door and said Jackie Robinson was there. I got up, brought him into the office, and introduced Branch Rickey to Jackie Robinson."

The famed meeting in Brooklyn created a relationship that would last with much emotion and little conflict until Rickey's death some twenty years later. Like most people around the Dodger leader, Robinson always referred to him as Mr. Rickey, and the ballplayer was Jack or Jackie. It seems to have some overtones of a teacher/student relationship until one understands that almost everyone, from players to Dodger executives to newspaper reporters to fellow owners, addressed the bushy-browed, cigar-smoking Dodger leader as Mr. Rickey.

With only Sukeforth still alive of the participants, the historic meeting now has taken on, in baseball circles, the significance of the Roosevelt-Churchill summits or the surrender of Lee to Grant at Appomattox. Rickey spoke for nearly three hours. His voice rose and fell in dramatic fashion. He came close to Robinson's face and backed off. He stood and he sat. He paced and he paused. He attacked Robinson and he defended him. He challenged his intellect. He tested his strength of character. At one point, as Rickey spelled out the rules for Robinson, the ballplayer asked, "Mr. Rickey, do you want a ballplayer who's afraid to fight back?" Rickey, a thespian to his shoe tops, bellowed, "I want a player with guts enough not to fight back."

SUKEFORTH: "I remember Mr. Rickey saying how he had looked for a great colored player all his life. He wanted more than a great player. He wanted a player who could turn the other cheek and fight back by exceptional play. He wanted a guy who could carry the flag of his race with his performance and his conduct. When a guy slides in and cuts you in baseball, you are justified in getting him back. What Mr. Rickey wanted was for Jackie to take it, soft-pedal it, keep his mouth shut, and play good baseball. Helping Brooklyn win was supposed to be satisfaction enough.

"The meeting finally ended, and Jack agreed to sign. By the time he got to Montreal the next spring we would have another black player [John Wright], and I warned Jack not to be caught in a photo just standing around with him. Make sure he moved among his teammates on the field. He understood.

"It was very exciting to follow Jack's career after that. I

admired him very much. He was one wonderful player and a very fine man. I remember a couple of years before he died there was a dinner in New York, at Leone's I think, honoring Jack, and I was invited to attend. They brought me down from Maine, and it was a wonderful evening. Jackie was already looking bad from the diabetes, and I was saddened to see how he slipped back. He had been so big and strong and fast and now he seemed so tired and old.

"When he died I felt very sad for his family. I didn't think much about the part I played in the situation at the time. I was just doing my job. Mr. Rickey sent me out to see a ballplayer, and I scouted him, same as I did with dozens of white boys. It wasn't that special to me. I guess forty years later it seems more special. I guess I have to say now that I was part of history. I was lucky. I was in the right place at the right time."

The next act in this sociodrama would be played out in the city of Montreal. Jackie Robinson had technically signed a contract with the Montreal Royals, the top farm club of the Brooklyn Dodgers. The announcement was made in the offices of the ball club at Delormier Downs on Ontario Street in this picturesque, cosmopolitan city in Canada. President Hector Racine of the Royals made the announcement. Rickey sent his son, Branch, Jr., called the Twig by the press, as his representative. It was October 23, 1945. Jacques Beauchamp, of the *Montreal Matin*, covered the press conference announcing the signing of Jackie Robinson.

BEAUCHAMP: "I was just nineteen years old then and I was beginning my career. Nobody knew what the announcement would be, but we were told it would be big. We thought it might be a new manager, a big-name manager for the ball club.

"Jackie Robinson was there, and it was announced that he had signed a contract to play for the Royals. He was a big fellow and certainly looked like an athlete. Black players had played in Montreal before. The previous season there had been a game between the Josh Gibson All-Stars with Satchel Paige and a local semiprofessional club. There were many blacks in Montreal. Nobody made a fuss over them. I'll tell you how big Jackie Robinson became in Montreal. Some people thought he was an athletic hero equal to Maurice Richard, the hockey star. Nobody was ever a bigger sports hero in Montreal than Richard.

"I think the people in Montreal have always been proud that Jackie Robinson broke into baseball here. There is a statue to Jackie Robinson in Montreal near St. Catherine Street, down from the site of the ballpark. It cost fifty thousand dollars to build, and the money was raised by public contributions. It was hard not to admire Jackie Robinson once you saw him play. And his wife, Rachel, what a warm and wonderful person she was. Everybody loved her around the ball club, and I think she helped make things a little easier for Jackie.

"The Royals started training in Sanford, Florida, but there were some racial problems because of Jackie, and the team was soon moved to Daytona Beach where the big club trained. Jackie stayed out in a private home, but he trained routinely and I don't remember any racial incidents around the club. These were minor leaguers who wanted to make the big leagues. They weren't about to make a fuss. Clay Hopper was the manager, and he was from Mississippi. I asked him once, a few days after Robinson reported, how his family back in Mississippi was taking it. He said, 'My father is dead. If he were alive he would probably kill me for managing a black player.' I never wrote anything like that because Clay was a nice man, and we all expected he would judge Robinson on his baseball ability. I think he did. Jackie had a great year, of course, just won the batting title at the end over Eddie Robinson [.349], and led the team to the pennant and the Little World Series. I can't recall one incident all year. He was a very humble man and a perfect gentleman. I think Jackie Robinson's name is still popular around Montreal. He may not be the equal as a hero to Maurice Richard, but he is certainly remembered by older people in Montreal. As for the youngsters knowing who he is, I'm not so sure. They may not know him. Nowadays young baseball fans in Montreal are interested in the Expos, not the Royals."

On April 18, 1946, Jackie Robinson played his first game of organized baseball. He was at second base for the Montreal Royals against the Jersey City Giants, the top farm team of the New York Giants. Marvin Rackley, a speedy center fielder from Senecca, South Carolina (baseball always seemed to have a disproportionate number of Southerners), led off with a ground out. Robinson worked the count to 3–2 against Giants left-hander Warren Sandell. Before a full house, including thousands of enthusiastic blacks, Robinson also grounded to short. He was thrown out easily. By the marvelous mathematics of the baseball diamond, through years of trial and error in the nineteenth century, no man, not even with Jackie Robinson speed, could beat a routine grounder to shortstop. If it was handled cleanly from normal fielding depth, a man with a professional arm would always throw out the hitter. Robinson was out.

On his next time at bat, Robinson crushed a high fastball for a three-run homer. He bunted for a hit his next time up. He singled his fourth time up. He bunted for another hit his last time up. He stole a base after his first single. He moved to third on a ground out and scored on a balk when his brazen dashes off third rattled the pitcher. After his second single, he scored on a triple by Spider Jorgensen. On his last hit he raced all the way to third on a scratch single off the second baseman's glove. He scored again on a balk. The Royals won 14–1. Robinson had four for five, scored four times, hit a three-run homer, knocked in three more runs, and drove the Jersey City pitchers wacky with his baserunning.

The crowd could not stop cheering. In the tradition of the day, he tipped his cap after the homer before ducking into the dugout. Today, that performance would call for a standing ovation from the crowd and a magnificent curtain call in the tradition of Mets catcher Gary Carter, who punches the air with vigor for every key blow. One of the most significant events of the day occurred after his home run. Manager Clay Hopper of Mississippi, coaching at third, patted Jackie on the back as he rounded the base, and outfielder George Shuba of Youngstown, Ohio, warmly shook his hand.

SHUBA: "I don't know how he performed so well under that pressure. The blacks wanted him to hit every ball out of the park, and some of the Southern whites didn't want him to hit at all. I remember that homer because somebody took a picture of it and it appeared in the paper. It was the first picture of a black player being congratulated by a white player for a home run. It was a piece of history.

"Jackie was a very special person and I felt honored to have played with him at Montreal and Brooklyn. I remember when the announcement of his signing was made in 1945. I was out fishing and somebody had a radio and said Brooklyn had signed a colored player, and he would be in Montreal. It wasn't something I thought much about. I was too busy trying to make my own way in baseball. We started out training that spring in Sanford and then went to Daytona, and it didn't take long to see Jackie was a fine athlete. He was pretty quiet at first, but by the end of spring training he was warming up to the guys and they were warming up to him. He used to come out every morning in a cab from where he was staying, and I don't ever remember asking him about it. Those kind of things just weren't discussed. We talked about what went on in the ballpark, not what happened before or after the workout or the game.

"Then we got to Montreal, and I think Jackie and Rachel got an apartment downtown. I used to ride the trolley out from downtown to the ballpark, maybe a nickel or so, and one day Jackie and Rachel ran after the streetcar as it was leaving. She was a gorgeous girl, and they seemed to get on together so well, laughing and talking together, with much affection. When he hit that homer opening day, and I shook his hand, we looked at the picture in the paper the next day and he saw it and just said, 'Thanks, George,' and I didn't even realize what he was thanking me for. I guess later on it dawned on me that he wasn't sure if any of the players would shake his hand or just make him uncomfortable at the plate. There wasn't anything to think about. He hit a home run for our team, he helped us win, and that was all there was to it.

"There were a lot more problems and incidents in Brooklyn and around the National League when he joined the Dodgers. There wasn't much of that in Montreal that I can remember. He was just a wonderful player there, did a grand job with that club, and earned that chance to make it to the Dodgers the next season.

I guess there is no question Jackie Robinson earned everything he got up there."

In some few weeks Robinson settled into a successful pattern with the Royals. He was hitting the ball hard and often. He kept his average above .340 most of the first half of the season. He was a line-drive hitter with good power to all fields. He was not, as Bob Feller had suggested, "tied up in the shoulders." He could get around on the fastball and he could wait on the curve. He had some trouble with off-speed pitching, but few in the International League could take advantage of that minor failing. His glove was smooth. He had played shortstop for Kansas City and was having some trouble adjusting to the intricacies of second base in Montreal. He needed help on his footing around the bag. He got help from his teammate, Al Campanis.

Campanis was a twenty-nine-year-old journeyman infielder with the Royals. He had been a football star at New York University and a baseball player of some note. Born in Kos, Greece, Campanis had arrived as a youngster with his family in New York. He grew up on Manhattan's West Side. He attended NYU before the Second World War, entered service, played part of the 1943 season in Brooklyn, and drifted back to the minors by 1946. Rickey saw some special ingredients in this intelligent youngster and watched him closely. Campanis helped the Dodgers immeasurably when he helped Jackie Robinson.

CAMPANIS: "I was the shortstop when he broke in as the second baseman. He hadn't played a lot of baseball. You could see that. He was a bit awkward around second base, but he was such a good athlete he seemed to pick things up easily. He got cut a couple of times, but he wouldn't budge. The blood ran through his socks once, and I came up to him after the game. 'I think I can help on the double play.' He said he would appreciate that. I told him to come out early the next day and we would work together.

"He was a fast learner. I taught him how to straddle the bag. I taught him how to pivot away from the base and throw. We worked on getting rid of the ball more quickly from his blind side. He became better and better and more confident as the season went on. Jack was also a very strong athlete. He could plant that leg and throw and the runner might hit it and just bounce off. This guy had played a lot of football and body contact was not upsetting to him.

"There were a few incidents from opposing benches. In the beginning the guys from the South weren't terribly friendly, but they came to respect him as a player. How could you not respect him? He played hard, all out, very smart baseball and was a winner. That's the biggest thing to remember about Jackie Robinson. He was one heck of a competitor. He wanted to win.

"There would be some name-calling from the opposing side, and when it got bad we would just holler back for him. Jackie never said a word, but a few of our guys—Herman Franks, Lew Riggs, Johnny Jorgensen, Dixie Howell—we raised some hell with the opposition. I used to let them yell a little, and then I would yell back. 'You wanna pick on somebody, pick on me.' They would yell, 'We don't have anything against you.' It was all ridiculous.

"In later years, after I went to work in the front office with the Dodgers (he is now the team's general manager), I was always proud that Jackie Robinson would tell people that I had helped him in Montreal. He didn't need a lot of help because he was a wonderful player. He was certainly the most exciting base runner I have ever seen. There was nothing more thrilling than watching Jackie in a rundown, the way he shifted back and forth. The fans in Montreal loved him and loved his adventurousness on the bases. Watching Jackie Robinson take a lead off third base was one of the most entertaining things any baseball fan could ever witness.

"We always feel that Jackie is part of the Dodger organization. His memory is with us, and there are photos of him all over Dodgertown in Vero Beach. We don't want anyone to forget Jackie Robinson. There is a Jackie Robinson drive in Vero Beach along with the streets named for Sandy Koufax and Pee Wee Reese and Don Drysdale and all our great players."

The crowds were almost universally friendly in Montreal and encouraging in most other International League towns. His most difficult visiting city was Baltimore, a border town in Maryland, but more Southern in its ways than many cities much further south. Spider Jorgensen, a third baseman on that team and later a teammate at Brooklyn, recalls one bad experience in Baltimore.

JORGENSEN: "Jackie was playing second and a slow grounder was hit to shortstop. The relay was slow, and Jackie was on the base and cut down. His legs were all bloody. He stayed in the game and a couple of innings later the guy who cut him was involved in a tough play at the plate. Herman Franks tagged him out on his head and it looked like a fight would follow but the umpires intervened and it remained quiet. The fans did some howling.

"When the game ended, Jackie was dressing in the clubhouse, and a couple of big guys were pounding on the door of the clubhouse yelling, 'C'mon out, you black bastard.' It was real ugly, and everybody was afraid of a scene. We just told Jackie to stay in the clubhouse and we would get the park guards to take care of these guys. I can't remember exactly what happened, but it finally quieted down and Jackie was able to leave. We still didn't want him walking those streets by himself. In those days we used to share cabs back to the hotel, and I got on one side of Jackie and Marv Rackley, an outfielder from down South, got on the other side of Jackie, and we escorted him to the cab and back to the hotel. I don't know if Jackie was afraid, but I sure as hell was.

"I'm from California and I had played with lots of black players around home before I went to Montreal. I was never bothered by it. If the man could play, he could play. Who was I to say who could play baseball and who couldn't? Everybody knows the pressure Jackie was under from the incidents, the name-calling from the stands, the crazy letters he got, all that stuff. More than that was the pressure to play well because the whole world was watching. That's what made it really rough. There was no such thing as just have a good day or a bad day on the field. Everything was measured against history."

Minor-league players are most ambitious for their own careers. Regardless of what personal animosity or racism they may have felt toward Robinson, very little of it was articulated that first season. Tom Tatum, an outfielder from Boyd, Texas, seemed typical of the attitude of Robinson's Montreal teammates. He is recently retired from the insurance business in Oklahoma.

TATUM: "You could see that Jackie was a battler from the beginning, and I think that impressed me the most. He was hit a lot at second and thrown at when he was at the plate and heard all kinds of things from the stands, but he just kept playing hard. He was sort of a loner in the early days, and I could understand that. A lot of guys were just holding back to see how things went. As the season went on we got more friendly, and I got to know him more as a person. He was a very strong man, on and off the field.

"We had a great year with that club and we won the pennant and the playoffs and then went down to Louisville to play in the Little World Series. He took a lot of abuse down there from the fans—booing, name-calling, people around the hotel yelling at him, just a lot of garbage. I think it made us more determined to win. We stood together and it helped us overcome a lot.

"I remember when we got back from Louisville after the series down there, and the snow was piled high on the ground at the stadium in Montreal. I think Jack was fascinated by that. He probably hadn't ever seen snow before. He certainly hadn't played in it, not any of us had.

"Jackie was a tremendous baseball player. I think if he was playing today, the way they let these guys run he would steal a hundred bases every year, maybe a hundred and fifty. There was nobody on the bases in baseball like Jackie Robinson, nobody.

"I remember when I got up to Brooklyn with him in 1947, and then I got traded to Cincinnati and I beat the Dodgers in a game with a home run. I accidently met Jackie in the hotel lobby where the Dodgers were staying, and we kidded about those Montreal days. I reminded him of how those fans in Montreal would yell for him in French and that was always fun to listen to that enthusiasm. Jackie Robinson was responsible for bringing out a lot of baseball enthusiasm everywhere he went, but Montreal was certainly one of the most thrilling. It has to be exciting when fans are standing up and cheering for you in two languages the way they did for Jackie Robinson."

Robinson, despite the burdens he carried, despite the focus of so many eyes on and off the field, had a dream year with the Royals. He won the batting title with a .349 mark. He was the defensive leader of the Royals with a .985 fielding average. He led the league in runs scored with 113. He terrified pitchers and catchers with his antics on the bases. He developed the bunt into a personal art form. Because of injuries, mostly to his legs from challenging runners, he played in only 124 games. Still, he was the force on the best team in the International League—one of the best minor league teams of all time. They won the pennant by 19½ games. The Montreal Royals of 1946 had earned a place in baseball history because of their collective skills, their poise, and their performance under pressure. The Royals had proven without a doubt that a black man could play on a white professional baseball team without the world coming to an end.

*Robinson family, shortly after arrival in
Pasadena: Mack, Jack, Edgar, Willa Mae, and
Frank, with their mother, Mallie Robinson*

House at 121 Pepper Street, Pasadena, California

Basketball star at Pasadena Junior College

Above: *football star at UCLA*
Opposite: *basketball star at UCLA*

Baseball star at UCLA

Lieutenant Jack Robinson

*Jackie in his rookie season
with the Brooklyn Dodgers*

Star of the film
The Jackie Robinson Story

*When Jackie stole home it
was a baseball thrill.*

*Rookie of the Year honors
at Ebbets Field*

Duke Snider refused to sign "anti-Robinson" petition.

Dodger Captain Pee Wee Reese, gentleman from Louisville, befriended Robinson early on.

*Hall of Fame great
Hank Greenberg
of Pittsburgh was
sympathetic to
Jackie's plight.*

*"Spahn and Sain and
Pray for Rain." Spahn
was tough on Jack's
base-running tricks.*

*Carl Furillo changed
his mind about Jackie
after he saw him play.*

*Bob Feller of the
Indians didn't think
Jackie could make it.*

Stan ''The Man'' Musial wanted no part
of the Cardinal's racist rebellion.

The Brooklyn infield of 1947 with Spider Jorgensen,
Eddie Stanky, Pee Wee Reese, and Robinson

CHAPTER

Six

THE BOYS
OF BROOKLYN

RACISM. ON PAGE 1184 OF THE
Random House Dictionary of the English Language it is defined
as "a belief that human races have distinctive characteristics that
determine their respective cultures, usually involving the idea
that one's own race is superior and has the right to rule others."
For some, it is an emotion more significant than the drive for sex,
money, or power. In the famed Broadway musical *South Pacific*,
Rodgers and Hammerstein wrote, "You've got to be taught how
to hate." [If so, the teaching begins at the stage of a toddler.] It
defies logic. It erodes reason. It cuts across economic, social, and
intellectual lines. It appears in every aspect of human life.

Racism takes on many forms. At its most violent, it is the
rationale for brutal murder. At its most subtle, it keeps people
from decent jobs, proper housing, healthy lives. In the South, it
was written into the legal system. In the North, it was ingrained
in the heart. It was the underlying cause of one American war.
Hundreds have been killed defending it. Hundreds more have
been killed defying it. It has been analyzed, intellectualized, and
generalized for decades. In a country more than eighty percent
white, it is the blacks who have suffered from it most. If the
population were reversed, few doubt that the whites would be the
victims. No ethnic group ever escapes it. The American South

has been most charged with it. Yet the American North has created the ugliest ghettos; those massive bastions of indelicate life, ugly homes, disease, anger, and frustration.

Decent men have made some indecent remarks regarding their attitude toward others of a different race. Clay Hopper once asked Branch Rickey, "Do you really think blacks are humans?" Alvin Dark once told sportswriter Stan Isaacs of New York's *Newsday* that, "Blacks didn't think as fast as whites, except for Willie Mays." Yankee teammates in the 1970s described Reggie Jackson as an "uppity nigger." In the baseball season of 1986 it would be fair to say that no more than a dozen white players had dinner alone with a black teammate.

The rationalization heard forty years ago for keeping Jackie Robinson out of organized baseball is still heard today. In 1986 there was no black baseball club owner, no black general manager, no black manager, no black public relations director, no black league presidents, no black baseball union full-time executives.

Blacks had proven in the forty years since Robinson that they were certainly not inferior athletic performers. It meant little off the field. Racism. Baseball was no less guilty of separate but unequal standards when it came to its postcareer hiring practices.

The impending arrival of Jackie Robinson in major-league baseball in 1947 would unleash emotions as strong as any seen in this country over the race issue in nearly a hundred years. Branch Rickey was gearing up with educational sessions in Brooklyn involving politicians, church officials, newsmen, leaders of the Negro community, and baseball executives. Robinson was winding down in Pasadena with his beautiful bride after a hectic Montreal season.

Baseball in 1947 was a semicooperative business of sixteen wealthy owners, eight in each league, bound together loosely by some never-tested laws in the awarding of franchises. No man ran a baseball franchise without understanding that financial loss might be the result. Creative bookkeeping kept many baseball executives in a lavish life-style.

These owners would meet on occasion and work out certain problems common to the game. They would then separate and attempt to get around the rules they had just written. They were, in some cases, honorable men, but they were, in all cases, competitive men. They wanted to win for money, glory, and vanity, and the bending of rules was not considered a major sin if the end result was a pennant flag and a hometown parade for the owner-hero. Robinson presented a unique dilemma. As did most white, wealthy, executive types in this country in 1947, baseball owners suffered from degrees of racism. None—except theoretically for Rickey—were completely free of it. Some were vicious about it, and the word "nigger" was heard as often around the meeting rooms of baseball owners, as in the locker rooms by their players.

They also sensed that Robinson would reach an untapped audience. The dollars of the blacks were as green as the dollars of the whites. But the arrival of Robinson would bring riffraff to the ballpark, foul odors, the bad elements, the drunks, and the rowdies. Niggers. Their beautiful, clean, famous old ballparks would be filled with niggers. When they rented out these same famous old parks for Negro league games at high fees, they never minded niggers in their parks. They themselves would not be there and on Monday morning the dollars would all smell clean.

Baseball had a single executive leader from 1920 to 1944, a former Federal court judge named Kenesaw Mountain Landis, an arrogant, pretentious, white-haired, officious jurist who had achieved incredible power as commissioner of baseball. His overall record in the game was a positive one. He rescued baseball from the scourge of the Black Sox scandal and made integrity synonymous with the game. He watched over contract violations and freed many players if he felt they were being secreted away by the conniving owners. He opened baseball to radio and television. He encouraged promotional features. He had one major blind spot. He was a racist. He would do nothing to encourage supporters of blacks in the game.

Landis died in 1944, and he was succeeded by a Kentucky politician named Albert B. Chandler. He lasted as commissioner from 1945 through 1951. Whether through any action or inaction on his part, blacks entered baseball as full-time playing partners. He also established the ground rules for a baseball pension. Last July 14—Bastille Day he points out—A. B. (Happy) Chandler, the ebullient former governor and United States senator from Kentucky and the second commissioner of baseball, celebrated his eighty-eighth birthday. Sound of mind and strong in will, Chandler may specialize in revisionist history in 1986, but he still feels he is one of the most significant figures in the arrival of Jackie Robinson on the baseball scene. He does not pretend he encouraged Branch Rickey to search the Negro leagues for a black baseball player, but he contends he was the commissioner and no such move ever could have occurred without his approval, active or implied.

CHANDLER: "Any time there was a hint of a black player being brought into the game, Landis had a standard answer. I've read the minutes of many meetings. Landis said, 'I've said everything that's going to be said on that subject. The answer is no.' Then he would move on to new business.

"Robinson had that great year in Montreal, and we all knew he would be moving up to the big leagues. Rickey was a little concerned about the reaction of his fellow owners. There was a secret meeting called by the owners. It was held in New York at the Waldorf-Astoria Hotel. No minutes were taken at that meeting. It was held for the purpose of letting the other owners know what Rickey was planning to do. I remember the meeting as if it was held yesterday. I'm eighty-eight years old, but I happen to be blessed with a very accurate memory. I can't say I can recall the exact comments of all the owners at the meeting. I can say I am very sure of the tone of the meeting. The owners were against Rickey doing this thing, and they implored him to forget the whole idea.

"He talked for a good long while about how bringing a Negro boy into the game was just the right thing to do and how Jackie Robinson had earned his chance by the fine year he had in Montreal and how he was going to bring him up that spring. There was a resolution of support proposed by Rickey. He wanted the owners to go on record as saying they endorsed his plan and would go along with it. I don't think he was looking for any help, but he was looking to see that his fellow owners would not get in his way.

"The vote was finally taken after a lot of talk and it was 15–1 against Rickey. I was at the head of this big table in one of the large meeting rooms at the hotel. I read the votes one by one and all of them were no votes except that single yes vote in Rickey's hand. He was very angry, and he got up and walked out of the meeting room.

"Babe Ruth was quite ill then, and I stayed in New York another day or so and I went to visit him. He was very grateful, and I told him I would do whatever I could for him. We arranged to have a day for him at Yankee Stadium with all sorts of other ceremonies honoring the Babe around baseball. I know he was very proud of that.

"I went home to Versailles, and a couple of days after the meeting in New York I got a call from Rickey. He said he was very bothered by the vote of his fellow owners and said he was concerned about the situation now more than ever. I told him to come down to Versailles and we would talk about it some more. We went out in my cabin and discussed the case for many hours. Rickey was as emotional as I had ever seen him. He said he didn't know if he could do this in light of the opposition of his partners. He said, on the other hand, Negro people expected Robinson to be brought up. 'There will be riots in Harlem,' he said, if he didn't do it. He also expressed fear there would be fires in Ebbets Field and in the Polo Grounds, and he also said his partners said there would be riots between blacks and whites in their parks if he did it.

"We talked back and forth for a long time about it, and he said he was also upset about the reaction of some of his players. He thought they were fair-minded gentlemen and would realize Robinson deserved a chance the same as anybody else. He was especially upset about something he had read about Dixie Walker. I think he respected Dixie very much, and he was one of his favorite players. Rickey looked at me with lots of emotion and said, 'I read where Dixie Walker says he will stay home and paint his house if I bring a Negro player to camp.' Then he asked me what I would do about all this. I told him he could do what he wanted with his ballplayers, same as everybody else, and if he brought Jackie Robinson up, he would be treated the same as anybody else. I think that is all he wanted to hear.

[91]

"I wasn't present when the Lord gave out colors, but I told Rickey I had been a senator from Kentucky on the Senate Military Affairs Committee during the war, and I knew a lot about the casualties during the war. Plenty of Negro boys had offered to fight and die for this country in those days, and if they couldn't engage in baseball after the war that just wasn't right.

"I told him to bring him in if he wanted, and I would have somebody from my office monitor every game, and if any other club made trouble for Robinson I would take action. I sent John Demoise from my office to every Dodger game with Robinson early in the season, and he gave me detailed reports of what was going on, and if his reports suggested things were not being done fairly I talked to the people responsible.

"I knew the history of the Negro situation in baseball before my time, and I knew how much Landis wanted to make sure they never entered the game. I didn't have to think very hard about what I did then because I knew it was right. When I meet my Maker I don't want to have to sit down and explain why I kept some people from playing baseball because of their skin color. If the Lord made some people black and some people white and some people yellow, he must have had a pretty good reason. It wasn't my job to decide who could play baseball and who couldn't. It was my job to see that the game was played fairly and that everybody had an equal chance. I think I did that, and I can face my Maker with a clear conscience.

"I can honestly say I never ran from my responsibilities, and I did what I thought was best. It wasn't always popular with the owners, the people I worked for, and a lot of them never forgave me for it. Some owners thought I would keep Jackie Robinson out. That was bad enough that I didn't, as they saw it. Then I also got involved in the baseball pension plan, and I encouraged the players to move ahead with that and set up a meeting with the owners which resulted in the forming of the first pension committee. That cost the owners some money and also made me unpopular. It wasn't long before they started agitating not to renew my contract, and by 1951 I was out of baseball. I went back to the governor's mansion in Kentucky and served my state as best I could.

[92]

"When I got in the Hall of Fame in 1982 it was a very satisfying moment. It reinforced my feelings that I was right all along in what I did. Yes sir, I'm proud of the part I played in bringing Jackie Robinson into baseball, and I'm proud of the part I played in establishing that pension plan for ballplayers. When I face my Maker some day I can honestly say I never ran away from anything, no matter how difficult it seemed."

Buoyed by Chandler's stance, Rickey moved quickly ahead. The commissioner would not issue a public statement that he supported Rickey's move, but he would not do anything to slow it down. The promotion of minor-league players to the big-league roster had always been the right and privilege of each individual club, and Rickey understood that Chandler wanted the Robinson matter handled in the same way.

To ease the social pressures on the move and to avoid overt racism against Robinson, Rickey contracted for a training site in Havana, Cuba, in the spring of 1947. Some twelve years before the overthrow of the Batista government by Fidel Castro, Cuba was truly an island paradise. Magnificent restaurants, late-night entertainment, easy, open sex, plenty of drink, and inexpensive prices all contributed to the lush life-style so much enjoyed by baseball players. Ballplayers, for the most part, were freewheeling young men, physical, macho, anxious for off-the-field fun, and unafraid of any serious consequences. As moral, religious, and temperate as Rickey was, he tolerated the bad habits of ballplayers if they could play. While Rickey's worst curse was "Judas Priest," and his stiffest drink was a sour glass of tomato juice, he was a pragmatist. Some of the heaviest drinkers and carousers in the legendary history of baseball played for Rickey that spring of 1947, including pitchers Hugh Casey and Kirby Higbe. It was Higbe who would set off a minirevolution in the Dodger camp when he talked about a petition Dixie Walker was having signed to ban Robinson from the club.

Higbe, who died in 1985, was from Columbia, South Carolina. He was with the Cubs and the Phillies before joining the Dodgers in a major trade in 1941—a move that helped Brooklyn win its first pennant in twenty-one seasons. He was 22–9 that year. He was a handsome man with big brown eyes that some ladies found irresistible. He returned once from a road trip to St. Louis and a package arrived at his home. He was out, but his wife opened the package to find a pair of pajamas he had left back in a woman's apartment in St. Louis with an accompanying, erotic note.

"What is this?" his wife demanded as he walked in the house unawares.

Higbe carefully read the note and studied the contents.

"This isn't for me," he replied without a grin. "This is for some other Kirby Higbe."

While Higbe did his drinking with teammates, Hugh Casey— the gutsy relief pitcher who had thrown a famous pitch that bounced past catcher Mickey Owen in the 1941 World Series, allowing Tommy Henrich to reach first after the supposed last out and the Yankees eventually to win—drank with writer Ernest Hemingway. The novelist was ensconced in Cuba then and found Casey to be a fascinating bar mate. Hemingway always had an affinity for courageous athletes from ballplayers to bullfighters. Hemingway never had quite the following or fame with ballplayers that he had with the literary public. The story is told of how he once arrived at Toots Shor's New York restaurant, a hangout for sports celebrities, and was introduced to Yogi Berra, then the famed Yankee catcher.

"Yogi, I want you to meet Ernest Hemingway, the writer."

"Yeah," said Yogi, "what paper does he write for?"

Robinson arrived in Havana as a member of the Montreal Royals. Rickey had made no move over the winter to promote him to the Dodger roster, as would be normal for an International League batting champion. He had earned the privilege of training with the parent club and working his way on to the roster. Rickey thought otherwise. He wanted Robinson to perform for his future Dodger mates so ably they would clamor for his addition to the team. It is impossible to believe now, some forty years later, that a man of Rickey's baseball acumen could be so naive. Even if Robinson were white, few players would suggest he join the club. Ballplayers don't often want minor leaguers on their big roster, no matter how talented. They are concerned about their own jobs, their own salaries, their own security. They are probably the most selfish of men, made so by the pressures to hold a job and the insecurities fostered on them by ownership. On top of that, ballplayers worry about their own careers, not anybody else's. The most common cry of ballplayers is "Look out for number one." The Dodgers of 1947 were no different than the Yankees of 1957 or the Cubs of 1967 or the Cardinals of 1977 or the Mets of 1987 in that respect.

Add to that the racial dimension. The Dodger players had read all about Robinson throughout 1946. Many had played against him the previous spring. Dixie Walker had been quoted as saying he didn't care if Robinson played in the Dodger organization as long as he wasn't on the same team. A lot of the Dodgers sincerely believed that taking a shower in the same large shower room with a black ballplayer would infect and contaminate them.

Rickey, making haste slowly, set the Brooklyn Dodgers up in the elegant Hotel Nacional, a playground for the rich and famous, where a prostitute could be delivered to the room as easily as a ham sandwich. The Montreal Royals were housed at the Havana Military Academy, a sprawling school grounds complete with its own huge baseball field and populated with the wealthy sons of many Batista government officials. Jackie Robinson, Roy Campanella, Don Newcombe, and Roy Partlow, the four blacks in professional baseball, were quartered alone in a small hotel away from the downtown area of Havana. Rickey had decided not to ruffle feathers in Cuba if he did not have to. Make haste slowly. Robinson was not pleased.

"I thought we left Florida to train in Cuba so we could get away from Jim Crow," Robinson told traveling secretary Harold Parrot, the man in charge of hotel arrangements. "So what the devil is this business of segregating the Negro players in a colored nation, Cuba."

Parrot explained to Jackie that it was Rickey's idea. He didn't want any incidents in the team hotel with other players. "Well, I don't like segregation but I'll go along with Mr. Rickey's judgment. He's been right so far," Robinson said.

Rickey seemed overly cautious. The Hotel Nacional was as integrated as a hotel could be with wealthy men from around the world, including many black Cubans and many other dark-skinned men from Asia and Africa, staying in its magnificent quarters. But Robinson went along with the program.

There were two major aspects to that first spring with the Dodgers in Havana. First off, Robinson was having his position shifted to first base. Secondly, some Dodger players, led by a Southern contingent including Walker, Higbe, Casey, Ed Head, and Bobby Bragan, were moving openly toward a confrontation with Rickey and Dodger manager Leo Durocher over Robinson.

Robinson knew little of the Dodger petition. It was taking place after workout hours, sometimes in the Nacional bar, sometimes in more sleazy places in Havana's night scene. Robinson knew a lot about the first-base situation. He didn't care for it very much. He had worked hard to become a skilled second baseman after being a shortstop with the Kansas City Monarchs. Another move, on top of all the given pressures of the situation, was not to his liking. General Manager Mel Jones of the Royals handed Robinson a first baseman's mitt on the day he reported.

"What is this?" asked Robinson.

"Manager Hopper will explain it later," he said.

Rickey had decided, along with Durocher, that Robinson's best chance to help the Brooklyn club was at first base. Durocher felt Howard Schultz, the big right-handed slugger—more renowned back home in Minnesota as a college basketball player—and Ed Stevens, a left-handed hitter, could not do the job. He had Eddie Stanky for second base, Pee Wee Reese at shortstop, and Spider Jorgensen for third. The only opening was at first. That's where Durocher wanted Robinson.

Jones instructed Hopper to have Robinson practice at first base while he played second in the games. George Sisler, a Dodger scout and a Hall of Fame first baseman, worked around the bag with Robinson. Robinson was being worked very hard to learn the new position. He also suffered from a sore toe and stomach troubles. His enthusiasm was significantly missing in the early days of spring training in contrast to the excitement he showed in 1946.

The Dodgers had flown from Cuba to Panama to play three exhibition games in that small country against their Montreal farm club. Robinson would be unveiled as a first baseman there. Rickey's hope was for the Dodger players to come clamoring to his hotel door, demanding Robinson's addition to the club. Fat chance.

The anti-Robinson petition, drawn up by Walker in concert with some of the others, was beginning to move clandestinely around the club. This was a dangerous situation because Walker, the veteran outfielder, was considered the team leader despite the title of captain bestowed on Pee Wee Reese. Almost single-handedly, Walker had kept interest high in Brooklyn baseball through the war years. He had won the league batting title with a .357 mark in 1944 as the team finished next to last, severely depleted by the loss of most of the best players to military service. Walker, deferred by a punctured eardrum, was the biggest hero in Brooklyn, rattling line drives off the scoreboard in Ebbets Field, hitting a career high thirteen homers—many of them over the fence into Bedford Avenue and across the street to a parking garage and service station—and earning the ultimate Brooklyn accolade: an inspirational nickname. Walker was called the People's Choice (in Brooklyn it was pronounced People's Cherce). Along with Casey Stengel, Babe Herman, Pee Wee Reese, and Pete Reiser, Walker was probably one of the most popular players to wear the blue Dodger cap up to that time.

Born in Villa Rica, Georgia, and raised in Birmingham, Alabama, Walker, then thirty-six, was an influential member of the team often consulted by Rickey on player deals. He had bounced around with the Yankees, White Sox, and Tigers before coming to Brooklyn. A sore arm had plagued him for several seasons, but once he breathed the clean Brooklyn air, he seemed to be rejuvenated. He hit .311 in the Dodgers' pennant-winning season of 1941 and would finish his eighteen-year career with a .306 lifetime mark. His father, also known as Dixie, and his Uncle Ernie, had played in the big leagues before him. His brother, Harry, had been a star with the St. Louis Cardinals and went on to win the 1947 batting title with the Cards and Phillies. Walker asked Higbe to sign the petition. Higbe decided to think about it. He visited his favorite local night spot in Panama and thought and thought. Harold Parrot was in the same bar. Higbe, his loyalty to the Dodgers severely tested, confided to Parrot, "Ol' Hig just won't do it. The old man [Rickey] has been fair to Ol' Hig. Ol' Hig ain't going to join any petition to keep anybody off the club."

Parrot reported what he had heard to Durocher. The manager, known as a guy who would knock down his mother if he thought it would help him win, exploded. He had two major reasons for his conduct, neither of which had to do with Robinson's color.

Durocher wanted the best team he could put on the field. To his thinking, a Dodger team with Jackie Robinson at first base was the best he could do.

Durocher was also aroused to anger by the idea that any-body—Rickey, reporters, and certainly not his own players—would tell him what to do. Durocher, a man of action, went forth to do battle.

Leo Durocher was a well-known pool hustler from Spring-field, Massachusetts—a bon vivant and slick-fielding shortstop for the Yankees, Reds, Cards, and Dodgers. He was also the creator of the Gashouse Gang identity of the Cards of the 1930s. He would later be immortalized in Bartlett's Quotations by his saying "Nice guys finish last." His fame came as a manager for the Dodgers, Giants, and Chicago Cubs. He is eighty-one now, lives in Palm Springs, California, counts Frank Sinatra and other show business names as close pals, and shoots from the hip, as he always did.

DUROCHER: "If I go to war I want Jackie Robinson on my side. What a competitor. What a fighter. Sure we had our feuds, because he wanted to win and I wanted to win. It was never racial. That garbage didn't mean anything to me. I had no trouble with him in Brooklyn when we wore the same uniform. I had a lot of trouble with him when I went over to the Giants and we wore different uniforms.

"About that session in Panama you're talking about, yeah, I got the players together after I heard about that damn petition, and I told them what they could do with their petition, and I don't think I got much back talk on it. I told the players that Robinson was going to open the season with us come hell or high water, and if they didn't like it they could leave now and we'd trade them or get rid of them some other way. Nobody moved. I just told them nobody could tell me who to play and who not to play, and if any of them thought they could they were in for a hell of a shock.

"I was suspended by Chandler before the season started, so I didn't see Robinson in 1947 except on television. He looked like a hell of a player to me. Then I came back in 1948, and he was much heavier than he had been in 1947, and he wasn't going to be able to run and stay strong with all that weight. He said, 'Leo, I'm 195, 200, the same as I was last year,' and I said 'The hell you are. Let's get on a scale because the scale don't lie,' and when he did it didn't stop until it got to 215, and then he started losing weight. It took him a long time which is why he wasn't the player early that year as he was later on when he got in shape.

"By the time I got over to the Giants we recognized how tough he was. I agitated him a little, and he agitated me back. He said some personal things about my wife [Laraine Day] and the Hollywood crowd and things like that, and we got hot a few times. Managers used to coach at third in those days, and I would yell things at him and he would yell back all game long. We didn't like each other because we were competitors on different sides.

"I respected Jackie Robinson, and I never questioned his integrity or dedication to the game. He was one hell of a player and he could play for me any time. As far as his standing in the game, he wasn't no Willie Mays. Willie was the best that ever lived. It's hard to judge ballplayers in different times, but I always liked DiMaggio and Musial and Clemente, and Willie, like I said, would be the first guy. Jackie wasn't in their class. Just say he was damn good, and he was one hell of a battler.

"The game was just tougher then, too. Now they don't play as hard with the big salaries and all. That's why I don't miss it. I remember once I was with the Cards and playing for Frankie Frisch, and a ground ball off the infield split the skin between my thumb and my forefinger. I had twelve stitches in it, and when I got back to the ballpark after being in the hospital, Frisch told me to spit some tobacco juice in it because I was in there the next day. The damn thing was still bleeding the next day, so he let me sit it out; but I was in there two days after it happened, and I don't think you would see that kind of thing now. That's twenty days on the disabled list for sure.

"A lot of things were written about me and Jackie through the years and not all of them true. They said I threw at him, and I had Alvin Dark go after him on a slide. That was part of the game, just trying to win. How about Jackie knocking my little second baseman, Davey Williams, out of a baseball game with a body block. That was part of the game, too. Jackie Robinson was tough and hard-nosed and a complete player, and I admired the hell out of him."

After Durocher met with the entire team and scolded them about their conduct, Rickey moved quickly. He took on the ring leaders of the petition in a heated hotel session. Emotions were running high. Most of the players—Walker, Casey, Ed Head, Higbe, Carl Furillo, a hotheaded Pennsylvanian who had been dragged along into the anti-Robinson group without much conviction, and Bobby Bragan—were determined to have their positions heard. Other Southerners, Ed Stanky, Pee Wee Reese, and Clyde King, stayed out of the petition problem, concentrating instead, as the others should have been, on preparing for the season. Some players—Ralph Branca, Joe Hatten, Hank Behrman, and Spider Jorgensen—claim now they never heard of the petition. Gene Hermanski, Arky Vaughan, and Pete Reiser knew about the petition but did not take it seriously.

Rickey was a radical revolutionary in the matter of Jackie Robinson. For some of these players, especially the ones from the Deep South, the matter was almost as emotional an experience as they had ever dealt with in their lives. They lived by the racial clichés of the time. They thought of blacks as slaves, a generation removed: maids, porters, local laborers, shiftless, dirty, unintelligent. Aged blacks were always called "boy" by most Southerners and were treated by whites as children. Dixie Walker was as kind, decent and gentle a man as ever played baseball. In his own heart he saw no question of hatred in the Robinson matter. He saw only culture and custom. He was a

God-fearing man who saw the separation of the races as part of the divine order. He never expressed any indication of violent behavior. He simply didn't want Robinson in the same locker room, the same shower, the same hotel, the same taxicab, or on the same team. Much of racism, sociologists explain, is based on sexual fears: fears of a black raping a white woman, marrying a daughter, ravishing a wife. Forty years after Jackie Robinson, much of the so-called baseball humor between blacks and whites, in a more tolerant time, revolves around sex.

All of the players on the Dodgers in 1947, especially the Southern players, carried this baggage with them. It was only a little more than eighty years after the end of the Civil War, and many of these players had heard tales of slave days from elderly parents and grandparents. Racism was close to their being.

Of all the participants in Rickey's lecture on equality, Americanism, fair play, and Jackie Robinson in March of 1947 in Panama, only Bobby Bragan survives.

Bobby Bragan, sixty-nine years old, is an executive with the Texas Rangers baseball team in Arlington, Texas. He was born and raised in Birmingham, Alabama, broke into the big leagues with the Phillies in 1940, came to the Dodger organization in 1943, and was a backup catcher to Bruce Edwards in 1947. He also could play short, second, or third. Bragan is a very intelligent baseball man, a former manager, a witty speaker, and a marvelous storyteller. He was a feisty player and later a combative manager.

BRAGAN: "I grew up in Birmingham. I'm one of seven boys and two girls. My father worked as a local contractor, and his biggest jobs were building streets in town where only dirt paths existed. He used blacks to do a lot of the manual labor on the jobs. They were good workers, and he paid them a fair salary. At the end of the week they would come to the back door of our house and get paid. They were friendly and I got along with them when I was a kid, but they never came to the front door. That was the custom of the times. Everybody understood the rules.

"There was one black in my youth, a quiet man named Frank, who did come into the house. He came to the back door, and I would greet him after school, and he would teach me piano.

I would have a lesson two or three times a week. I got to be very good. I didn't know where my folks met him, but he taught several of us to play. I still can play the piano and enjoy singing and did a lot of entertaining of my teammates in the old days in spring training whenever I could find a piano.

"With all that background of my upbringing, you could imagine what a shock it was for me when I found out Jackie Robinson was going to be on our ball club. I didn't have anything personal against Jackie Robinson. I didn't know the man. I just felt my upbringing, my attitude, would not allow me to play on the same team with him. The guys started talking about it. Dixie got up this petition, and we all thought about what to say. I can't actually remember what it said. The Southern players were the ones who were the leaders in this, but I can honestly say I heard a lot of the other players, the guys from the North, say one time or another that spring, 'I'm not playing with a nigger. They can't make me play with a nigger.' It got out that it was four or five Southern players, but I think it was much more than half the ball club felt the same way.

"Anyway, we got ushered into Rickey's room, and he reads the riot act to us. I told him how I felt, that I didn't feel I could play with a black ballplayer, and that if need be, he could trade me. There were several players involved, and one way or another they seemed to give in to Rickey. I stood up to him. I repeated how I felt. I told him I just didn't feel comfortable playing with a black and didn't want to do it. I also told him I didn't want to be the scapegoat in this episode, and if he traded me I wouldn't take all the blame. I would tell the press I thought other Dodgers felt the same way. Rickey understood my feelings clearly and that was it.

"I stayed with the Dodgers, and I think I gained some respect in Mr. Rickey's eyes. He didn't agree with my position but he understood me. He paid me the ultimate compliment when he hired me after my playing days were over to work in the Dodger farm system.

"Those early days were awfully tough on Jackie. I remember times on the train when nobody would sit with him or talk with him. Pee Wee always seemed to be the first to break the tension.

He kidded Jackie before anybody else did and made him a part of the team. He was probably the first Dodger to have a meal with him off the field. Pee Wee was a real leader on our club, and when he started being friendly with Jackie, everybody started being friendly. In the beginning Jackie was alone at the dining table. By the middle of the year you couldn't get a seat at the dining table with him, there were so many guys.

"When I was a manager in the Dodger organization I helped Tommy Davis, and later on I really worked hard with Maury Wills. I made him into a switch hitter, and he got to the majors and became the great base stealer and fine player he was. I'm very proud of that.

"Jackie was a great player, a Hall of Famer, of course, and an outstanding man. He was the only player I ever saw in a rundown who would be safe more often than out. He ran as if his head was on a swizzle, back and forth, back and froth, until he could get out of it.

"In 1965 I went to Mr. Rickey's funeral in St. Louis, and I sat next to Jackie Robinson in that church. We shook hands warmly. I don't think either of us thought anything of it, or of the past. It was a new time. I changed. Jackie changed. The world changed."

Robinson continued to work out at first base before games that spring, to play second base in the games against the Dodgers, to hit hard and run well, and clearly to earn a spot on the big team.

While Rickey considered the best method of bringing Robinson to Brooklyn, he lost his manager. Leo Durocher—involved all spring in a controversy surrounding two alleged gamblers, his former boss Larry MacPhail, and actor George Raft—was being hit hard in the papers almost daily. He also suffered some bad publicity as a result of his marriage to actress Laraine Day. His pugnacious personality exacerbated the situation with damaging statements in the press. Finally, Commissioner Chandler, forced to choose between Rickey and MacPhail in this battle over alleged gamblers who supposedly knew Durocher, settled the question by suspending Durocher for "conduct detrimental to baseball," one of the loosest definitions of a crime with one of the strongest penalties. It shocked Rickey, upset the Dodger scheme of things, and actually lessened the impact of Rickey's move the next day when he told Robinson he would be on the ball club.

The Dodgers and Yankees traditionally played a three-game series at Yankee Stadium and Ebbets Field before the season. To some Brooklyn fans this was almost as important as beating the Giants.

In the sixth inning of a game between the Dodgers and their Montreal farm club, on April 10, Robinson bunted back to the mound, into a double play. At that instant, his Montreal teammates had been informed of the move. They applauded as the chagrined Robinson returned to the bench. He would finish out the game as a member of the Royals and then pack his baseball belongings and move over to the Dodger clubhouse at Ebbets Field for the series against the Yankees.

Clubhouse man Babe Hamburger assigned Robinson uniform number 42 when he reported the next morning, gave him a locker in the middle of the right side of the clubhouse between Ralph Branca and Gene Hermanski, and showed him where to lock up his valuables.

Jackie Robinson, Negro, was a Brooklyn Dodger.

CHAPTER

Seven

EARLY
DODGER DAYS

*C*ASEY STENGEL, THAT NOTED elocutionist, managed the Brooklyn Dodgers for three years. He was later paid almost as much not to manage the Brooklyn Dodgers for one year. That's the way things seemed to be done in Brooklyn. "Brooklyn was the borough of churches and bad ball clubs, many of which I had," Stengel said years after his Brooklyn tour.

New York was divided into five boroughs, separate and unequal. Only Queens, now the home of the New York Mets, and Staten Island did not have a major-league team from 1923—when the Yankees moved into Yankee Stadium in the Bronx—until 1957, when the Brooklyn Dodgers moved out of Ebbets Field to Los Angeles and the New York Giants moved out of the Polo Grounds to San Francisco.

Brooklyn fans were the most passionate. Few could identify with the lordly success of the Yankees from the time Babe Ruth arrived in 1920 to the time Mickey Mantle departed in 1969. The Giants, under John McGraw, were almost as equally successful. They were also arrogant, as exemplified by manager Bill Terry's crack about the Dodgers in a hot pennant race. "Brooklyn. Is Brooklyn still in the league?" he asked. What joy when Stengel's Dodgers knocked his Giants out of a pennant.

To most people growing up in New York in the 1930s and

1940s, the city meant Manhattan. "I'm goin' to the city," a Brooklyn kid would tell his parents before boarding the BMT for a movie in Manhattan; a chance to see the Roxy, the Strand, or the Paramount; a chance to listen to the skinny singer, Sinatra, in person or hear the big bands or walk those famous streets mentioned on the radio.

The only Brooklyn streets mentioned on the radio were Bedford Avenue, the border street to the right-field wall in Ebbets Field, and Montague Street, where the Dodgers maintained their offices. Brooklyn baseball was a symbol of enormous status. The Dodgers had been a bad ball club from 1920 through 1940. They won in 1941, and the corner was turned. Everybody was in love with 'Dem Bums, the euphemism for the Dodgers, used only by Dodger fans. For a Giants fan to call them Bums was derision and cause for fisticuffs from Flatbush to Bensonhurst, from Williamsburg to Bay Ridge.

All Brooklyn felt protective of the Dodgers. The park was small and intimate. The team was often populated by strange or rowdy players from Babe Herman to Leo Durocher, from Dazzy Vance to Van Lingle Mungo. The many New York and Brooklyn newspapers covered the team thoroughly. The Brooklyn Dodgers were a link between all the people in the borough, a source of enormous pride and togetherness, a catharsis that soothed all ills.

In lower-middle-class Bensonhurst and East Flatbush where I grew up, kids imitated the stance of Dixie Walker in stickball games or argued the merits of Pee Wee Reese against Phil Rizzuto or packed salami sandwiches and pickles for a Dodger game. The Dodgers were a magical bond that tied some two and a half million people together as a family. In my neighborhood it was simple. You were a Dodger fan or a dope.

On April 10, 1947, Jackie Robinson was given his Dodger blue cap with the large white letter *B*. His uniform fit loosely as they all did in those days, and his face appeared in the one-column cuts in the papers, to be clipped and pasted and saved in all our scrapbooks. He was of us. We were of him. We were all Dodgers and Dodger fans. We were bonded.

I have searched my memory faithfully. I cannot remember much fuss being made in my neighborhood of the fact that our newest first baseman was, what we called then, a colored man. A Negro. A Dodger, yes. That seemed all that mattered.

There was a black man who swept up in the local drugstore and another black man who showed up on the moving truck when one of our neighborhood families would move down the street or across the block (because they had been promised one free month of rent) or a black man languishing on the street in front of the large chain grocery store, often sleeping there on lazy summer afternoons. There were no black classmates, no black police officers breaking up our stickball games, no black storekeepers, no blacks taking tickets in the neighborhood movie theater, no blacks delivering blocks of ice to the two-family homes, no black schoolteachers, and no blacks in the playgrounds where we acted out Dodger games by summer or played violent, sweaty three-man basketball all fall and winter.

Into this narrow, traditional, segregated world of small businessmen, salesmen, white-collar workers, lawyers, doctors charging half a dollar a visit, and insurance men and their housewife women and school-age children, came the black face of Jackie Robinson. For many of us in 1947, it was the first black person we recognized by name.

We knew that blacks lived mostly in Harlem, and on languid summer Sunday afternoons we might drive over the Manhattan Bridge and up the West Side of Manhattan. We would ride around Times Square by car and continue as far north as 125th Street and Seventh Avenue to drive through the area for a look at this other world. In the late 1930s or early 1940s we thought of driving to interesting sites as an entertainment we could afford. The squalor we saw was used as a point of reference. "If you don't do your math homework," my mother might say, "you will wind up living like the colored people."

The colored people. We were modern, progressive, Roosevelt democrats. We never used the term "nigger" in our set. We certainly heard it. We did nothing about it.

When Jackie Robinson arrived in Brooklyn, those few Giant fans in our neighborhood called him a nigger. "You're crazy. He's a Dodger, ain't he?" We defended him with all our might. Many of us proudly showed off a black eye or a welt on the cheek, sustained honestly in a street battle defending Jackie Robinson.

Finally, the day arrived. A new baseball season, the 1947 opener. The Dodgers had come as close to winning without winning in 1946 as a team could do. They had lost to the Cardinals in a pennant play-off with Eddie Stanky and Howard Schultz, the big home-run hitter, leaving the bases loaded in an 8–3 loss. Dodger fans knew, they just knew, that Stanky would walk to make the score 8–4 because he had walked 148 times in 1946. He was the Walking Man, his Red Barber nickname, though the papers often called him the Brat or Muggsy, two names he detested. He struck out. So did Schultz. That set the stage for the 1947 season. It was notable for many things, not the least of which, of course, was Robinson. For those less socially oriented or color conscious, it was the year baseball returned in its full flavor. The war had ended late in the 1945 season, and many of the servicemen returned for the 1946 campaign. Some still had battle fatigue and sea legs to shake. It would be 1947 before all the prewar stars would reach the full potential of their skills.

No less than six starters were ex-servicemen. Robinson, Pete Reiser, Carl Furillo, Gene Hermanski, Johnny Jorgensen, and Pee Wee Reese. Veterans Stanky, Dixie Walker, and Bruce Edwards, the catcher, were back from the successful 1946 squad.

Durocher had flown to California as a result of his suspension, and Burt Shotton—the Durocher surrogate brought in by Branch Rickey as a counterbalance to the furor of Leo—had not yet arrived. It was coincidental that Clyde Sukeforth, now a Dodger coach and the man assigned to bring Robinson to Brooklyn, was the manager on that first day Robinson's name appeared in a Brooklyn big-league box score.

Stanky led off and Robinson, playing first, batted second. Then came Reiser in center, Walker in right, Hermanski in left, Edwards catching, Jorgensen at third, Reese at shortstop, and Joe Hatten pitching.

Joe Hatten, seventy years old, is a retired letter carrier living in Shingletown, California. He was born in Bancroft, Iowa, played semipro baseball around Iowa before signing with the

Dodgers, won fourteen games with the 1946 team and seventeen in 1947. He was traded to the Cubs in the famous 1951 deal that sent Andy Pafko and Rube Walker to Brooklyn—a deal that was supposed to wrap up a Dodger pennant. He lasted in the big leagues through 1952 and played until 1960 in the minors. He then went to Bakersfield, California, and started delivering the mail as he had delivered left-handed pitches.

HATTEN: "I was excited about starting the season for Brooklyn. That was quite an honor. There wasn't much of a fuss about Jackie Robinson playing his first game. We had all followed the story in the papers, of course, and when he joined us we had played against him a lot that spring with the Montreal ball club. If there had been any petition on our club to keep him off the ball team, I didn't know anything about it. Maybe the Southern boys had something like that among themselves, but I never heard it. I wouldn't sign anything like that anyway. I was just trying to make a living, and so was everybody else.

"It wasn't anything special to play with or against black players for me. I had done that around home in those semipro leagues. I had played against everybody: those black barnstorming teams and those teams from New York like the House of David, the guys with the beards, and just about everybody else who would come through Iowa with nine guys and a few bats and balls. I didn't have any feelings one way or another about Jackie being there. If he could help us win, great. If he couldn't, they would get somebody else. That's the way it was with me and every other player.

"I think Leo really pushed hard for him. He really thought he could help us win, especially with his speed, and if you want to know the truth, when Leo got suspended I think we talked more about that than we did about Jackie."

Spahn and Sain
And Pray for Rain

That ditty was penned by a Boston sportswriter late in the 1948 season. The Boston Braves were making a run at the pennant, and the only successful starting pitchers they had were Warren

Spahn, the hard-throwing left-hander, and Johnny Sain, the curve-balling right-hander. With an occasional rain out, an occasional strong game by an extra starter, and a strong bullpen, the Braves managed to win the pennant.

Sain, sixty-nine years old now, born in Havana, Arkansas, is the pitching coach of the Atlanta Braves. He pitched for the Braves, the Yankees, and the Kansas City A's before turning to coaching and managing. He won twenty or more games four times. He was the starting pitcher for Boston on April 15, 1947, at Ebbets Field when Jackie Robinson made his big-league debut.

SAIN: "I'll tell you why I remember that game so well. I had been in the Naval Pre-Flight Program down at Chapel Hill, North Carolina, during the war, and I played on the base baseball team. One day we had a big event with a fund-raising game for the armed forces. Our base team, which had a lot of pro players, got to play a Babe Ruth all-star team. It was somewhere in the middle of 1943. Babe managed that team, and all of a sudden here he comes up to the plate. He was big then, really overweight, and I didn't want to embarrass him, so I threw two or three pitches well wide of the plate, and he just took them. Then I walked him. The crowd was a little upset that he didn't get a chance to swing, but I knew he couldn't get a real good swing off me then. Buddy Hassett was our first baseman, and I just watched as Babe walked down to first base, touched the bag, and jumped straight in the air and clicked his heels. I threw the ball over to Buddy for fun, and he tagged the Babe, but he was on the base. Then they brought in a pinch runner. That was the last time Babe Ruth ever appeared in a ball game in uniform.

"Then in 1947 I was the first pitcher to face Jackie Robinson, so I made some history again: the first to face Jackie and the last to face the Babe.

"I don't remember any commotion that first day. It was like any other opener. I can't say for sure how I pitched him because it is forty years ago, but I know I almost always threw a lot of curve balls to young hitters. I think he grounded out the first time against me."

Robinson grounded out, flied out, sacrificed, and hit into a double play that first day against the Braves in a 5–3 Brooklyn win. There were 26,623 fans in the stands, a slightly better than average opening-day crowd for Brooklyn on a cloudy, chilly April afternoon.

SAIN: "I don't remember our bench getting on him at all that day. We had a good ball club and thought we had a chance to win and didn't want to start the season with a fuss. Robinson was just another player to us, maybe another Dodger we disliked because we disliked all of them. The Giants and Dodgers were the big rivalry because of New York, but I think there was a lot of intensity in those games with Brooklyn and Boston.

"Jackie was an outstanding ballplayer. He could steal second any time he wanted. I always had trouble holding men on, and I think he got some easy steals against me. He was a tough hitter because he didn't try to hit home runs. He hit the ball where it was pitched. He liked the ball out over the plate, and I tried to pitch him inside and then give him a big curve away. He had this knack of hitting balls back up the middle, and I didn't like that very much.

"I came from a little town in Arkansas called Havana, about five-hundred people, and there were a few black families, and we all got along well. I don't remember any incidents in school down there, and I don't remember any incidents in the big leagues with Jackie Robinson. He was a real fine gentleman, and I probably would have liked him even better if he didn't hit so many balls up the middle."

Another Boston player, a witness to the conduct on the opposing bench that day, was Tommy Holmes. Holmes, seventy years old, was born in Brooklyn. He played for the Braves from 1942 through 1951. He was a teammate of Robinson's with Brooklyn in 1952. He had a lifetime .302 average. He is now director of the New York Mets amateur baseball program.

HOLMES: "Billy Southworth was our manager, and he was a very fair man. He just wanted everybody on the ball club to play hard. He didn't think bench jockeying was a big part of the game. I don't think you can have any of the stuff Jackie heard from other clubs without the manager allowing it.

[113]

"I only got into that opener as a pinch hitter, so I was on the bench all game. It didn't seem like anything special, just an opener, the same as all the others. We were excited to be starting the season after spring training, but I can't remember any discussion about playing against Jackie Robinson, the first black or anything like that. Much of that stuff seems to become important years later.

"Our pitchers probably knocked him down a few times that year, but they knocked everybody down. In those days that's the way the game was played. I think he went down once and started out for the pitcher, but Campy stepped in.

"I used to go up to Grossinger's in the wintertime for some skating and some fun in the snow. Jackie was there once and we started talking. We hadn't been good friends on the field. Nobody in a Dodger uniform was ever our friend. But he was nice around the hotel, and we chatted easily. He seemed to be different off the field, not as intense, not as competitive as he was when he put on that Dodger uniform.

"I was traded to Brooklyn in 1952 where I always wanted to be. Jackie was one of the first guys to come over and say hello. He was a leader on that team, and when he welcomed me they all welcomed me. It was an honor playing with Jackie Robinson."

From strictly a baseball perspective, what may have been the most significant aspect of the arrival of Jackie Robinson as a member of the Dodgers that April day in 1947 was his birthday. Born January 31, 1919, Jackie Robinson was twenty-eight years and seventy-six days old when he walked out of the Dodger dugout in Ebbets Field. Very few rookies ever have been older. Satchel Paige was supposedly forty-one when he was a Cleveland rookie in 1948 (and supposedly fifty-nine years and seventy-eight days when he pitched his last big-league game on September 25, 1965). But most ballplayers will break into the big leagues before their twenty-fifth birthday or not at all.

The Dodgers were rebuilding their organization from the ravages of the war years. The 1947 season would be the start of one of the most successful decades any team would experience with six pennants in ten seasons, one play-off loss in 1951 to the

Giants, and no finish worse than third. Jackie Robinson and Jackie Robinson's teams were winners.

One of the brightest stars of the great Dodger teams of the late 1940s and 1950s was Edwin Donald Snider, known throughout the baseball world by the boyhood family nickname of Duke. Duke Snider played eighteen years in the big leagues, batted .295, hit 407 home runs, was the single everyday left-handed batter on the powerful right-handed Dodger teams, and was named to baseball's Hall of Fame in 1980. He sat on the Dodger bench that April day in 1947.

SNIDER: "I don't know why everybody was making a fuss over Jackie. I broke in the same day and did not even get my name in the paper. Maybe it was because I didn't even get my name in the box score. I don't know if Jackie was nervous that day, but I was scared to death. I was twenty years old and only a couple of years out of high school. I always thought Jackie was helped by his age. He had been around. He was very mature.

"I had grown up in Compton, California, and I went to Enterprise Junior High School, and one day a few of my buddies decided to go to the USC-UCLA baseball game. This guy came walking across the field in a baseball uniform, and he was walking toward the track. We were out there fooling around, and we knew who he was. His name and picture had been in the papers a lot, and I knew it was Jackie Robinson. 'Where you going?' I asked him. 'I have to jump,' he said. 'In that uniform?' He said he was playing in a baseball game across the field, and his team had just come in from the field, and he had time to take a broad jump, and he had promised his coach he would. We asked if we could tag along and he said we could and we watched him jump. He jumped just once, wearing his baseball spikes, and won the broad jump.

"The next time I saw him was in that Dodger camp in Havana in 1947. He was with the Montreal ball club, and I had just been put on the Brooklyn roster. One night, one of our pitchers, Hugh Casey, I think, came up to me with this piece of paper and said, 'We have this petition about Robinson, read it and sign it.' I had heard some talk and I knew what it was. I didn't bother to read it. I just said, 'The guy is one of my heroes from California.

You must be kidding me.' I just walked away, and that was the last I heard about the petition.

"Jackie was the keenest competitor I ever saw in baseball. He knew he had to do well. He knew that the future of blacks in baseball depended on it. The pressure was enormous, overwhelming, unbearable at times. I don't know how he held up. I know I never could have. In the beginning, because of those promises to Rickey about behaving, he was playing with one hand tied behind his back. That wasn't Jackie. Jackie was an all-out, no-holds-barred kind of player. That was his nature. That's why those early years had to be so tough on him, when he had to take all that garbage.

"In the beginning I didn't even know where he went after games. I just noticed I didn't see him around the hotel. I figured he was out with friends, and he just showed up in the park. He was staying in those rat traps in the colored section while we were out in those fancy hotels, and that galled him. He never said anything, but you could see him seething when the guys complained how slow the room service was or how the porters lost a bag or how the asparagus wasn't just right. He would just take out that anger on the opposition.

"I remember one game we were playing against the Cubs in Chicago. Sam Jones was pitching, and we were down by a run, and he was throwing hard, and we weren't hitting him. Jackie came up, and he threw a close pitch, and Jackie started jawing at him, calling him gutless and screaming that he would beat him by himself. Jones got real hot and he hit Jackie with the next pitch. Jackie just got up laughing and jogged to first base. He couldn't hit the guy that day and now he was on base. That's all Jackie needed to turn a game around again. 'I'm gonna steal, I'm gonna steal,' he's yelling at him. Sure enough he steals second. 'I'm gonna steal third, I'm gonna steal third.' Then, in a flash, he has third stolen. By now you can fry an egg on old Sam's face, he's so mad. 'I'll steal home, I'll steal home,' and he makes one of those breaks, and Jones bounces the ball into the dirt. Jackie scores and we win the game by a run.

"After those early years Jackie was as fiery a competitor as I ever saw. He fought for everything he got. He had a bitter relationship with Leo. They were similar in a lot of ways. Leo would cut his own mother's throat to win a ball game. He knew Jackie was just as determined, and they screamed at each other a lot. I think Jackie was upset with Leo at the start of 1948 because Leo was making cracks about his weight. Leo had this way of putting you in his doghouse and burying you even if you had a good year the season before if he felt you weren't doing the job. That really angered Jackie and certainly livened up a lot of our games against the Giants.

"Jack loved any kind of competition. He was the greatest athlete ever produced in southern California, and I'm sure he could have been just as good in pro basketball or pro football if he went that way. One time we had Charles Goren, the bridge expert, come into our clubhouse before a game, and he would play a few hands of bridge. If you beat him he would give you this little button reading, ''I beat Goren in bridge,' and Jack played him one time, and I guess Jack thought he was a pretty good bridge player and wanted that button. But Goren beat him. Jack was really upset and walked on that field angry. I think he had a big day in the game but was irritated when he didn't have his button, especially when Pee Wee or Gil needled him by showing off their 'I beat Goren in bridge' buttons.

"I think the toughest part for Jack in his later years was spring training. He didn't enjoy it, and he hated the conditions. They still stayed in black hotels, and Jack found that galling. One time we played in Miami, and Jack was in the black hotel, the Sir John in Miami, and Ray Robinson, Joe Louis, and Archie Moore were staying there. Jack brought them over to the workout, and Sugar Ray suited up. He got in the batter's box, and he was bailing out before the pitch was thrown. Jackie was all over him. He yelled, 'How come you're bailing out?' and Sugar Ray yelled back, 'That thing can cut like a knife. You guys must be crazy to stand up there and take that.'

"Jack knew a lot of people and the big people all wanted to know him. Our clubhouse in Ebbets Field was a hangout for some important stars, and they would all gravitate to Jack. We had everybody in there at one time or another—General MacArthur, President Eisenhower, Vice-President Nixon,

Jonathan Winters, Danny Kaye—and they all wanted to meet Jack.

"Jack changed a little at the end. He got a little sour, and he was paying some people back. He always felt the umpires gave him a hard time, and when he was called out on a close play he would scream at them from the bench, 'I know why you called me out,' suggesting it was because he was black. Campy and Gil or Pee Wee would have to walk over and calm him down. Jackie could be stubborn about those things. I admired him so much. He was such a great competitor, such a hard-nosed player. Jackie Robinson taught me mental toughness. I don't think you can play this game, take the pressures, unless you are mentally tough. If I had that I owe it to Jackie Robinson. Nobody was mentally tougher.

"I remember the last time I saw him. We were at some banquet in New York honoring him. Bev and I came in from California, and we were at this cocktail party before the dinner, and the four of us—Jack and Rachel and me and Bev—just sat down together for a few minutes and talked about the old days and some things we remembered when we were young, and it was just so wonderful to reminisce. We kidded about some games and some of our old teammates, and Jack put his hand on my knee as I was telling some old story, and he just kept it there for a few minutes and I really felt close to him, and it was a real special moment for me. Every once in a while somebody on our team [Snider is a broadcaster for the Montreal Expos] comes up, usually a black player, Hubie Brooks or Ron LeFlore, and asks me about Jackie Robinson. I just tell them he was one hell of a player, one hell of a man."

The Dodgers had won that first 1947 game against Sain and the Braves with the black first baseman scoring his first National League run when his sacrifice bunt was messed up. First baseman Earl Torgeson hit Jackie with the throw as he attempted to advance a runner. Pete Reiser doubled off Sain for two runs and the 5–3 game. Brooklyn won again the next day as Jackie got a bunt single. He was very tight at the plate, swinging at bad pitches, and showing some of the signs of nervousness expected of any rookie, especially an elderly twenty-eight-year-old carrying around, oh, maybe fifteen million of his dark brethren on his back.

The Dodgers moved over to the Polo Grounds for a series against Mel Ott's hated Giants. If love is impossible to explain if you haven't been there, the hate between the Dodgers and Giants was even harder to explain. No player was immune. No fan was excused. It started with the first school-yard hassle in kindergarten and continued without a stop until those horrible days of 1957 when both clubs moved west. The worst day in Brooklyn history was October 3, 1951. It is too painful to spell out why.

The Giants had assembled a fine ball club under Mel Ott. The Giants manager was one of the few New York players tolerated, even admired, in Brooklyn. His story was one of those charming baseball legends. He had arrived in New York as a sixteen-year-old out of Gretna, Louisiana. His swing was so unique, his front foot thrust high in the air before uncoiling a flashing bat, that manager John McGraw, pugnacious and pompous, had placed Ott on the bench next to him to save him from some sloppy minor-league manager who would damage the natural beauty of that swing. Ott sat quietly and learned. At seventeen he played 35 games and hit .383. At eighteen, he hit .282. At nineteen he hit 18 homers and batted .322. At twenty he hit 42 homers and batted .328. What if Jackie Robinson had been allowed to sit on a big-league bench at sixteen, break in at seventeen, and have over 400 games in the big leagues before he turned twenty-one? Ott hit 511 home runs, a figure every fan in New York had memorized, was elected to the baseball Hall of Fame in 1951, and died in an automobile accident in 1958. He was called Master Melvin for his youth when he arrived and derided with that title for his gentle nature as manager of the Giants—succeeding crusty Bill Terry, McGraw's successor—in 1942.

Ott thought he could win with the powerhouse lineup he had assembled in 1947 led by Johnny Mize, Willard Marshall, Bobby Thomson, Sid Gordon, and Walker Cooper. Buddy Kerr, a gangly shortstop from Astoria, Queens, New York, was on that team. He is sixty-four years old today and is scouting for the New York Mets.

KERR: "Everybody was a home-run threat in the Polo Grounds. We had a big-hitting club but didn't have the pitching to win. The Dodgers got a new dimension out of Robinson. He was a terror when he got on base. He'd drive you crazy when he was on third base. Nobody could start and stop on the bases the way Jackie could. He had that great year in Montreal in '46 so we knew all about him.

"Ott was a Southerner, but he was a very quiet man. He didn't get on anybody, and he certainly didn't get on Jackie. I never heard one nasty word about him on our bench. We wanted to beat him because he had Brooklyn on his shirt, but it was no factor that he was a Negro. At the end of the year I got to know him a little when I barnstormed with him a bit. Charley Dressen had put together this team with Jackie, Campy, Sid Gordon, Stanky, Jim Russell, Red Barrett, Virgil Trucks, Rex Barney, Ralph Branca, and some others. We played in Brooklyn, and I made six hundred dollars for the day, and that was quite a pay day then. I played cards with Jackie, and he was good at that, too.

"In the early days we used to knock him down a lot, not because he was black, but because he was new. Who didn't go down in those days? Then after a while, Ott told us to forget it. 'I think it's the worst thing we can do. The guy is fearless.' It was a little different after Leo took over. Jackie went down again, but I never thought it was very smart. The guy was just a tough hitter, and he simply couldn't be intimidated.''

William Walker Cooper is seventy-two years old and lives in retirement in Buckner, Missouri, outside St. Louis. He ran an antiques business after retiring from baseball after the 1957 season. He played for eighteen years, mostly with the St. Louis Cardinals and the Giants. His Cardinal battery mate for several years was his older brother, Mort, who died in 1958. Walker Cooper was a brute of a man, 6 feet, 3 inches tall and 210 pounds, and the anchor on the great Cardinal teams of the early 1940s. He was sold to the Giants in 1946 for the whopping price of $175,000.

Cooper: "I remember one time after I was traded over to Boston by the Giants, and Robinson was on third base. Warren Spahn was pitching and I went to the mound. 'Now don't go into your windup with this fellow on third.' Spahn was a pretty headstrong fellow, and he told me I should go back behind the plate, and he would take his chances. Damned if he didn't go into his windup, and Robinson stole home on the first pitch. I don't think Spahn ever did that again.

"Jackie took a lot of heat from a lot of people in those days, but he had courage, had a big heart, and just kept playing ball. I think after a while you just had to admire him, no matter what your feelings were about the black and white thing. He was just one terrific player. He was tough, he was fast, and he was smart. That's a pretty good combination for a ballplayer."

The coverage of Robinson's deeds was extensive. Kids hung around the Brooklyn candy stores at ten or eleven o'clock at night waiting for the pink edition of the *Daily News* or the early, gray *Daily Mirror*. They read Dick Young, Jimmy Powers, Harold Weissman, Dan Parker, and so many others on the doings of Robinson and the Dodgers. For most young fans, the racial aspect of Robinson's persona seemed lost in the baseball aspect. The man could play. He was fast becoming a vibrant force on the Dodgers. With Stanky walking and Robinson bunting or hitting to right behind him and Reiser and Walker driving in runs, the Dodgers seemed as strong a team as they had been in their last pennant-winning season of 1941. There was one element of excitement Robinson provided that few baseball observers had ever seen: Jackie Robinson on third base was an incredible thrill.

He never stood still at third. He dashed down the line. He bounced around the base. He made full runs toward home, just stopping at some perfect time so he could return without being caught. The fans were caught up in this ritual. Ty Cobb had been the last great baseball base stealer in the early 1920s (he had set the stolen-base record of ninety-six in 1915), and now Robinson had brought this electrifying element back into the game. To the roar of the crowd, the squeal of the women on Ladies Day, and the proud howls of blacks inundating baseball fields in the early days of the 1947 season, Robinson quickly became the most entertaining part of the game. For a fifty-cent bleacher seat, a fan could have a close-up of this audacious game-breaker.

Robinson, almost with a show of arrogant guile, would get caught in a rundown between bases. He would take too long a lead at first, and the pitcher would throw behind him. The first baseman would throw to the second baseman, and stopping with instant timing, Robinson would head back toward first. One throw. Two throws. Three throws. The fans were caught up in the chase. Four throws. Robinson, still alive, twisting and turning away from the tag. Five throws. Then, finally, a dropped ball or an errant throw. Robinson was safe. Baseball is a game of statistics, but the written evidence of how many times Robinson escaped rundowns to be safe does not exist. Witnesses will swear it was endless.

It was only two or three weeks into the season when Robinson's unique skill began etching itself on Brooklyn playgrounds. As he did this more and more, encouraged heartily by Branch Rickey who knew a crowd-pleasing act when he saw one, the rundowns became part of the ritual of a Dodger game. Nothing could be more disappointing than attendance at a Brooklyn game with Robinson not making it to first base safely, not giving the fans a chance to see this baseball ballet. Soon, in street corners and empty lots of Brooklyn, the act was being repeated by boys clothed in tattered garments with well-worn blue Brooklyn baseball caps. In Brooklyn it was not called a rundown, the technical baseball term for a runner being hung up between two fielders until he was erased from the bases. In Brooklyn, it was a pickle. Robinson was being caught in a pickle. Kids all around the borough were practicing their escapes from a pickle. If the truth be known, Jackie Robinson was responsible for more cut pants and torn kneecaps in Brooklyn that spring than anyone else.

Robinson's baserunning had become part of the daily rituals of many Brooklyn kids. By summer, no Coney Island or Long Island beach would be free of youngsters engaged in baseball rundowns with daring headfirst slides. Swallowing sand as they slid, the kids took turns being Robinson. "Spaldeens" were substituted for baseballs. Cutouts in the sand substituted for big-league bases. Bathing suits substituted for Dodger uniforms.

None of these kids could know or appreciate the pain Robinson was undergoing to provide them with this pleasure.

CHAPTER

Eight

HINDSIGHT
TO HISTORY

*H*ATE. IT IS AN EMOTION that defies logic, common sense, reason, and justice. No scholar can really explain it. No therapist can really destroy it. No servant of God can adequately exorcise it. For the blackness of his skin, this grandson of slaves was reviled, threatened, harassed, and abused. Jackie Robinson was attacked verbally and physically as he tried valiantly to find a place for himself in baseball. He had experienced some prejudice, some anger, some degree of hatred most of his life, but nothing prepared him for the vile intensity of hatred he would experience in his earliest days as a Dodger.

Robinson had been spat upon as a youngster in Pasadena. Robinson had been called a dirty nigger more times than he could count as an athlete in southern California. Robinson had seen hatred and anger in his prewar jobs, in his time in the military service of his country, and in his year of learning with the Montreal Royals. Nothing matched the viciousness of the early days as a Dodger.

"I don't remember exactly when it was. I know it was in the early days in Brooklyn that first year," says Jackie's sister, Willa Mae. "The phone rang and it was Jack calling from Brooklyn. His voice was very choked, and we knew some more bad things had happened. We had been reading the papers. We knew what was going on. He just blurted out, "I can't take it anymore. I'm quitting." I just told him to hold on, and I put my mother and then my brother Mack on the phone, and they talked him out of it, I guess. I know he meant it. I could tell just how bad he felt. He was fed up fighting it every day of his life then."

Robinson had gone through the opening series against the Braves at Brooklyn and the series with the Giants at the Polo Grounds. The Polo Grounds was located on 155th Street and Seventh Avenue, the heart of New York's black ghetto of Harlem. Thousands of blacks, some scraping their last few cents from the cookie jar, had turned out to watch Robinson play. There had been some catcalls from the stands, a few racist remarks filtering down on the field, but relative acceptance from the opposing dugouts. Everyone was interested in seeing what Robinson was made of as a player, not in his African heritage.

Then came a series at Ebbets Field against the Philadelphia Phillies. The manager was Ben Chapman. The general manager was Herb Pennock. The owner was Bob Carpenter. It is important to consider how baseball operates to understand the events of the next several days.

Baseball in 1947, before the strength of the Players Association, salaries in excess of two million dollars a year, and constant national exposure through television, was run as a benevolent dictatorship. Players were treated as lackeys. When a player held out for more money, he was considered an anathema to the ball club; it was often relayed to the fawning press as a venal act. The press almost always sided with the club in salary squabbles because sports reporters were the profession's chosen people. They got to travel with ball clubs on luxury trains, stay in luxury hotels, eat fine meals, get free game tickets, take their sons to spring training fields, hobnob with famous athletes, and receive gifts at holiday times. What manner of man could not be swayed by telling a friend in the 1920s, "I had lunch with the Babe yesterday, and I told him . . ." If Joe DiMaggio, Ted Williams, and Stan Musial were major heroes of the early 1940s, they were no less heroes to the men who wrote about them. Few sportswriters would last long if they were extremely critical of the actions of the ball club. Few accepted the confrontations. Life was too sweet. It is the same environment that gives Ronald Reagan a honeymoon press. Why point out a president's inadequacies at the cost of blowing a cocktail party with the Duke of Windsor?

Bob Carpenter, an heir to the Duponts of Delaware chemical fortune, was among the nation's elite in 1947. His wealth was enormous. He ran the ball club more for fun than for fame or fortune. He could hardly be expected to have any social connection with a black. Black people shined shoes at Carpenter's country clubs. They didn't play golf with him.

Herb Pennock, fifty-three that February of 1947 (he would be dead less than a year later), was born outside Philadelphia in Kennett Square, Pennsylvania. He pitched for the Philadelphia A's and the Boston Red Sox before reaching his true fame with the Babe Ruth–era Yankees from 1923 through 1933. For some unexplainable reason, Pennock had more animosity toward Jews and blacks than most players of his time. Reports indicate he was a leader among a group of players harassing the occasional Jewish or dark-skinned Latin player of his time. He would certainly condone any action taken from his team's bench to ridicule Robinson.

William Benjamin Chapman was born in Nashville, Tennessee, and grew up in Birmingham, Alabama. He was a talented outfielder and a fine hitter. He joined the Yankees in 1930, was a teammate of Babe Ruth and Lou Gehrig, and was the regular Yankee center fielder for four years until Joe DiMaggio joined the team. Chapman was soon traded to Washington. He played for several teams, including Brooklyn, in a playing career ending in 1946. He was the manager of the Phillies from 1945 through 1948. His teams finished last, fifth, seventh, and sixth before he was fired. He was involved in amateur and professional baseball coaching until his retirement. At the age of seventy-eight, he remains chipper, talkative, and healthy at his Birmingham home.

Some players, Chapman among them, used bench jockeying as a significant baseball weapon. Some players, Dick Williams of the Dodgers was one, lengthened their careers and ingratiated themselves to management, despite minimal skills, because they would scream at opposing players. Nothing was too ugly. Players would be taunted for physical characteristics. Babe Ruth was called, on occasion, nigger lips, though the culprit would generally hide and offer the ugly taunt in a false voice. Tall players would be criticized for their size. Thin ones would get it for lack of girth. Fat ones would hear food jokes. Noses were a special target with players such as Ernie Lombardi, nicknamed Schnoz: Billy Martin, Casey Stengel, and Warren Spahn also heard it about their noses. Players would be wonderful targets if they happened to have bad skin. Bullet face, pock face, and sandpaper face were some of the more gentle code words. Bald men could never escape: cue ball, skinhead, or old-fashioned baldy were commonly heard. One player, Dick Groat of the Pirates, bald at an early age, was so sensitive to his bare head that he even took his cap with him into the showers. Players were attacked for their strange stances, for a hint of femininity in their walk or voices, for their big ears (when Walt Disney made Dumbo famous he destroyed many ballplayers), for the way they wore their uniforms, or for their lack of intelligence.

Players were most attacked for their ancestry. Phil Rizzuto, Joe Garagiola, Yogi Berra, Tony Lazzeri, and Frank Crosetti heard much about their Italian ancestry; Joe DiMaggio was called Dago. Stan Bordagaray and Lou Boudreau were razzed about their French backgrounds. Frank Frisch was the Dutchman, Charles Risberg was Swede, Emil Meusel was Irish, and Herman Schaefer was Germany.

And Jackie Robinson was nigger. He was also snowflake and Little Black Sambo. He was accused of sleeping with the white wives of his teammates. He was told he was spreading contagious diseases among his teammates, and his teammates were browbeaten with that time-honored phrase of bigots—nigger lover. The intensity of the attacks were beyond what anyone had ever heard. Chapman vilified Robinson every chance he had. It was difficult for Robinson to keep turning his other cheek. Some of Robinson's teammates bristled at the unfair attacks. Second baseman Ed Stanky, a Philadelphia native who had settled in the South, bellowed to Chapman and the Phillies bench, "You yellowbellied cowards, why don't you yell at somebody who can answer back?"

The language was so vile that National League president Ford Frick ordered Chapman to cease and desist. When sportswriters, led by black sportswriters on black newspapers, quoted and revealed some of Chapman's language, the public rebelled. Letters of sympathy poured into the Dodger clubhouse for Robinson. When the teams next met in Philadelphia, Robinson, under orders from Rickey, was asked to pose with Chapman. He was supposed to shake hands with the Phillies manager. Chapman would only agree to a picture with Robinson holding one hand on his bat and Chapman holding two hands on it. Robinson would later say that that experience was the low point of his tumultuous year. He was, he later said, "tempted to stride over to that Phillies dugout, grab one of those white sons of bitches, and smash his teeth with my despised black fist."

CHAPMAN: "I didn't like the idea he was pushed in the game. There were other players more qualified to be in the big leagues that year. Rickey wanted Robinson. That wasn't right. He should have been made to earn his chance.

"Sure, we rode him. We rode everybody. They rode Babe Ruth and Lou Gehrig when I went to the Yankees. Nobody said anything about that. Everybody in baseball understood that was part of the game. We knocked him down. We knocked everybody down. I didn't tell my Phillies ball club to ride him more than anybody else. I just told them to treat him like they would treat any other rookie. We got on every new player to see if he could take it.

"I'd been around colored people before I saw Robinson. We saw colored people in Birmingham. They had their schools and things, and they would come downtown to shop and nobody thought anything of it. I think a lot of what happened was caused by the newspapers up there looking for a scapegoat for Robinson. I wound up as the bad guy, and they wrote a lot of things about me that caused me a lot of trouble. I don't want to go into detail now because it's so many years ago. Look, I had a good career and played fifteen years and even came back during the war to pitch in Brooklyn. I had a lifetime average of .302 and played on one of the greatest teams of all time, the 1932 Yankees, and I never get mentioned for the Hall of Fame. Do you know why that is? I think it is because of all the bad publicity I got involving all that business. I think Jackie Robinson kept me out of the Hall of Fame.

"I got to admire the boy after I saw him play a few times. He was one of the best competitors I ever saw. He could beat you more ways than you could curry a mule.

"I coached a lot of amateur teams around Birmingham and did real well. We turned out a lot of players for the big leagues. Britt Burns was one of my pitchers. I had a good career, helped a lot of young men, and didn't treat Jackie Robinson any different than I treated other rookies. I'm not ashamed of anything. I think the press should be ashamed of making me a scapegoat."

The escalation of public disclosures about the ridicule and hatred heaped on Robinson by the Phillies unearthed more snakes. Hate mail increased. Death threats were plentiful. Scribbled letters came in daily with vulgarities. The crazies were on the loose. In 1986, protected by laws against discrimination and public bigotry, Robinson would have been better defended. In 1947, only common decency and custom helped soothe his hurt.

Robinson had decided early on that he would not push himself on his teammates. That was the way he operated in Montreal. That was the way he operated in Brooklyn. He spoke to his mates when spoken to. Pee Wee Reese began speaking to him regularly and casually. Eddie Stanky discussed positions of hitters. Spider Jorgensen talked with Robinson as easily as any men who had been teammates and winners a year before. One day there was an even more significant breakthrough. Dixie Walker approached Robinson during batting practice.

"Ah think you'd be better able to handle that curve ball if you didn't stride so far," Walker said.

"Like this?" Robinson said, as he shortened his batting stride.

"That's about it. A little shorter. A little quicker."

"I'll try it," Robinson said.

That afternoon Robinson had a line drive double, a bunt single, and a single up the middle.

"Thanks, Dixie," Robinson said quietly later in the clubhouse.

Dixie Walker, the People's Cherce, would be traded to the Pirates at the age of thirty-seven that December, along with Hal Gregg and Vic Lombardi in one of the best deals Rickey ever made. He got Preacher Roe, a wonderful left-handed pitcher, Billy Cox, a marvelous third baseman, and Gene Mauch. The joke was that Mauch was included in the deal to carry the money. Walker would hit .316 and .282 for Pittsburgh but would be gone in two years. He was another example of Rickey's theory that "it was better to trade them one year too early than one year too late." He had gotten great value for Walker. It might not have happened if he had waited another year.

Walker, also, was one of the most outspoken of the Dodgers against Robinson before he came to the club. He said little about Robinson after he joined Brooklyn. Walker became a distinguished batting instructor for the Dodgers, helping players for years, including prize pupils Tommy Davis and Maury Wills, both black players. On two or three separate occasions when the old teammates were reunited, Robinson and Walker talked animatedly together. Walker died in 1982.

Harry Walker, Dixie's younger brother, was a hitting star for the Cardinals, Phillies, Cubs, and Reds. He managed the Pirates for seven years. He is considered one of the most gifted hitting instructors in baseball history. He lives in Leeds, Alabama, and is still called on at the age of sixty-eight to help young hitters.

HARRY WALKER: "Dixie and I used to go fishing together at some lakes about three hundred miles away from Birmingham. We spent a lot of time together alone in those days. Dixie never brought up Jackie's name. I was playing for the Phillies that year, won the batting title with a .363 mark, and I asked Dixie what it was like batting behind Jackie. He said he didn't like that jumping back and forth Jackie did on the bases. It was very distracting.

"I know there was a lot written then about Dixie and Jackie, and I think you have to understand the times. We didn't have much contact with black folks, and when Dixie said what he did it was like a man seeing a green door and not wanting to open it because you didn't know what was behind it. I think we just didn't know what it would be like when the blacks came into baseball.

"After a while we all got to playing with the colored players, and there was no fuss made about it. The Cardinals and the Dodgers had a great rivalry and so did the Phillies and the Dodgers when I went over there. Jackie was a great player, and you had to be real alert to play against him. He had catlike ability, and he could accelerate so fast. He never shut that motor down.

"Jackie was always fired up in a game. It was great to play against him because he made you play your best. What was interesting from the standpoint of drawing fans was that Jackie drew fans all over the league in those days, but the other colored players didn't. Even when Willie Mays came into the league in 1951, he never drew fans the way Jackie did. Willie wasn't as hungry as Jackie was. He didn't play with that same fire day in and day out.

"I think those days are behind us now. Nobody feels angry about what happened then. It was all so new. How could anybody know how to act. I remember a couple of years ago I was at an old-timers game in Los Angeles, and I saw Campy on the field in his wheelchair, and I went up to say hello to him. 'Hi, I'm Harry Walker, I used to play . . .' He stopped me. 'I know you. You used to hit a lot of line drives against us.' We had a real nice conversation, talked about some of those great games we had with the Dodgers, and talked about a lot of the old players. We had a real nice conversation, and before we had to break it up, I was telling Campy about my grandchildren."

Pressures on Robinson mounted. He wasn't hitting much. The big-league curve ball, an ever-present torment for young ballplayers, was giving him fits. The hate mail was intense. The racial remarks were still being heard from the opposing benches and from the stands. In Philadelphia, Robinson was refused admission at the Benjamin Franklin Hotel. The Dodgers moved to the Warwick. Robinson's teammates were pleased. The food was better, they were allowed to sign for meals, and they would enjoy the luxury of the establishment for many years afterward. In St. Louis, as expected, Robinson was denied access to the Chase Park Plaza Hotel. When access was finally allowed some seven years later, Robinson was told he and his black teammates had to eat in their rooms. The next trip, he simply sat down in the dining room, was served, and broke another barrier.

On May 9 a story broke in the *New York Herald Tribune*. It was a blockbuster. Sports editor Stanley Woodward, a crusty curmudgeon, described a rebellion he said Cardinal players were leading against Robinson. He said the Cards had been urged on by some Dodgers—the inference was that it was Dixie Walker talking to Harry Walker, an event heatedly denied now by Harry— to strike against Robinson. Enos Slaughter, Terry Moore, and Marty Marion were the supposed ringleaders. The scenario in Woodward's story suggested that these players would refuse to take the field against Robinson, and as leaders of their club, others would follow. According to Woodward's tale, owner Sam Breadon got wind of the plot and squashed it after informing NL president Frick. Happy Chandler was also told.

Woodward wrote that Frick took swift action, delivering an ultimatum to the Cardinals saying, "This is the United States of America, and one citizen has as much right to play as another."

No documentation of the supposed plot exists. All living Cardinals contacted deny it. The best explanation seems to be that of *St. Louis Post* sports columnist Bob Broeg. He was the beat reporter covering the Cardinals then.

BROEG: "Rud Rennie was the beat reporter for the *Tribune*. He was close to Bob Hyland, the Cardinal team doctor, and he had a drink with him one night during the Dodger series. The Cards had won the pennant and the World Series in 1946, and now they had lost eleven of thirteen. Typical of any ball club in that situation, there was a lot of grumbling and a lot of pointing of fingers.

"Breadon was a fan type owner, sort of the George Steinbrenner of his day. He fired managers on a whim. He had about six before Eddie Dyer. He knew the club was struggling, and he was upset. He was looking for a reason, a good excuse. He jumped on the Robinson thing. He probably mentioned it to Hyland and told him his club was so upset at having to play against a Negro they were talking of going on strike. Hyland repeated this theory to Rennie and Rennie told Woodward.

"What probably happened next was that Woodward wrote

the story and then called Frick at his home in Bronxville. I don't think Frick knew a damn thing about it, but he probably told Woodward if the Cardinals were thinking of striking they'd better not because he would suspend all of them.

"Then the story is on the street. I'm resting comfortably in my hotel room and I get a call from Tiger Murray. Murray tells me to run out and get the Tribune; I was shocked. [Murray, a Princeton grad who covered baseball for the *New York Post*, died in a fire caused by his smoking in bed. I succeeded Murray after getting a call from *Post* sports editor Ike Gellis. 'Do you smoke?' he asked me. 'No,' I answered. 'Good—you're hired.']

"Then I started chasing after the players. I caught up with Moore in the lobby. He was the team captain, and he would know if anybody did. He said he hadn't heard anything like that. I talked to Marion, and he said there was no truth at all to it. I chased after Dyer, and he denied any knowledge of it. Dyer sort of liked Robinson when he saw him play because he had this deep admiration for multisport athletes. Dyer had been a multisport star from Lousiana at Rice, and the first time he saw Robinson he yelled, 'How you doin', pal?' and always got on with him. Dyer admired Frankie Frisch and Alvin Dark because they had each played three or four sports in college. Dyer used to say baseball was a game of loose wrists and football is a game of tension. Few people can play both sports well. That's why he was so interested in any player who could, like Robinson. He said that he thought Robinson would be like Frisch. If you got him mad he would kill you six ways. I think he had the Cardinals low-keying all of the Robinson stuff because he admired him so much as an athlete. He felt Robinson would be tough to beat and didn't want to get him riled up. He wouldn't encourage any kind of strike talk, I'm sure of that.

"I remember the first time Jackie played in St. Louis. The pavillion was the only place they allowed blacks and it was filled. They charged seventy-five cents and it was some event. I got friendly with Jackie later and interviewed him many times. He was a great interview. One time he told me that his favorite snack was day-old bread dunked in milk and sugar. I thought about that later when I read that he died of diabetes at the age of fifty-three.''

In a magazine article written some forty years after the incident, Broeg writes, "The story about the Cardinals' planned 'rebellion' against Robinson early in 1947 is a barnyard vulgarism. Some players grumbled about having to play on the same field with a black, just as did some of the Dodgers. Maybe here and there one popped off about how he didn't care to play against Robinson, but no one paid attention to it. Certainly not the captain of the Cardinals, Terry Moore, nor his infield alter ego, Marty Marion, the man to whom ballplayers are most indebted for their tremendous pension plan. . . .

"The *Herald Tribune* broke a copyrighted story and the monkey was on the Cardinals' back. I've always resented the story, not because I had to scramble at night to follow it up, but only because it put so many fine players in an unfavorable light.

"The truth is, to repeat, the Cardinals did *not* plan a strike against Robinson even though a few players grumbled in their beer about the athlete of a different color. But baseball history has labeled them unfairly.''

What is most intriguing about the supposed Cardinals strike story of 1947 is that it gives far too much power to the players. Baseball players in 1947—unlike their unionized counterparts of 1987—had very little collective strength. They could hold out for a few more bucks as individual talents. They could report late to spring training. They could sit out an occasional game with a fake injury. But they most certainly could not forge a strike that would cost their team a gate. The average salary in 1947 was barely over $10,000. Stan Musial, the best player in the National League, was paid $31,000 for the 1947 season after asking for $37,000. No better example of the relative weakness of the players' position in the late 1940s or the early 1950s is a story Ralph Kiner likes to tell about Branch Rickey, who had moved on to Pittsburgh in 1950.

"I had won seven home run titles in a row," Kiner says. "I

had just hit thirty-seven homers in 1952. I went in to meet with Rickey and asked for a big raise.''

Rickey replied, ''We finished last with you, we can finish last without you.''

Kiner had to accept Rickey's final offer.

Members of the 1947 Cardinals all seem to indicate, despite Woodward's story, despite the general anti-Negro tone of the time, despite some basic unhappiness on a losing St. Louis team, that no organized strike decision was ever made.

Joe Garagiola, the NBC baseball broadcaster and game show host, has parlayed a bald head, a fast smile, and a quick wit into a marvelous career. Born in the St. Louis section called Dago Hill, Garagiola, now sixty-one, grew up as a buddy of one Lawrence Peter Berra. He began calling the stumpy youngster Yogi after a movie character they had seen together. It was Garagiola, using his Berra-isms, who helped make Yogi a national folk figure. It also helped make Garagiola baseball's resident wit.

The younger Garagiola was a hot-tempered, minimally talented big-league ballplayer. He hit .316 as a Cardinal rookie catcher on the 1946 Series team after a .237 season average. Two years later, confined to twenty-four games, he actually batted .107 for an entire Cardinal season. He'd better be funny. He played with four teams and batted .257. He had a couple of notable scuffles with Jackie Robinson. He now praises him highly.

GARAGIOLA: ''I don't remember any strike talk on the ball club about Jackie. I can't say that the older fellows on the team might not have had a meeting by themselves and had something to say about Jackie. I just didn't know anything about it. I don't think anything could have happened on that team without Dyer, and I don't recall him ever discussing it with us.

''I had a couple of run-ins with Jackie. Maybe we disagreed on the call of pitches, and I might have said something to the umpire, and he probably said, 'Why don't you get in there and catch?' and I probably said, 'Why don't you mind your own business and get in there and hit?' That stuff went on all the time in those days. Maybe there was some yelling from the bench, and

I guess the word nigger was used. I think Jackie heard that from every ball club.

"He was simply the most exciting player I have ever seen on the bases in baseball. In the clubhouse meetings we not only went over how to pitch to him, we went over how to defend against him on the bases. 'If Jackie is on first we do this. If he is on second we do this. If he gets to third, watch out, he'll steal home.' He was the only player we ever went over like that. When he got in a rundown he would have everybody involved, including the vendors. The park would be in an uproar. He was the most daring player I ever saw.

"Jackie had inner conceit as a player. He drove pitchers and catchers crazy. He would actually yell at the pitchers 'I'm going, I'm going. Do anything you want, pal, you can't stop me.' Then he would go and steal the base. When he got on, it was like the Jackie Robinson hour, he would so dominate the play while he was on. Everybody would be caught up in his antics—the pitcher, the catcher, all the fielders, the bench, everybody in the ballpark. He was the most intimidating player on the bases I have ever seen.

"Jackie was also a tremendous clutch player. In a big game, in a big spot, he seemed able to do whatever had to be done. Jackie Robinson was very tough with or without a bat in his hands.

"You don't think that way about many players.

"Jackie took an awful lot of heat in those early years. I don't know of another player who could have handled that and not exploded. I mean they called him every name you could imagine and threw at him and cut him and did everything to run him out of the league. There should be a special place in baseball recognizing Jackie for more than just his baseball ability. He was a very special man."

On one occasion Garagiola spiked Robinson on a close play at first. On another occasion outfielder Joe Medwick slashed Robinson. Enos Slaughter, the aggressive outfielder called Country, caught Robinson at first with his spikes. The play got a great deal of publicity. Slaughter would spend a good part of his postbaseball career denying racial intentions to the spiking.

Slaughter, seventy-one, now a gentleman farmer in North Carolina, was elected to baseball's Hall of Fame in 1985.

SLAUGHTER: "You have to remember Robinson was an inexperienced first baseman that year. I played hard and I ran hard. He didn't know how to get his foot off the base in time to avoid a runner. I'm sure I wasn't the only player who spiked him that year. The Dodgers put him over there without much training, and anybody who cut him was blamed for it. Nobody said nuthin' when a white first baseman got cut.

"I remember a couple of years later Monte Irvin was playing first base for the Giants. There was a close play, and I jumped on the bag and just missed his leg. I told him after the play he had better learn to get his foot off the base. He thanked me for that because he knew I saved him from a cutting. [Irvin agrees the story is accurate.] I had a tough reputation, but I never went out of my way to cut anybody, Jackie Robinson or anybody else. That's not the way I was taught the game.

"The thing about me supposedly cutting Jackie, that kept me out of the Hall of Fame for years. I played nineteen years and hit .300, and the writers kept passing me up every year. I know why. It was because they believed that story about Jackie Robinson being cut intentionally and that was it. Nobody ever asked me about it. They just said I did it and that was it. I think they were being prejudiced against me.

"I waited a long time, and I finally did make it, and it was very satisfying that I did. I'm not going to go into details of why I didn't make it and what happened with Jackie and me. I just know I played hard baseball and tried to win, and that's what I want to be remembered for."

One legend that has existed for forty years is disputed by Stan "The Man" Musial, the famed slugger of the Cardinals, a seven-time batting champion, a lifetime .331 hitter, and one of the nicest, most decent men ever to put on a baseball uniform. He was so well loved by fans everywhere that even as he belted line drive after line drive against and over the right field wall along Bedford Avenue in Brooklyn's Ebbets Field, he was honored by opposing fans. It was in Brooklyn where he was first called the Man, an endearing term for his great skills.

MUSIAL: "There was this story during that time that Slaughter was one of the ringleaders of that supposed strike. The legend had it that he came to me and asked me to sign a statement or a petition or something to keep Jackie Robinson out of baseball. It never happened. First of all, everyone who knew me knew I would never consider anything like that. My parents were immigrants from Poland, and they came over and got a chance to make a living, and I certainly couldn't deny any other person a chance to make a living.

"But more importantly, Slaughter and I never had any words over Jackie that I can remember. Somebody wrote that Slaughter came to me and asked me to sign, and I refused and we got into a knock-down, drag-out brawl in the hotel room. That was complete nonsense. As a matter of fact, that season I couldn't fight my own shadow. That was the year I had an appendicitis attack, and I think I was in the hospital in Brooklyn during our first visit there. I was weak a good part of that season and never could regain my strength until late in the year. I had an off-year [he hit .312, which would be his lowest average until he hit only .310 in 1956, and he would not drop under .300 until he hit .255 as a thirty-eight-year-old in 1959], so I wasn't too worried about Robinson or Slaughter or anybody else. I just wanted to regain my strength and my batting stroke that year.

"I never had any trouble with Jackie. He was a fine ballplayer, a very tough competitor, and a very decent man. I enjoyed playing against him. Heck, I enjoyed playing against everybody. I just enjoyed playing."

Then the man they called "The Man" in Brooklyn smiled that infectious smile of his, went into his famous corkscrew batting stance, and walked away laughing.

If any Cardinal player would know of any team unrest it would be Terry Moore. At seventy-four, he is the same handsome, soft-spoken, stylish gentleman he was as a leader of the Cardinals from 1935 through 1948. He lives in Collinsville, Illinois, across the Mississippi from St. Louis, attends an occasional game, and spends his spare time bowling, fishing, and hunting.

MOORE: "A lot of my spare time is taken up traveling to Slaughter's weddings. He's been married five or six times, and I think I've been to about four of them. He is fixin' to get married again, and I told him he may not be too old for that marryin' nonsense, but I'm probably too old for attendin' them.

"As for Jackie, to me he was just another Dodger to get out like the rest of them. He was a great player, a daring base runner, a complete player, and I enjoyed the challenge of playing against him. I remember the first time we played against him in Brooklyn. We talked about defending against him. I think earlier that year Dr. [Robert] Hyland, the team physician, had told us that Brooklyn was bringing him up. I had played against colored players in barnstorming games and played against them in the Army, so it was no shock to play against them in the big leagues. Slaughter was my roommate and maybe we talked about defending against him because he was a good hitter and a very fast runner, but I don't remember any talk of a plot to strike against him. No sir, I don't remember anything like that.

"I was a pretty good outfielder in my time because I practiced as hard at that part of the game as I did with the hitting. Maybe today they don't practice that part of it, so not as many of them can catch the ball or throw it the way we could in our day. I just liked to win, so I worked on every part of my game. My most satisfying year was 1942 when the Dodgers had a real big lead on us through August, and then we got hot and caught them at the end, and that was a season I won't forget. I went away to service, was in the Caribbean for a couple of years, and when I came back I just wasn't the same ballplayer anymore. I was thirty-four, thirty-five years old, and I couldn't cover ground the way I did before. If you can't cover ground, you are not about to be too good a center fielder.

"Everybody knows Jackie was a great player. He could do everything you could ask a ballplayer to do, and he was the best I ever saw at stealing home. He sure could turn a game around in a hurry when he got on bases. I had nothing against Jackie Robinson. Just say he was on the Dodgers, and I wanted to beat the Dodgers more than I wanted to beat any other team, and I think if you ask the old Cardinal players they will all say that."

One of the best pitchers on that 1947 St. Louis team was a big, red-headed right-hander named George Munger. He is sixty-eight years old now, recently retired from his job with the environmental service in Houston. Red Munger was 16–5 in 1947. He laughs now when asked about a Cardinal strike against Jackie Robinson in 1947.

MUNGER: "Hell, I was too busy feeding my family to think about anything like that. I wanted to win and I wanted to keep on pitching as long as I could. I wouldn't get involved in anything like that strike talk because it was none of my business. Players didn't have any say on who was on your own team, let alone any say on who was on somebody's else's team.

"Maybe the game was tougher and more batters were knocked down then. I guess Jackie was thrown out the same as anybody else. They didn't wear skullcaps like they do today, so everybody was a little more serious about things at the plate.

"I tried to get Jackie out with good sliders and a cut fastball. I would pitch him up and in and then go away with the slider. Mostly, I wanted to keep him off base. As good as he was then, he'd be better now. He hit down on the ball, and he would get a lot of hits through the artificial infields. I think that is the biggest change in the game. I can't say I was a pal of Jackie Robinson's. I talked to him a few times but that was it. I kidded around with Campanella a lot though. He was a real good guy. I never hated anybody when I played ball. It was just a good job then, the best time of my life. I'm glad even to be talking about it now. I didn't get involved in any strike business like I say because I just liked that paycheck too much."

Now, forty years later, with memories not as clear, the idea of a Cardinal strike in 1947 seems a little farfetched. A significant reality was present in those days after World War II. The United States was embarking on some successful economic times. Ballplayers wanted their share of this new prosperity and postwar growth. It was probably the main reason that strike talk—if it existed—never got very far.

It was certainly the reason the players on the Brooklyn Dodgers were fast becoming fond of Jackie Robinson. He was helping them win. A lot of Dodgers no longer saw him as black. They saw him as green, as in the color of money.

CHAPTER

Nine

ROOKIE
OF THE YEAR

HEIR EARNING YEARS ARE FI-
nite. They die twice: once on that feared day when their careers
end; and then again, less emotionally for most, on the day their
mortal lives are ended. Baseball players may well be as selfish a
group of individuals as ever gathered in a single occupation.

In Jackie Robinson's rookie year of 1947, there were eight
teams in each league, four hundred ballplayers total in the big
leagues, survivors of a list of millions of youngsters who envi-
sioned themselves as big-leaguers when they were under the age
of ten. The competition was fierce. The salaries then were not
outrageous. The prestige was not overwhelming. Many played
six, eight, ten years and went on to pump gas in service stations,
work on construction crews, toil in grocery stores, drive buses, or
sweep streets.

Robinson soon showed his teammates he could help them
win. Winning would lengthen their careers, increase their earn-
ings, possibly provide them with a postcareer job, add to their
potential, and soften the later years of their lives. His ability on
the field, his quick bat, his fierce sense of competition and desire,
his good glove, his clutch play, and his ability to bring victory
with his fleet feet, all contributed to soothing the pains. It was
difficult for a Dodger teammate to criticize "that nigger" when
Robinson was winning games for his mates almost every day.

The reality of economics did more to break down barriers than all the goodwill offered by dozens of teammates and opposing players. Ballplayers understand the emotion of winning and making big bucks.

After the early season slump and the slow start, Robinson got into high gear. He was running bases with abandon and would lead the league in stolen bases with 29. Only Pete Reiser with 34 the previous season had stolen as many since Kiki Cuyler stole 37 in 1930. He broke a record for sacrifice hits with 28. The flair, bravado, brazen style of his running could truly be said to have revolutionized play in the National League. He hit 12 homers to lead the club, had 5 triples and 31 doubles, scored 125 runs to lead the team in that significant department, and batted .297 after spending most of the second half of the season over .300. The Dodgers won the pennant by five games, and the team outdrew every other club in the league. On and off the field people were beginning to notice him not as a black but as one fine player.

There were still incidents, some significant, some trifling, in almost every first visit of the Dodgers to a town. Some of these incidents brought out the best in people. In Pittsburgh, the crowd was on him early with racial slurs. Hank Greenberg, the Jewish star who had come over from Detroit to finish his brilliant career, chatted amiably with Robinson after he drew a walk.

"Hang in there, Jackie, you'll be all right," Greenberg said.

"I'm trying," said Robinson.

"I know what you are going through," Greenberg said.

When Greenberg made his big-league debut as one of the rare Jewish players in the big leagues, he heard every anti-Semitic attack he could imagine.

"Then one time I heard one of my teammates tell another how Jews were so cheap and controlled the banks and all the money in the country and wouldn't spend a nickel. I laughed to myself. That was coming from a teammate of mine who used to sit around the hotel lobby all morning waiting for somebody to drop a newspaper so he could pick it up without paying. Do you know what a newspaper cost in the early 1930s. Maybe a penny or two at the most."

One of the Pittsburgh players who also had a kind word for

Robinson in 1947 was a handsome slugger from California by the name of Ralph Kiner. He was the NL home run king for seven straight years. He broadcasts the New York Mets games now.

KINER: "I remember playing softball against Jackie in Pasadena under the lights before the war. It was at Brookside Park and he was the shortstop on this team. Everybody knew Jackie. He had this big reputation for football and basketball and track. Actually I think baseball was his worst sport. His brother had been on the 1936 Olympic team, and Jackie got a lot of attention as soon as he started playing college sports at Pasadena Junior College.

"I had played against Negro players in California, and I had played against Negro league teams around Pittsburgh after I came to the Pirates. The Homestead Grays were the local Negro league team, and it was a real fine ball club. We had some good games against them.

"Jackie had this wide-open stance when he first came up and had a lot of trouble with the curve ball. He couldn't hit a curve ball with a paddle, but he shortened his stance and his swing a bit and he became a real good curve-ball hitter. You can't last ten years in the big leagues without becoming a decent curve-ball hitter. If you can't hit it, that's all you will ever see. Those pitchers are that mean.

"I was close to Hank Greenberg, and I remember talking to him about Jackie. Hank thought Jackie would make it if he remained calm. That was the big thing, not to lose self-control. I think he was a very disciplined player, but he had that fire burning inside.

"I didn't have any social relationship with Jackie. In those days you didn't mingle the way they do today. It was a much more intense game. People disliked each other if they wore different uniforms. Jackie Robinson was a tremendous player, especially on the base paths. You know what I remember now about him, his eyes—those deep, intense eyes that always seemed to be staring at you."

As the 1947 season moved forward, the Dodgers visited some towns for the second or third time. The crowds remained huge.

There was still some overt racism from the stands, but the players seemed more and more to treat Robinson as an effective opposing player and less as a freak. He was welcomed on the field with huge cheers in most places, especially from the new clientele in the cheaper seats, the black fans. They had been told by their political and religious leaders to low-key Robinson's arrival, not to be overtly demonstrative, not to showboat his successes for fear of creating jealousies and tensions. It was hard for them to follow these suggestions.

Everything about him demanded attention. He walked to the plate pigeon-toed, carrying two or three bats, moving slowly, throwing away the excess bats, digging in with his back foot on the outside line of the batter's box. He would pump the bat back and forth, back and forth, high over his shoulder as the pitcher went into his motion. He would often take his front hand off the bat just before the pitcher let go of the ball to dry it on his baggy pants leg. His entire body seemed to rock in some rhythmic connection just before he exploded on the ball. His escape from the plate after striking the ball with his bat seemed instantaneous. When he was safe on first, he would stretch out his lead as far as any man had ever done. He would get back safely most of the time when the pitcher threw over, but if he was caught, it was in a cloud of dust, umpire, first baseman, and a sliding Robinson all coming together at the heart of the action.

By the time he broke in with Brooklyn he was twenty-eight years old and had lost some of his explosive college football speed. But he had lost none of his timing or ability to change direction or balance his large body. He was a big man, a bit under six feet, weighing anywhere from 195 pounds to 225 pounds during his career. He ran with short strides, seemingly not running fast at all, but most often beating the throw by a step as he slid. His sense of athletic timing and coordination was impeccable.

As his ability and dynamic style took hold, teammates began more and more to like and appreciate him as a friend and a winner, and opposing players began dealing with him as they would with any Dodger. Warren Spahn, the winningest left-hander in baseball history and the first half of the Spahn-and-

Sain-and-Pray-for-Rain Boston combination, remembers how he felt about Robinson.

SPAHN: "We disliked Robinson because he wore that Dodger blue, and the Braves disliked Dodger blue as much as Tommy Lasorda [Los Angeles Dodger manager] says he loves it. The Dodgers always got more attention than any club in baseball in those days, and we enjoyed knocking them off. When we won in 1948 it was very satisfying to finish first, and it was just as satisfying to beat Brooklyn.

"I had pretty good success with Jackie. I just wanted to keep him off base. When he got out there he was like an eggbeater, just moving and bouncing around and disturbing the pitcher's concentration. I remember once I picked him off in a game, and he got on again and jumped around and faked stealing, and finally I got one over there to first and picked him off a second time. I don't think anybody else ever did that. I can't remember Jackie ever trying to steal on me again.

"Of course they would skip my turn a lot against them because they were mostly a right-handed hitting club, except for Snider, and I was supposed to have trouble with clubs like Brooklyn. I was angry about that because I really didn't have any more trouble with them than with anybody else, especially after I developed my screwball in later years.

"Jackie was what I called a front-foot hitter. He leaned into the pitch, and if you threw him off-speed stuff, you could tie him up. He was a very muscular guy, and he was vulnerable to off-speed stuff outside and a good hard fastball inside. You couldn't make a mistake on him because he was a strong hitter, a contact hitter, and he could hit the ball hard somewhere most of the time.

"I didn't have any concerns about playing with black players. I had grown up in Buffalo, went to South Park High School, and played with and against black athletes. When I became a professional player in 1940 I played some games in the wintertime down South against black barnstorming teams. I remember facing Satchel Paige quite a few times, and that was always fun.

"As he got more established in the league, Jackie got to be quite an agitator. He had a lot to say about a lot of things, racial and otherwise. He was a little bit of a crybaby, and when things didn't go his way he was quick to suggest it was because he was a Negro. Baseball's a tough game, and if a hitter leans over the plate, he is going to taste dirt whether it is Jackie Robinson or anybody else. I think Jackie never quite understood that. I think Jackie had a little more immunity than most players on a lot of things. They wanted to protect him. I didn't think that was right.

"I think it was a very good thing that Jackie Robinson made it big in baseball. It is the country's number one sport, and we deserved the best athletes, and until Jackie made it we didn't always have the best athletes getting a chance to show what they could do. The most significant thing about baseball, I think, is how democratic it is. There's no grouping according to age or race or nationality or anything like that. You make it on ability. I went away to fight in World War II, and when I came back the game was open for everybody, and that was a very good thing."

His teammates soon got to know Robinson as a friendly fellow with a good sense of humor. He could kid and be kidded. Ralph Branca, the star pitcher on the Dodgers in 1947 with twenty-one wins at the age of twenty-one, had some good times with Robinson.

BRANCA: "We used to go to the racetrack together a lot, me, Jack, Gilly, Pee Wee, and there was a lot of needling back and forth about picking winners. Jackie liked to gamble on the horses, and he liked to gamble at cards. He was a very good cardplayer, and he would play hearts, a little poker, and gin rummy on some of the longer trips.

"Our relationship really began in spring training when he was not yet with the big club, and I was pitching against the Montreal ball club. Jackie hit a grounder wide of the bag, and I ran over to cover first and got him out. When we crossed paths after the play he said, 'Thanks, Ralph,' I said, 'What for?' He said, 'For not signing the petition.' He was still concerned about the reaction of some of the Dodgers, especially the ones from down South. He seemed to appreciate any kind word he could get.

"I think what was important was how we showed the fans and the opposition he was just part of our team. One time the

Boston bench was giving him a hard time, and Pee Wee just walked over and put his arm on Jack's shoulder out on the field. That did a lot to tell people we were a team. One time I was pitching in St. Louis, and somebody hit a pop-up, and he came racing over from first base to catch it, and just as he did he tripped on the mound. I caught him before he could fall and held him up for an instant. It was no big deal, but I guess people saw it as an act of a teammate, the same as any other teammate.

"Jack was the best competitor I ever saw on a ball field. He could intimidate the opposition and never felt we were out of any ball game. It seemed at times he could almost will things to happen. I was twenty-one that first summer Jackie broke in with us, and I had been around the big leagues four years by then. Jack was twenty-eight and he was just starting. He knew it was late in his career, and I think that had a lot to do with the intensity with which he played. He knew that he just didn't have a lot of time to make it."

For many Southerners, born and trained in the traditions of segregation, playing with or against Robinson was difficult. For many Northerners, with extensive experience in sports with or against blacks, playing with or against Robinson was fairly routine. For a good many players, Robinson's presence on a big-league club was a litmus test of their own attitudes.

Larry Jansen was 21–5 with the 1947 New York Giants. The handsome right-hander had come out of combat service in World War II to establish himself as one of the best pitchers in the league. He was from a small town in Oregon called Verboort and lives in retirement now in the same area, in Forest Grove.

JANSEN: "I didn't know how I would feel about Robinson. I grew up in a town of only two hundred people, and there were certainly no blacks in Verboort. I was more curious about my own reactions than I was about him. He was an excellent player, and he certainly had a lot of pressure on him as the first colored player. I just wanted to get him out and beat Brooklyn. That's all we ever thought about on the Giants, beating Brooklyn.

"One thing I didn't like about Jackie is that he liked to show you up, bunting all the time, jumping around on the bases, stealing when he didn't have to. I don't think that sat well with a lot of players on opposing teams, and it didn't have anything to do with Jackie being colored.

"I never had been around any colored people, like I say, and the first time I faced Robinson I got two quick strikes on him. Then I pitched him tight like I did everybody, and I knocked him down. He was yelling, 'You haven't got the guts to hit me. You haven't got the guts to hit me,' and so I hit him in the ribs with the next pitch. He stole a couple of bases, and the Dodgers were all hollering from the bench that I was going to kill my arm throwing over to first so many times. When Leo became our manager the next year, he had a good way of stopping him. He said I should just hold on to the ball, and that would slow him down. I did that a lot, and when Robinson yelled over at me I didn't say anything but just held on to the baseball. I don't think he liked facing me very much."

No one seemed neutral about Robinson, teammates or opponents. Some came to him with preconceived opinions and never changed. Others changed dramatically. Carl Furillo, the fine Dodger outfielder and one of the toughest competitors on those great Brooklyn teams, came full cycle. He was the only non-Southerner to be involved in the 1947 spring training anti-Robinson petition. He became a staunch Robinson supporter. Furillo played with Brooklyn from 1946 through 1960 with a .299 average and seven Dodger pennants. When he was released after an injury, he became bitter and sued the Dodgers. He could never get a postcareer baseball job. He worked as a construction laborer and ran a meat market around his home in Stoney Creek Mills, Pennsylvania, for many years. He is retired now at the age of sixty-five.

FURILLO: "I was lying in my bunk in the barracks in Panama in the spring of 1947. Some of the older players, Ed Head, Hugh Casey, Dixie Howell, came over to me and said they had this petition to keep the nigger off the team, and I should sign it. They told me if I didn't sign it the niggers would have my job. I signed it. I was an innocent bystander, a kid, the only Italian boy involved in all of this. What the hell did I know? I had watched him play that spring, and it looked like everybody was trying to cut off his legs.

"Rickey took care of the petition thing, and Jackie joined the ball club, and it didn't take long to see he was a natural ballplayer. The other teams screamed all kinds of garbage at him, and we would scream back at them, and they would yell at us for protecting the nigger. You know why they didn't like him? Because he could beat them. If he was a bum ballplayer, you would have seen how quick they liked him. Nobody could compare with Jackie, and it didn't take me long to realize he was going to help me feed my family. Salaries weren't all that big in those days, and I wasn't going to make a big fuss over what color a player was if he was helping me win. You can bet about that.

"I remember Ben Chapman calling him those horrible names, and I remember Enos Slaughter getting all over him, and we gave it right back to them, me and Gilly and Pee Wee and the rest. By the time Jackie could answer back a couple of years later, he didn't need any help. He could take of himself with his mouth or his fists or anything else they wanted.

"Jackie got a little sassy later on, and some guys didn't like that. He had a tough time getting along with Walter Alston. I think he didn't have much respect for Alston as a manager. I didn't have much respect for him myself. I didn't think he was much of a manager. Alston was afraid of the players because most of us made more money than he did, and that galled him. He only liked the brownnosers on the team, and the guy he got along worse with than Jackie was Pee Wee. He kept hearing and reading in the papers how Pee Wee was going to take his job. That caused some friction between Alston and Pee Wee.

"I can't say I got real close with Jackie. Of the black players, I liked Campy better because he wasn't so sensitive and you could kid more with him. Jackie was just a tremendous ballplayer, and he could beat you in so many ways. He was one of us, and I think he did an awful lot to eliminate discrimination just by the way he played and the way he handled himself.

"The best times I ever had with Jackie were just listening to Jackie fight with Leo. When Leo managed Brooklyn in my first year there, he treated me like dirt. Leo was in love with himself and didn't care about young players. I never had much use for Leo, and we finally went at it in the Polo Grounds. Jackie was right there. He didn't have much use for Leo, either. Jackie had a real sharp tongue. It was fun playing with him. The guy was good for us, good for baseball. Where the hell would the big leagues be today without Jackie Robinson?''

The Dodgers won their first pennant since 1941 in Robinson's rookie season. He had become a national figure, and his people walked with more pride down more city streets in the North and the South. Rickey had even allowed some black politicians and church leaders to honor Robinson with a day at Ebbets Field late in 1947. Jackie Robinson had overcome turmoil and torment. He had maintained his dignity through gritted teeth. He had proven, most importantly, that he was a wondrous athlete capable of playing on big-league ball fields with the best of them.

Baseball has an ebb and flow through any season. It has been that way for well over a hundred years, as the game has survived many of the people who ran it, to bond itself in some mystical, unexplainable way with the American public. We are forever young as we root for our favorite teams—a collection of young men from across our nation who are tied together for six or seven months because their uniform shirts read Dodgers, Giants, Cubs, or Cardinals. In March 1947, Robinson was a curiosity and a figure of much animosity. By May he was a promising rookie and a figure of major interest. By July he was an established big leaguer with certain unique skills. By September he was a key Dodger on a pennant-winning team. He was the first baseman on the National League champions and manager Burt Shotton counted on him as he counted on Reese, Reiser, Stanky, Branca, or Edwards.

The New York Yankees and the Brooklyn Dodgers met in the 1947 World Series, one of the most exciting ever played. Baseball fans would long argue the relative merits of the two teams even though the record books show the Yankees as the winners four games to three. It was a Series notable for Bill Bevens's near no-hitter and then a loss to Cookie Lavagetto's pinch-hit double off the wall in right field. It is remembered for the near no-hitter of Rex Barney through five innings until Joe DiMaggio homered. It is recalled today because of one of the greatest outfield catches ever made when backup outfielder Al Gionfriddo caught DiMaggio's huge wallop in front of the Yankee Stadium left center field bullpen fence. It is discussed by baseball fans because of the rare strategy by Yankee manager Bucky Harris of walking the potential winning run in the seventh game—a move Yankee owners would still be upset about a year later when Harris failed to win with the powerful Yankees. He was soon fired.

Probably what was most memorable about the 1947 Series was the minimal interest in the appearance of the first black player in a World Series. The curiosity seemed to diminish greatly by late September when the "Fall Classic" began, and the questions were not about Robinson's color but about his speed.

Robinson got only seven hits in twenty-seven times at bat for a .259 average, but he stole three bases, threatened to steal every other time he was on base, and kept the Yankees in constant turmoil. A young Yankee catcher named Yogi Berra was so embarrassed by his inability to handle Robinson on the bases that he was pleased when Harris removed him from the position and replaced him with a veteran catcher by the name of Aaron Robinson. It was Aaron Robinson and pitchers Spec Shea, Bill Bevens—in a relief role—and left-handed fireballer Joe Page who halted Jackie in the seventh game. He did not get on base, and the Yankees won the game 5–2. It took a lot of heat off Berra.

"I hadn't done a lot of catching then," says Yogi Berra. "Robinson was very tough to control on the bases. We did better with him when we kept him off the bases."

The 1947 baseball season was over. Robinson had lived through it. He had survived hurt and harassment. He had proven he could play with anybody. More importantly, despite some bigots, haters, racists, and snakes, the majority of American baseball fans— the majority of American people—had enjoyed seeing Robinson make it on the fields of the great American pastime.

Discrimination would not end in baseball at the end of the 1947 season. Many might argue that though there are black players everywhere, there are black executives in baseball almost nowhere. That makes the segregation in baseball as serious as it was forty years ago. Jackie Robinson was an exceptional athlete, an exceptional man, and black baseball players in 1987 might quietly examine what their lives today would be like if Jackie Robinson had failed.

Robinson had broken baseball's unwritten color barrier with a vengeance. It would be so ordained officially soon after the 1947 season ended, when Jack Roosevelt Robinson was named baseball's first Rookie of the Year.

How fitting if the powers of baseball in 1987, from Commissioner Peter Ueberroth on down, could see fit to name this award in his honor. The Jackie Robinson Rookie of the Year award. Did any man ever have a tougher rookie season?

CHAPTER

Ten

THROUGH
THE OPEN DOOR

*L*ARRY DOBY JOINED THE
Cleveland Indians in July of 1947 as the first black in the American League. Then the parade of blacks gaining their baseball rights would follow with Dan Bankhead, the second black Dodger, and Satchel Paige, the second black Cleveland Indian. Paige would join the Indians in the middle of 1948, in time to help them win the pennant. He became the first black to pitch in a World Series. Paige, an enormous talent, was always slightly cool when discussing Jackie Robinson. Paige thought, despite his age—judged to be anywhere from forty-one to forty-eight, if the legends were accurate—that he deserved the honor of being first.

Lou Boudreau was the player-manager of the Indians when Paige was brought in by owner Bill Veeck for a tryout. "I was asked by Bill to come out early. I didn't know why. When I got to the ballpark he took me down into the corner of the field and introduced me to Paige. He said he wanted me to catch him. He bragged about the man's control. I put a handkerchief down on the ground, and Paige went back to throw. He pitched over the corner of that handkerchief nine times in nine tries. 'I believe you, Bill,' I said. Paige really helped us win that year."

The Indians had a marvelous pitching staff with Bob Lemon, left-handled knuckleballer Gene Beardon—who would later win the famous play-off pennant game in Boston—and Bob Feller. Known as Rapid Robert, Feller had pitched against Paige in many barnstorming games. He had also opposed Robinson in a couple of exhibitions.

"When I was asked about Robinson I said he had big football shoulders, and I didn't think he could hit good big-league pitching. I had nothing against Jackie or having blacks in baseball. I had made a lot of money on those barnstorming tours against Negro teams. I just said what I felt," Feller says.

It was always difficult for Robinson to accept criticism if he thought it was racially motivated. He thought Feller's remarks were racially motivated. He never stopped criticizing Feller every chance he got.

Ironically, they entered the Hall of Fame together on the same July day in 1962. There was only perfunctory conversation between them. The animosity between Feller and Robinson was not due to race as much as it was economics. Feller was the drawing card in those barnstorming tours. Robinson, according to Monte Irvin, wanted more integrated seating made available and a larger portion of the gate for the black players. Nothing makes a ballplayer madder than sharing money. Feller answered Robinson's demands the only way he knew how: he threw at his head during one game.

With Paige and Doby on the Indians, Roy Campanella soon joining the Dodgers (Durocher *made* the ball club when he put Campanella behind the plate and moved a big catcher named Gil Hodges to first base shortly before moving to the Giants in 1948), Hank Thompson on the Browns, Sam Jethroe with the Braves, and other blacks in almost every big-league club, the arrival of a black player soon became a nonstory. It remained a big story in only two places: New York, where the Yankees waited until 1955 to integrate with Elston Howard, and Boston, where Pumpsie Green joined the club in 1959. The next time color made big news in baseball was in the early 1960s when the Pittsburgh Pirates fielded nine black players.

It was a different Jackie Robinson who reported to the Dodger camp in 1948. Durocher was back in all his feisty persona (the fatherly Burt Shotton had been dispatched again) and the team was still riding high from the 1947 win.

"I wasn't there in 1947, but I saw Jackie that spring. He had ballooned up a hell of a lot by the time I saw him the next spring," Durocher says.

Jackie had gone Hollywood. He had played himself in *The Jackie Robinson Story,* and when he reported to camp he was grossly overweight. Durocher went wild. He needled Jackie every chance he got. He grew livid when Jackie insisted he was in shape. The manager pointed out that Robinson was ticketed to play second base now, with Eddie Stanky traded to Boston, and needed all the speed he could gather.

It would be midseason before Robinson would finally lose those extra winter pounds. He would finish the year with figures almost identical to his rookie season, a .296 average, 85 RBIs, 12 homers, 22 stolen bases, 170 hits, and a league-leading .983 fielding average in his first big-league season as a second baseman. The Dodgers had fallen out of the race early, and the Braves ("Spahn and Sain and Pray for Rain") were the winners. St. Louis finished second.

At Pasadena Junior College, at UCLA, and with the Monarchs and the Royals, Robinson had always been a leader. He helped younger teammates. He rallied his colleagues. He led by word and deed. In 1947, he was just too busy playing well and too involved with the caution of his conduct to express his true leadership personality. That began to surface more in 1948.

A young pitcher by the name of Carl Erskine saw that characteristic early that season. Erskine, sixty, is a banker now in his hometown of Anderson, Indiana. He pitched twelve seasons for the Dodgers, won 122 games against 78 losses, played in 5 pennant winners, owned one of the wickedest curve balls in baseball history, and was forced to retire at the age of thirty-two when his arm gave out.

ERSKINE: "I was pitching in the Dodger organization for Fort Worth in 1948. I got a chance to go three innings against the big club and did real well. When the game was over, I was doing my running in the outfield. I could see Jackie Robinson walking across the field toward me. I didn't know what he wanted. I had never met the man. He stuck out his hand and introduced himself. Then he said, 'You won't be here too long. Your stuff is too good.' You could imagine how that made me feel.

"They had just made Shotton the manager again after Durocher went to the Giants, and they called me up from Fort Worth on July 25. The first guy to come over to my locker to say hello was Jackie. 'I told you that you wouldn't be at Fort Worth long.' He congratulated me for making the ball club. I didn't have any hang-ups over race. I grew up playing with blacks in Anderson, Indiana. One of my teammates and best friends at Shadeland High was John Wilson, a black. Jackie did everything he could to make me feel comfortable, part of the ball club. Here I was, a scared twenty-one-year-old from Indiana, and the famous Brooklyn Dodgers were welcoming me. I remember Jackie and Rachel really being kind to my wife and me when we were trying to learn our way around Brooklyn.

"Jackie never could relax over the race thing, though. He was really marked by that experiment. One time the Dodgers had a birthday party for Pee Wee, and they gave all the fans at Ebbets Field birthday candles, and on a signal they turned out the lights in the ballpark, and everybody held up their candles and sang Happy Birthday to the captain. It was real sweet and touching. Pee Wee was from Louisville, and the Dodgers raised a Confederate flag in his honor and Gladyce Gooding played "Dixie." Well, I looked at Jackie's face, and his skin was pulled tight. He was as angry as I had ever seen him. He took that whole scene as a personal insult and let everybody know about it.

"Jack also felt so strongly about the racial question. I think he had a strained relationship with Campy over it. Campy was just glad to be in the big leagues, and Jackie would say, 'Just because we are here, it doesn't mean the problem is solved.' When Jack would make a fuss in the papers over something, Campy would say, 'Why don't you just keep your nose clean?' It was never easy for either of them because they saw things from a different perspective.

"I remember one time Jackie was in the dugout and some black fan leaned over to ask for his autograph. He was obviously drunk and when Jack saw him he just looked at him and said, 'Go home, clean yourself up. Come back when you're sober.' Jack just sat down in the corner of the dugout. He just felt responsible for everybody.

"There were some racial remarks here and there through the years from some players on our club. I don't recall any open confrontations, but not everybody always agreed with Jack. When he got it from the opposition we always defended him. Things were tense a couple of times over race. In Atlanta, during an exhibition, the hotel was picketed by the Ku Klux Klan because Jackie was staying with us there, and that was a difficult situation.

"The worst thing I can recall was in Cincinnati when Jack received a death threat by mail and turned the letter over to the ball club. Shotton read the letter because he wanted the entire team to know the danger he was playing under. The clubhouse was real quiet as he read these nasty things about how Jackie was going to have his head blown off if he walked on the field. You could feel the tension in the room. It was still. Then Gene Hermanski got up and said, 'If we all go out on the field wearing number 42 on our uniforms, they wouldn't know which one of us to shoot.' It broke the tension and everybody laughed.

"As Jackie got older and a little heavier, his hair began turning white, and some of the guys used to kid him about that. Gil called him Uncle Remus. He wasn't the player in 1955 and 1956 he was when I first joined the club, of course, but he still had that incredible fire, that desire, that burning passion to win. My arm started going bad about 1956. I needed more rest between starts. The Giants had always been a tough club for me and their scout, Clancy Sheehan, had watched us for a week. A reporter interviewed him on what he saw, and he said one thing he noticed was that Erskine was 'throwing garbage. He can't win with that garbage.' I went out to pitch on May 12 and had real good stuff. It was so good I pitched a no-hitter. Jack was playing third that day and made a great play on Willie Mays's bullet to save the no-hitter. I get the last guy out for the no-hitter, and Jackie runs over to the stands where Sheehan is sitting and watching the game. He pulls a newspaper article out of his back pocket. It's the story quoting Sheehan. 'How do you like that garbage; how do you like that garbage now?' He really made me laugh.

"The last time I saw Jack was at the Tavern on the Green in New York. They were making a television program out of Roger Kahn's *The Boys of Summer,* and a lot of us had come over to be honored. Jack was there and looked old. We were kidding about the old days, and he had a copy of the book and said to me, 'Start my hand on the page about me. I can't find it.' When I got home I sat down and wrote Jackie a letter about how much he meant to me and to my career and how kind he and Rachel had been to us. He sat down and sent me a warm, wonderful letter in return. When I got it I just cried."

With a big right-hander in the farm system by the name of Don Newcombe, and with the addition of Erskine on a staff led by Ralph Branca and Joe Hatten, the Dodgers seemed one pitcher away from having a solid starting rotation for the next several years. They added that man in left-hander Preacher Roe, obtained in a deal with Pittsburgh involving Dixie Walker. Roe, a skinny left-hander from Ashflat, Arkansas, weighed 170 pounds on a 6 foot-2-inch frame. He had a good fastball, a good curve, and threw an occasional spitter. He would reveal all about his spitter after his 1954 retirement. He said he thought it would help legalize the pitch again—or eliminate it. It did neither. He is seventy-two and lives in retirement in West Plains, Missouri.

ROE: "I faced Jackie in 1947, and he got a few hits off me, and I got him a few times. He had this open stance and liked the ball away. I wasted that pitch and tried to get him out inside. Most pitchers did, but you couldn't always put it where you wanted it.

"When I came to Brooklyn in 1948, all that racial talk was about over. It didn't mean anything to me. I just wanted to play ball. I grew up on a farm in Viola with about 180 people. There weren't any blacks around there except for the sharecropper farmers, but my father did about the same thing, and he wasn't any better off than they were.

"I enjoyed playing with Jackie. He was like an alley fighter, he wanted to win so bad. He wanted to win at everything: baseball, cards, shooting pool, everything. He also had the most confidence of any ballplayer I ever saw. He made an error one time in a close game I was pitching. A guy does that, he usually stays away from you on the bench the next inning. 'Don't worry, I'll win it for you.' Then he gets up the next inning, hits the ball out of the park, and we win it 3–2. That was Jackie Robinson.

"I think we got along just fine. We had dinner together on occasion, once with Jake Pitler [Dodger coach], and Robby [Robinson] and Jake got to talking about bridge. Jack thought he was a real good bridge player, and Jake kidded him about it, and I think he got a little hot. I think you have to remember this about Jackie Robinson. He had a lot of weight on his shoulders to carry around. He just wanted to win all the time at everything he did."

Robinson was gaining more and more respect around the league for his playing as the 1948 season moved along. A year earlier, the press had concentrated on Robinson as the first black in the game. Now they concentrated on him as the most exciting player in the game.

Robin Roberts was a rookie Philadelphia pitcher in 1948. Before his first start against Brooklyn, he was told by Cy Perkins, an old Philadelphia scout and former American League catcher: "Jackie Robinson is the closest thing I've ever seen to Ty Cobb." Roberts, sixty years old now, is a Hall of Fame pitcher who won 286 games in his brilliant career. He coached college baseball for many years and now does some big-league scouting.

ROBERTS: "By the time I got to the big leagues in 1948, Robinson had convinced everybody he was for real. Ben Chapman was still the manager, and he would yell some ugly things at Jackie, but he was about the only one. Jackie had proven he was too good a player by then, and that stuff started to disappear. I think the game was enhanced by him and there's no doubt in my mind he made it a lot easier for the black players who followed him whether they knew it or not.

"He was among the greatest ballplayers and competitors I ever played against. He was fun to play against because he made the game so exciting. His baserunning was incredible. One time I picked him off first, and he thought he was safe. He got into a big argument with the umpire about the call. The next time up he got a base hit, got to third on another hit, and then stole home. That made up for the bad call for him.

"He won that great game off me in the fourteenth inning in 1951 after knocking himself out catching that line drive. I think that was the best example of the competitor he was. Not too many guys would have survived that shot he gave himself in the stomach. I enjoyed facing Jackie. He was always a great challenge. That whole team was a challenge. I don't think there were many better teams in the history of baseball than the Brooklyn Dodgers around that time."

The Phillies were building a ball club that would challenge the Dodgers in 1949 and beat them in 1950. The Phillies of 1950 were known as the Whiz Kids since so many of their players were youngsters. Roberts was the best pitcher. Their go-go guy, their Jackie Robinson, was a blond-haired Nebraskan by the name of Richie Ashburn. He played fifteen years with the Phillies, Cubs, and Mets and acquired two batting titles and 2,574 hits. His absence in the Hall of Fame is a glaring omission. Ashburn retired as an active player after a .306 season with the original New York Mets to go into broadcasting. He is now a baseball broadcaster and sports columnist in Philadelphia.

ASHBURN: "I never saw a black until I was eighteen years old and playing professional baseball. I never even saw a Catholic. They hadn't too many of either back in Tilden, Nebraska, where I grew up. I heard Chapman and a couple of our Southern players get on Jackie when I first came up. I think it was because he was killing us. One time Chapman was yelling at him, and Jackie came over to our bench after the inning, stuck his face in Chapman's face and said, 'Now, let's see how tough you are.' Chapman never moved. Jackie was a big guy, an intimidating presence, and not too many guys wanted to challenge him directly.

"We were in a close game once and Monk Meyer was pitching for us. [Russ (Monk) Meyer was considered a baseball flake, an oddball, a character. He later came to the Dodgers, was removed from a game by manager Charlie Dressen, and angrily heaved the resin bag high in the air. It landed smack on his head as he walked from the mound.] Monk had Jackie on third and all of a sudden Jackie began dancing off the base. He was driving Monk crazy. Monk finally threw over and Jackie was caught in a rundown. Andy Seminick [Phillies catcher] had Jackie out by a mile, but somehow he reversed direction and he got past Seminick. Monk was halfway between third and home, and when he got the ball back he just chased Jackie, and he chased him all the way across home plate. He was screaming at Jackie when the inning ended, and he was so embarrassed he threatened to take Jackie on in a fight. 'I'll meet you in the tunnel.' Robinson got up from the Dodger dugout. I leaned over to Monk and said, 'Forget it, Monk, he'll kill you.' Cooler heads prevailed.

"We had been told to slide hard into him as often as we could. We wanted to put him out of the game, and we thought that his legs had taken a lot of punishment. I slid into him this one time and really cut him badly. The trainer rushed out to second base, and I could see he was bleeding the same color blood as me. I just stood there and felt ashamed of myself, like a real jerk. There was no reason for that. It wasn't part of baseball. The next game we played I walked over to him and apologized for cutting him and told him that it wouldn't happen again. It never did.

"He was an absolutely fearless player at the plate and on bases. There was no way to intimidate him. You just hoped if the pitcher knocked him on his ass, he wouldn't hit a line drive at him the next time.

"Jackie was a very proud person, and I know it was galling to have to go through so much stuff, especially in those first few years. I think he was pretty angry about what had happened and what he had to take early in his career. He was bitter about it later on in his career, after he had achieved so much. It made me sad to see him leave the game so unhappy."

Not even his continued success on the field in his second season could relieve Robinson of the pressures of representing his race. He had become a spokesman, a national hero, a figure of history in those two seasons—a man other men wanted to emulate. Blacks across America were inspired by his success. They began to think in terms of their own success. The first measurable movement began, of course, in baseball. That was the avenue Robinson had used and blacks across America wanted to follow.

"The most significant thing besides just opening the door for us," says Ed Charles, "was that the entire black population of America became Dodger fans."

Bright, articulate, and willing to engage in verbal combat with the press, Robinson soon became the focus of the Dodger locker-room interviews. Some sportswriters, not terribly attuned to the changing social patterns in the country, wanted no part of that. All they wanted from Robinson was discussion on hits, runs, and errors. Robinson wanted to use his fame for a format for serious social discussion. This was probably best expressed by an aggressive reporter for the *New York Daily News* by the name of Dick Young. He would later command enormous influence, fame, and money for his sports column, but in the late 1940s he was just establishing himself as the best baseball writer in the country. He covered the Brooklyn Dodgers for the *Daily News*. Young once told Robinson, "When I talk to Campy I almost never think of him as a Negro. Anytime I talk to you I am acutely aware of the fact that you're a Negro."

Robinson would explain later why he disagreed with Young's analysis, and why he wanted to discuss issues, not just stats. "People thought of Campanella as a Negro when he was Jim Crowed at the Adams Hotel down in St. Louis. They think of him as a Negro when he goes to spring training in the South. They think about him as a Negro when he goes to buy a house." His fight was for others even more than for himself.

A young broadcaster out of Fordham University in New York would soon join the Brooklyn Dodger broadcast team. He had played a little baseball there, but his true appeal was his shock of red hair, his good looks, his beautifully modulated voice, and his hard-working style of in-depth baseball broadcasting. His name was Vince Scully, and he would be associated with Dodger broadcasts for more than a quarter of a century. He currently broadcasts NBC baseball with Joe Garagiola.

SCULLY: "This was around 1950, 1951, in Philadelphia. It was one of those blistering hot Philadelphia summer days. We were playing in old Shibe Park, and when the players came out of that small exit from the ballpark to board the team bus, an old, disheveled fan was outside waiting for them. He had huge slices of watermelon on a tray. As each player passed by, this old guy gave them a slice of watermelon. They thanked him and got on the bus with the cool, refreshing fruit. Finally, Jackie comes out of the clubhouse. The guy smiles at him and thrusts a piece of watermelon in his hand. Jack goes wild. He thinks he is being mocked, ridiculed, and made fun of with the watermelon. He tells the guy off in very harsh tones. Then he gets on the bus. He looks up to see most of his teammates sitting there eating slices of watermelon.

"Jack took great pride in what he did. He wanted to be the best at everything. One winter we were both invited to spend a weekend at Grossinger's in the Catskills. I had grown up in New York, so I was pretty good on ice skates. Jackie had grown up in southern California. He had never been on skates before. He comes over to the skating rink. He sees me there and says, 'Want to race?' I looked at him and laughed. 'Can you skate?' He says, 'No, but I can race.' We kidded around a little more about me beating Jackie Robinson in anything, and he laces up his skates and we race. I beat him, of course, because he didn't really know how to skate, but Jack didn't think not knowing how to do something was much of a handicap.''

Another Dodger broadcaster also saw Jackie Robinson under a lot of pressure. Ernie Harwell was broadcasting games in Atlanta before he came to Brooklyn. He was actually "traded" as a broadcaster to Brooklyn for a catcher. Atlanta owner Earl Mann needed a catcher and Branch Rickey needed a broadcaster. Harwell came to Brooklyn and Mann received catcher Cliff Dapper from the Dodgers.

HARWELL: "I was in Atlanta when the Ku Klux Klan decided to picket the hotel where the Dodgers were staying. This was a very serious situation. Those people were not the kind to make idle threats. Their leader had been quoted as saying he would see to it that Jackie didn't play in Atlanta. When he did play, it was a very scary thing.

"Atlanta was my home, and I understood the customs there. That was a very difficult time. When I came to Brooklyn I got along fine with Jackie. He was a great player and a gentleman. We always chatted warmly when I was in Brooklyn and afterwards when I moved over to the Giants."

Robinson's presence in Brooklyn meant increased crowds around Ebbets Field. The Dodgers sold out more often, and the people selling banners, pennants, baseballs, and photos also sold out more often. Robinson had a distinct influence on the economy of youngsters hustling around Bedford Avenue and Sullivan Place. Even the ticket sellers working for the Dodgers appreciated Jackie Robinson. John Downey, employed now by a power company, was a ticket seller at Ebbets Field.

DOWNEY: "I started with the Dodgers in 1940 as a stile boy. Those are the kids who turn the stiles when people pay their way into the park. My salary was fifty cents a day and after the third inning I could go inside for free and watch the rest of the game. I always worked the bleachers. It was fifty-five cents and a dollar ten in later years. By that time I had become a ticket seller and there was always a lot of business and a lot of tickets sold when Jackie Robinson joined the club. We used to sell out most of the time in a big series against the Giants before he came, but we started selling out against the Cubs and Cards and Phillies and just about everybody after he came. I think Jackie Robinson had a lot to do with increasing the Dodger business. I don't know the figures because I was only interested in my own take."

By the end of his second season in Brooklyn, Robinson had become a big part of the Dodger team. He had helped increase business. He had made the team better. Across America he had become an athlete of equal standing to heavyweight champion Joe Louis. He had become a godlike figure to blacks. To whites, he was also significant and slightly awesome.

Robinson had a home in the Flatbush section of Brooklyn, not too far from Ebbets Field. He rented the home and lived there during the season with Rachel and Jackie, Jr. One day he was walking down Utica Avenue in Brooklyn. Every head turned as he walked slowly with Jackie, Jr. I spotted him, pulled a page from my looseleaf school folder, and approached him.

"Could I have your autograph, Jackie, please?"

"Sure," he said. "What's your name?"

I gulped out my name. He signed the paper, said he was on the way down the street to the post office, and took off. That was my first autograph. And my last.

CHAPTER

Eleven

"ERSKINE BOUNCED
A CURVE"

*M*ANY ARGUE STRONGLY that the most glorious years in all baseball history were the seasons in the early 1950s. In the five years between 1949 and 1953, the Brooklyn Dodgers won three pennants, lost out on the final day of the 1950 season when Cal Abrams was thrown out at home by Richie Ashburn, and tied for the flag in 1951. They lost the third game of the pennant play-off when Bobby Thomson hit his heroic home run off Ralph Branca.

The Dodgers lost to the hated Giants in 1954 and came back to win again in 1955. This time they also won their only Brooklyn World Series. They won again in 1956.

Jackie Robinson, at the age of thirty, had his peak season in 1949. He won the batting title with a .342 mark. He led the league in stolen bases with 37. He hit 16 homers and batted in 124 runs. He had 203 hits and played all 156 games. He played a brilliant second base and emerged as the key figure on a strong Dodger team.

He would follow that marvelous year with five straight seasons over .300 with marks of .328 in 1950, .338 in 1951, .308 in 1952, .329 in 1953, and .311 in 1954. He hit only .256 in an injury-filled 1955 season and .275 in his final year of 1956. He was a heavy-legged thirty-seven-year-old that summer.

Perhaps even more importantly, Robinson's 1949 success,

including the coveted Most Valuable Player award, the most prestigious honor in all sports, allowed him even greater freedom to speak out off the field as well as on. Branch Rickey had freed Robinson from the bondage of his early years, no longer fearing that a Robinson outburst would result in a ballpark riot. Jackie argued with umpires, opposing players, the press, and sometimes his teammates.

"I think Jack was one of those guys who just enjoyed arguing," says Pee Wee Reese.

He carried his fight for racial freedom everywhere he went, to the still-segregated hotels in the National League, to the segregated, insufferable conditions he found every spring in Florida (the Dodgers had built their own spring training camp complex at Vero Beach by 1949), to speaking engagements he accepted each winter, to congressional committees, to radio and television interview shows, and to political platforms when candidates would agree to the conditions of his support.

Unlike Joe Louis, a charismatic figure mainly for his athletic skills, Robinson was an intelligent, articulate, forceful man off the ball field. He could debate anybody. He would debate anybody. He was unafraid to prick sacred cows. He found the New York Yankees a comfortable target as they were constantly unable or unwilling to integrate. Under the conservative, country-club mentality leadership of Dan Topping and Del Webb, with general manager George Weiss clearly uninterested in a black player, and with manager Casey Stengel a victim of his early twentieth-century racist upbringing in Kansas City, the Yankees lagged behind Brooklyn, the Giants, and most other teams in their own league in this matter. They won so easily and so regularly (five straight World Series triumphs from 1949 to 1953 under Stengel) that the white fans put little emphasis on the matter. There were few black fans. While thousands of blacks passed through the gates at Ebbets Field, the rare black face at Yankee Stadium was usually a token government official or business executive. Racism was clearly part of the Yankee core.

Bill McCorry, a crotchety, old retired pitcher who was the Yankee traveling secretary, once said, "No nigger will ever have a berth on any train I'm running." It may have been tasteless, but it was probably indicative of the attitude of the Yankee management.

When pressed by Robinson, by the NAACP, by progressively bold civil rights groups, the Yankees would suggest they were not prejudiced at all. "We're just looking for the right man," farm director Lee MacPhail said. That was a euphemism for "a Campanella, not a Robinson, a grateful black, not a boat rocker." They found their man in Elston Howard, who starred as a Yankee for twelve seasons from 1955 through 1967 before moving on to Boston. He returned to the Yankees after his playing days, worked as a coach and front-office assistant without specified duties, and died in 1980 without ever being given a chance to manage: the new Yankee regime, echoing the old, avoided blacks off the field. Howard was the perfect black Yankee. He was a wonderful player, loyal, obedient, quiet, dignified, a perfect boy scout. Even though Stengel liked Howard personally and valued his skills, he often repeated the same line. "When I get a nigger," he said of the heavy-footed Howard, "I get the only one who can't run."

Led by Robinson, most of the early black players could run. Willie Mays, Hank Aaron. Sam Jethroe. Larry Doby. They could all hit. The pitchers could all throw hard. They had to be, as other blacks had to be to get into law school, medical school, engineering school, executive positions, higher military rank, just that much better. One of the best was Don Newcombe.

Newcombe joined Brooklyn in 1949. He won 17 games. He won 19 in 1950. He was 20–9 in 1951. He was 9–8 in 1954 before entering military service. He was 27–7 in 1956, the first Cy Young Award winner and the National League MVP. Mention the name of Don Newcombe today to most baseball fans and they know two things about him. He is a recovered alcoholic, and he never won a World Series game. "He choked against the Yankees," so many said. Racism? Newcombe is a drug and alcohol counselor for the Los Angeles Dodgers.

NEWCOMBE: "I was the 1956 MVP and Cy Young winner, and I think that entitles me to a spot in the Hall of Fame. They have a place for great players and for writers and for broadcast-ers, but they don't have a place for MVP winners. That's not right.

"It was a thrill playing on the same team as Jackie Robinson. He was just such a tremendous competitor. I had a tendency to let down a little some days, to lose my concentration. Jack would come to the mound and get all over me. He would call me every name you could think of. I would get pretty angry at him, and I would take it out on the hitters.

"If there was no Jackie Robinson, there might not have been a Roy Campanella, a Don Newcombe, any of us. Who knows what would have happened if Jackie failed? I owe everything I have, everything I have made in my life through baseball, to Jackie Robinson. I want young people, especially young black people, to know the history, to know the battles he fought, the racism, the turmoil he went through. It hadn't changed much by the time I got there. I was from New Jersey and never saw segregation. When I had to go to Florida and couldn't eat in the same restaurants with my teammates or sleep in the same hotels, that was very difficult for me to take. We fought it every minute. Jackie never stopped fighting.

"Jack was a forerunner, a leader, in what happened later, the civil rights progress of the late 1950s and early 1960s. People saw what he could accomplish under such odds. They could accomplish much in their own fields."

After a marvelous season in 1949, Robinson had a miserable World Series. He got only three hits in sixteen at bats for a .188 average. The Yankees won it in five games. Newcombe pitched the opener for Brooklyn and lost a terrific 1–0 game when Tommy Henrich broke up a scoreless battle in the bottom of the ninth with a home run. Preacher Roe came back the next day to win a 1–0 game. The Dodgers scored their lone run in the second inning when Robinson doubled and Gil Hodges singled him home.

Ralph Branca, who had consistent bad luck in postseason play, pitched into the ninth of a 1–1 game before the Yankees drove him from the mound and won the game 4–3. Eddie Lopat beat Newcombe in the fourth game with relief help from Allie Reynolds.

Don Newcombe always
considered Jack his hero.

*Jack and Roy Campanella
at an awards dinner*

Stanky, Robby, and Reese at Oldtimers Day
at Yankee Stadium

Hank Aaron, all-time home-run king, is the highest-ranking black in the baseball front office.

*Jackie's last Oldtimers Day at Yankee Stadium
with Billy Cox, Pee Wee Reese, and Eddie Stanky*

*Dodger General Manager Al Campanis befriended Jack
as a Montreal Royals teammate.*

*Jack at home with his family, Jack, Jr.,
Sharon, David, and Rachel Robinson*

*Branch Rickey and Rachel Robinson with Jack
at 1962 Hall of Fame induction*

Jack was inducted at Cooperstown with Edd Roush,
Bob Feller, and Bill McKechnie.

*Shea Stadium Oldtimers Day with
Pee Wee Reese, Dizzy Dean, and Bob Feller*

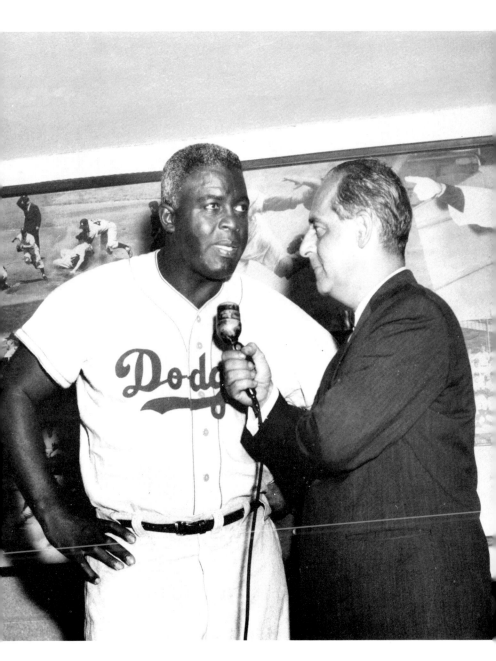

Broadcaster Ben Grauer interviews Robinson.

Jack is honored at "Little Rock Park"
Opposite: *Mallie, Willa Mae, and Rachel,*
with Jack at Little Rock ceremony.

Jackie at U.S. Senate
hearings in 1970

Willa Mae Robinson Walker and her brother Mack standing in front of their homes in Pasadena. The location of the original family home on Pepper Street is marked as an historic site by a sidewalk plaque.

*Mack Robinson holding his 1936 Olympic medal
with photo blowups of his running days
and brother Jack's Dodger days*

"Allie didn't like black people," says Lopat. "He just came in and knocked Robinson down. That was it. The Indian was a pretty tough fellow."

Vic Raschi beat Rex Barney in the fifth game, Robinson had a single, and the Yankees had their second World Series victory over Brooklyn in three seasons.

Robinson had another strong season in 1950 with a .328 year, but it would end as a downer. Cal Abrams was on second in the final game of the season. Duke Snider singled sharply to center. Richie Ashburn, playing shallow, picked the ball up quickly and fired a strike home. Abrams, trying to score with nobody out as coach Milt Stock inexplicably waved him home, was thrown out at the plate. Reese, who had singled, followed the play at the plate and raced to third. Snider, hustling all the way, ran to second. Robinson was next. Forget it. With one out and two on and first base open, Robinson was purposely passed. Robin Roberts, almost always magnificent in the clutch, retired Carl Furillo on a pop-up, and Gil Hodges on a fly, to end the inning.

Dick Sisler hit a tenth-inning three-run homer off star-crossed Don Newcombe to win the game 4–1. The Philadelphia Whiz Kids went to the World Series that year instead of Brooklyn and lost four straight games to the Yankees.

Six weeks later Branch Rickey resigned as president of the Dodgers. Walter O'Malley, a tough, aggressive New York attorney, took over. It ended Robinson's honeymoon with Dodger management. From that day forward the special relationship, the father-son, teacher-student association Robinson had had with Rickey was not repeated. His relationship with O'Malley was probably no better, no worse, than O'Malley had with Pee Wee Reese, Gil Hodges, Duke Snider, or any other big-name Dodger. Robinson would leave the Dodgers after the 1956 season, after an aborted trade, to O'Malley, just another in his large group of Dodger high-salaried stars. In fact, before he left he was the highest paid star on the team at $43,000 per year.

If William Shakespeare were a sportswriter in 1951, he would have well understood the tragedy of Coogan's Bluff. No single swing ever delivered so much pain. Some thirty-five years later, the pain lingers.

The Dodgers had a thirteen-and-a-half game lead in August. How could they lose? The Giants began the month winning sixteen in a row and gained only two games on Brooklyn. Then, day by day, the big lead shrunk. Ten, nine, seven, six games separated the two teams. The Dodgers needed only five wins in their last ten games to clinch, even if the Giants won them all. The Giants won them all. The Dodgers won four of nine and needed to win their last regular season game to tie.

The Giants had already won in Boston and waited breathlessly for a radio report on the Dodger game at Philadelphia. Brooklyn fell behind 6–1 to the Phillies. They closed to 6–5 and then it went again to 8–5. Rube Walker doubled for two runs, and Carl Furillo singled to tie it at 8–8. In the twelfth inning, with the bases loaded and two out, Eddie Waitkus rifled a line drive toward right field. Robinson, playing deep for the left-handed pull hitter, ran to his right and dove full out. He caught the ball stretched out, fell to the ground hard, and caught his right elbow in the pit of his stomach. He was woozy for several minutes and finally walked off the field with help from Pee Wee Reese and trainer Doc Wendler. Robinson was still wobbly as he sat in the dugout. He started to move to the clubhouse. Reese looked at his teammate and said, "We need you." Robinson said, "I don't think I can help the team." Reese had been through too many tough games with Robinson not to know better. "If you can't," said Pee Wee, "I don't know who can." Robinson struggled back to second base for the bottom of the thirteenth inning. Bud Podbielan, the new Dodger pitcher, retired the Phillies.

In the top half of the fourteenth, Robinson came to the plate to face Phillie ace Robin Roberts. "The one thing I didn't want to do was give him a ball he could pull," remembers Roberts. "I made sure the pitch was outside."

Roberts threw a high outside fastball, a ball that, at best, could have been lined to right for a single. Robinson snapped that quick bat, caught the pitch in full flight, and drove it over the left-field wall for the game-winning home run.

In the bottom of the inning Podbielan, a footnote in Dodger

history, gave up a single to Ashburn. He moved to second on a sacrifice bunt. There he stayed as the Dodger right-hander retired slugger Del Ennis and Eddie Waitkus (fully recovered now from the gunshot wound inflicted on him by crazed Ruth Ann Steinhagen—a legend that became the source for the book and movie *The Natural*) to win the game.

Brooklyn was on a train home for the showdown against the Giants. They had blown the 13½-game lead, but they had rallied in the final game to show their courage. It would be the best two of three.

Unlucky Ralph Branca lost the first game. The big blow for the Giants was a home run by Bobby Thomson. A rookie sinker baller named Clem Labine was given the second game start because the rest of the Dodger staff had been blown out in the final week of the furious race. Labine, now sixty years old, is in the banking business in his hometown of Woonsocket, Rhode Island. He pitched thirteen years in the big leagues, mostly as a relief pitcher. He finished up his career with three appearances with the original Mets of 1962.

LABINE: "I remember when I first pitched a spring exhibition with the St. Paul club against the Dodgers. I sat down that night and wrote a letter home. It began, 'Guess who I pitched against today. Yes, Jackie Robinson.' He was the most exciting player I ever saw, and he gave me goose bumps almost every game I played with him.

"Jackie not only was a great player as everybody knows, he was also a great individual. He took a lot, always held his head high, and fought back. He had this high-pitched voice which got higher when he got mad. I remember him yelling at umpires and opposing players from the bench, and it was never any question about which of us it was. There was no voice like Jackie's voice.

"After we both retired, I didn't see him. Then one day, in 1963 I think it was, I got a letter from him. He asked me to participate in the March on Washington. I had never been very political. I was in business then, and I thought about it a great deal. I knew how much that meant to him. Jackie had very strong feelings for his race. I had a couple of sleepless nights, and then I wrote him back a letter saying that no matter how much I supported his goals, I just couldn't participate. I thought that would be the last time I'd ever hear from Jack. A few days later, well before the march, I received a letter from him. He said he respected and admired me, was truly unhappy I felt that way, but understood completely. It was a letter with much feeling.

"I pitched that shutout over the Giants to tie up the play-offs. I was a rookie that year and it was some thrill. Then we played the third game, we got beat unfortunately, and the season was over. Bobby Thomson hit the home run. One of the first guys in the Giants clubhouse to congratulate them was Jackie Robinson. I was in there a few minutes later. I walked up to Bobby Thomson, stuck out my hand, shook his, and wished him well in the Series. He had this funny look on his face. 'Fine, thanks. What's your name?' "

October 3, 1951. Ask any Dodger fan over the age of forty, and he'll tell you where he was that day. "The Giants win the pennant, the Giants win the pennant, the Giants win the pennant," bellowed radio announcer Russ Hodges. The sordid details went something like this: Brooklyn had driven Sal Maglie from the mound in the eighth inning with three runs to break open a 1–1 game. The Dodgers were howling from their bench at Leo Durocher's Giants. Brooklyn manager Charlie Dressen led the torment. The Dodgers went wild as Don Newcombe blew the Giants away in the eighth.

Larry Jansen pitched a quiet Dodger ninth. Newcombe started the bottom of the ninth. He faced Alvin Dark. The Giants short-stop slapped a ground ball between Robinson and Hodges into right. One on. Don Mueller was next. He was a left-handed hitter nicknamed Mandrake the Magician for his bat control. Hodges held Dark closely on first base—silly strategy as things turned out in a 4–1 game. Mueller hit a sharp grounder toward right. Hodges, off the bag quickly, broke sharply to his right. The ball just whizzed by. It could have easily been a double play. Two on. None out. Monte Irvin, the first black Giant, popped out. "If I didn't pop up," he says now, "nobody would have heard of Bobby Thomson."

Whitey Lockman, a blond North Carolinian, doubled to left

center. Dark scored and Mueller, with a twisting slide, broke his ankle coming into third. While Dressen walked to the mound to rescue Newcombe, Clint Hartung came on to run for Mueller.

Activity was furious in the Dodger bullpen. Four pitchers— Labine, who had pitched nine innings the day before, Carl Erskine, Branca, and Clyde King—were there. Branca and Erskine were throwing. The most rested and talented Dodger pitcher, Preacher Roe, was on the bench. He had not pitched since the previous Saturday. This was now Wednesday. "I was rested," Roe says, "but Dressen wanted me for the World Series opener."

Labine had tried to lob a few pitches. He was too stiff. King, a reliever, had been ineffective Sunday against the Phillies. "When you were ineffective," says Erskine, "Charlie could bury you." Erskine had bounced a curve ball into the dirt in front of the bullpen plate just before Dressen had checked with bullpen coach Clyde Sukeforth. "Are they ready?" Dressen had asked.

"Erskine just bounced a curve," Sukeforth said.

"How about Branca?"

"He's throwing hard."

Dressen walked to the mound with the phrase "He's throwing hard" in his mind. He signaled for Branca.

"That was probably the best curve ball I ever threw," laughs Erskine now. "'I probably would have come in and given up the home run, and I'd have to carry that all these years instead of Ralph."

Erskine continued to throw as Branca walked to the mound. Thomson was up. Willie Mays was on deck. Dressen decided to have Branca pitch to Thomson. Branca threw a fastball for a strike.

"The next pitch was supposed to be a fastball inside," says Rube Walker, catching that day in place of the injured Roy Campanella. "It was supposed to be too inside to hit, or if he did swing, he couldn't hit it good. The next pitch was going to be the good curve. With one out and two on. We needed a pop-up or a strikeout or a ground ball."

The pitch was out over the plate, the proverbial baseball meatball. Thomson hit a low line drive into the short left field stands for three runs and the ball game.

"All I could think of," Thomson said years later, "was that I had beaten Brooklyn."

"The home run in Brooklyn that Thomson hit would have been an out in the Polo Grounds," says Branca, "and the home run in the Polo Grounds would have been an out in Brooklyn."

Thomson ran to first base with a hopping stride. He moved to second. Jackie Robinson watched him touch the base. He bounced toward third. Robinson, ever hopeful of a misstep, kept an eye on him. He ran home, took a two-footed jump on the plate, and created the Miracle of Coogan's Bluff. Robinson finally turned away and walked slowly to the center-field clubhouse. For the Brooklyn Dodgers and Jackie Robinson, the 1951 season was history.

While Branca lay prone on the clubhouse steps, tears streaming down his cheeks, Robinson showered and dressed. Then he walked across the small hall separating the home clubhouse from the visitors and walked through the crowded room. He went straight to Leo Durocher's office.

"Congratulations, Leo, and good luck in the Series," he said.

Durocher says now, "That was one of the hardest things any man ever had to do, and I really appreciated that. Jackie Robinson had class. He was some man."

The 1951 play-off loss to the Giants, one of the most bitter defeats in baseball history, seemed to have a strange, positive effect on the Dodgers. With the 1950 loss on the last day of the regular season, and the horrible play-off loss, the Dodgers were bound together in some mystical way. Dick Young, the clever baseball writer for the *Daily News*, had led one of his stories with a stinging insult. "The tree that grows in Brooklyn," Young wrote, "is an apple tree." No insult hurts more for a professional athlete than the suggestion that he or she is not equal to the emotional pressures of the game. Young suggested the Dodgers were a bunch of chokers, the most vile description of a sports team.

It was an insult that galled Robinson more than any of the others. His entire life was built on respect. His entire aura was as a winner. The leaders on the Dodgers—Reese, Gil Hodges, Carl Erskine, Robinson—often spent much time discussing this manly aspect of their professional lives. While Roy Campanella was as determined a competitor as the rest, he took losses with less despair than Robinson. He was always certain there would be another day. Robinson never seemed sure.

As the personality of the group dynamics of the Dodgers was being blended early in the 1950s, Robinson seemed more bonded with Reese and Hodges and Snider than with Campanella, Newcombe, or later the black infielder Jim Gilliam. Robinson, the militant black, seemed closer to his white teammates than to the black ones. He played cards often with them. He was seen at dinner in the newly opened hotel restaurants with white teammates. He engaged in clubhouse banter more with Reese, Snider and Hodges, not Newcombe or Campy. Robinson seemed on a different wave-length than Campy. In spring training, Campanella could sit with the black cooks and kitchen help at Dodgertown for hours—singing, laughing, telling stories. Today that location is called Campy's Kitchen. Robinson felt this menial work of his racial brothers was demeaning. He would not add his presence to that scene.

When Stanley Woodward, the sports columnist of the *Tribune,* attacked Robinson after his retirement for a racial bias in favor of blacks, especially involving a Floyd Patterson–Ingemar Johansson fight, he received a strange letter from Roscoe McGowen, the *New York Times* baseball writer who covered Robinson's entire Dodger career:

"It seems mandatory that I voice my agreement with and appreciation of your comments on Jackie Robinson," McGowen wrote. "He has been annoying to me for years, although I doubt more than a couple of instances could be found where I adversely criticized him in print. Even so, he has said (by expedient of omitting my name when mentioning other writers, such as Dick Young, who were not anti-Negro) that I am anti-Negro.

"I'll admit I'm anti-Robinson and with what seems to me to be good reasons based on personal contact, not heresay. I question his sincerity—which you don't—so far as his having any deep feelings about other Negroes doing well.

"He had no Negro pals on the Dodgers. In the clubhouse he could always be found in conversation with Reese, Snider, Hodges and other of the more outstanding white players. As for my anti position, I was never anti-Campanella, anti-[Charley] Neal, anti-Gilliam, anti-[Sandy] Amoros or anti-[John] Roseboro."

No one, it seemed, could be around Robinson for long without forming strong opinions about him. The man was electric off the field as well as on.

Two new pitchers joined the Dodgers in 1952. One was a white man from Morehead, North Carolina, named Ben Wade. The other was a black man from Plainfield, New Jersey, named Joe Black.

WADE: "I grew up on a street in Morehead with black families. We were poor, and my family was one of three white families on a street which was mostly black. I didn't think anything of it. When I came over to the Dodgers in 1952, I just wanted to make the ball club. I didn't care who else was on it.

"I was in shape when spring training started in 1952. I pitched a couple of good games, but I didn't know my status on the team. I knew the Dodgers could use pitching. One day Jackie came over to me and said he thought I could help the ball club. I didn't know if it was just his opinion or what it meant. 'You've got this team made.' When he said that I just relaxed and pitched well and made the ball club. I won eleven ball games that year for Brooklyn, and I don't know if I even would have been there if Jackie Robinson didn't help me relax in the spring."

BLACK: "I first met Jackie in the Negro league when I was with the Baltimore Elite Giants. He had apparently heard some talk then, late in 1945, that there were white scouts around looking at colored ballplayers. He said, 'We're gonna get up there. Just keep your nose clean.' He knew I could throw hard.

"When I was a kid I was a big baseball fan, cut out pictures from the papers. Hank Greenberg was my favorite player. Maybe colored kids did this as a defensive measure against hating white people. They wouldn't let us play with them, but through the papers and their pictures we could imagine it. You couldn't find anything in the New Jersey papers I read about black players.

"I went to Morgan State on an athletic scholarship in 1947, and people started telling me I looked like Jackie. He was getting a lot of attention then as the first one, and I could even run well then.

"When I joined Brooklyn they roomed Jackie and me together for a while. I got to know him real well, and I could see how much pain he went through in those early days. We were still going through it in 1952. They called me coon and nigger and old black Joe and all that garbage, and every time I felt like fighting when it came from the stands, Jackie would just put his hand on my shoulder and say, 'You can't fight. Maybe someday, but not now. You can't fight.' It was hard to take.

"Jackie developed this internal defense system, this thick skin, and he just didn't let it bother him. Sure, he was dying inside, but he felt the real answer was just playing well and beating the other guys. Campy's idea was to win. Jackie's idea was to win and gain respect. He used that word a lot. He wanted respect as a man as well as an athlete.

"He took me with him on a couple of barnstorming tours, and I made some extra money. As a kid that was very important. I think he helped out the black players as much as he could. One time in the winter he called me at home and asked me if I wanted to make fifty bucks for a few minutes' work. I said I sure did, and he set me up with an autographing session at some store. Fifty bucks was big money for that in 1952. They wanted Jackie, but he said he couldn't come and they should take me.

"Maybe some players, black and white, didn't like Jack. I'm sure that's possible. He didn't buddy around with everybody. The biggest thing in his life was just playing ball and being with Rachel and the children.

"I was really hurt when I read what Vince Coleman had said, and I had to write that letter. Not know Jackie? Wow. Unfortunately we tend to forget about people who stick their necks out for all of us. They get chopped off but we get the benefits. That's the way it was with Jackie. I think all black players should understand today what they owe Jackie. I think all of baseball should know that. Jackie Robinson changed the game and changed America for the better."

Wade won eleven games, Black won fifteen games, Hodges hit thirty-two homers, Campanella hit twenty-two, Snider hit twenty-one, and Robinson tied his career high of nineteen with a .308 batting average. The Dodgers won the pennant in 1952 by four and a half games. It didn't make up for the 1951 play-off loss, but at least they were in the World Series against the Yankees and the Giants were not.

The Series was another good one. It went to the seventh game. The score was 4–2 in the seventh with the Dodgers up in Yankee Stadium. They quickly loaded the bases on a walk to Furillo, a single by Billy Cox, and a walk to Reese. Vic Raschi, a right-hander, was removed from the game, and Bob Kuzava, a hard-throwing left-hander, replaced him. The next two scheduled Dodger batters were left-handed-hitting Duke Snider and right-handed-hitting Jackie Robinson.

"While Kuzava was warming up I was talking to Jackie. I told him I had faced Kuzava in the minors and always hit him well. He was an overhand hard thrower, and those were the kind of left-handers I always hit. 'I'll get him.' Then Jackie looked at me and said, 'If you don't get him, I will.' He was that confident."

Kuzava threw hard, but he was wild. He ran the count to three balls and two strikes. He threw Snider a high fastball. The Dodger center fielder reached out for a pitch that was out of the strike zone and popped it up.

Robinson swung his three bats, let two fall away, and moved to the plate confidently. Kuzava went to three balls and two strikes on Robinson. The runners moved. Kuzava threw a curve ball outside and Robinson swung. He lifted a high pop fly between first and second base. First baseman Joe Collins never saw the ball. Second baseman Billy Martin charged in from the deep second base position, lost his cap, and caught the ball near the mound. It snuffed out the rally. Kuzava retired the Dodgers in the eighth and ninth to save the game and the Series for the Yankees.

As he turned back toward the dugout to get his glove after Martin caught the pop-up, Robinson caught Snider's eye.

"I guess we didn't get him," he said with a small smile.

The Dodgers won the pennant in 1953 by thirteen games. Some people consider this 1953 team the best Brooklyn team ever, even better than the 1955 Brooklyn World Champions. Furillo won the batting title. Four players—Hodges, Furillo, Snider, and Campanella—hit over 20 homers each with Snider hitting 42 and Campy collecting 41. Erskine won 20 games. Robinson, at 34, hit .329 with 95 RBIs. Campanella had 142 RBIs and won his second of three MVP titles.

Almost more importantly for the Brooklyn fans, the Giants had a horrible year under Leo Durocher and finished fifth. Sal Maglie had an off year. That was enough joy for any Dodger fan. The Barber was the borough's bad guy.

Sal Maglie was born in Niagara Falls, New York, on April 26, 1917. He was a journeyman high-school and semiprofessional pitcher. He made it to the New York Giants in 1945. He was 5–4. Then he disappeared into the bowels of the Mexican League. When he returned from pitching in that light air, he had a marvelous curve ball and an intimidating fastball. At the age of sixty-nine he has fought off a serious brain operation and a stroke. "Jack was utterly fearless at the plate," says Pee Wee Reese. "I think Sal was one pitcher who really tested him."

"I loved pitching against Jack," admits Maglie. He was a very tough hitter, and you couldn't move him off the plate. I would throw inside the way I threw to everybody. He would go down but he would get up again. We had a lot of battles. Sure, we hated each other, but it wasn't because he was black and I was white. It was because he had Dodgers in front of his uniform and I had Giants. When I got traded over there to Brooklyn I didn't know how it would be. I came to that clubhouse early, and I was concerned about the reception. Two guys welcomed me in a hurry, the two guys I had the most trouble with: Carl Furillo and Jackie Robinson."

Maglie would help Brooklyn win another pennant in 1956, but in the 1953 season he was no factor. The Giants were down, the Dodgers were up, and the Yankees, again, were the team to beat in October. Once again, Brooklyn failed to do it. Robinson, now playing left field with the faster, flashier Jim Gilliam at second, batted .320. Billy Martin batted .500, knocked in eight runs, and helped the Yankees win the Series again.

"The Dodgers had a lot of right-handed power, but Robinson wasn't the guy I worried about," said Whitey Ford. "The real tough right-hander for me was Furillo. In Ebbets Field you had to watch out for Hodges and Campanella. They could hurt you with a long ball. All the Dodgers were tough, but you could beat them in the Stadium by getting them to hit straightaway. In Ebbets Field, those were home runs. In Yankee Stadium, Mickey caught all those fly balls."

As a left fielder, Robinson was more than adequate. He was not exceptionally fast anymore. The years and the pressures were beginning to take a toll. Jackie Robinson was approaching his thirty-fifth birthday. He had become a baseball senior citizen.

CHAPTER

Twelve

ROBINSON
OF THE GIANTS

$\mathcal{R}$ACISM BEGINS WITH A LACK of education," says Bill White, who began his career with the New York Giants in 1956, starred later with the Phillies and Cardinals, and is now a broadcaster with the New York Yankees. "When I was a kid going to East High School in Warren, Ohio, they never taught us about anything blacks ever did. I was a grown man before I knew that George Washington Carver was black. The whites practice racism by hiding the positive deeds of blacks in American history.

"I don't remember reading much about Jackie Robinson in the white papers. I heard about him when I was thirteen or fourteen from the black papers: the *Pittsburgh Courier,* the *Cleveland Call-Post.* We followed more football than baseball anyway out my way in Ohio. Our hero was Joe Louis. We listened to all his fights on the radio. I went to Hiram College after high school, and I wanted to be a doctor. Blacks could be doctors if they were good. Nobody thought they could be big-league baseball players."

With the Supreme Court ruling on desegregation of May 17, 1954, in the case of Brown versus the Topeka, Kansas Board of Education, the revolution for civil rights was on. Did it begin, really, with Jackie Robinson versus his future teammates in Havana and Panama in 1947, with Jackie Robinson and Ben

Chapman, with Jackie and the Cardinals, with Jackie Robinson and the New York Yankees? Whatever the answer, by the year of this historic ruling, 49 black players had followed the path that Robinson had carved into the majors.

Despite the strides made in American society and baseball, Robinson was restless in Brooklyn. 1954 was the first year of his professional career when he would have less than 400 at bats. He played in only 124 games. He did hit .311, but he was never a regular, playing 64 games in the outfield, 50 at third, and 4 at second. He stole only 7 bases, and it was clear his career was on the downside. He was slipping, but he wasn't quite ready to leave. It caused a major problem.

The Dodgers had won back-to-back pennants in 1952 and 1953 under manager Charlie Dressen, a feisty former infielder with a massive ego. It was Dressen who told his players in a tight game, "Keep it close and I'll think of something." At the end of the 1953 season, in cahoots with his wife, he thought to demand a two year contract. The O'Malley policy was one year at a time, just in case things didn't work out. When Dressen insisted, the Dodgers invited him to a Montague Street press conference and fired him. The new manager was the Montreal manager, Walter Alston. His experience in the big leagues up to that time was one at bat, one strikeout. One paper headlined, "Walter Who?"

Walter Who was a bit overwhelmed at the team he inherited. Alston was a big, laconic, introverted personality. He knew baseball, as most people who spend their lives in the game do, but he was not a communicator. He won seven pennants in twenty-three seasons with the Dodgers and was named to baseball's Hall of Fame because O'Malley, the most powerful of baseball executives, wanted it so. He got little respect from his veteran players.

Duke Snider says, "Walter was a little intimidated by the veteran players. Jackie was the most outspokenly critical of the move to fire Dressen and hire Alston and their relationship was never very good."

Robinson, by the spring of 1954, was feeling his oats. He was not only the father figure of all black players—his hair was starting to turn white—but he was clearly the outspoken leader of the Brooklyn club. Pee Wee was the captain, but he was a gentle man. Snider was too busy fighting charges that he couldn't hit left-handers. Hodges struck out too much. Furillo was too hot-headed. Campy was too soft. Robinson became the focal point of all anti-Dodger fury in the league, and he may have felt, right-fully so, he was more important to the success of the Brooklyn club than Alston.

Though he never expressed publicly any desire to manage the ball club, he was possibly thinking along those lines.

"Jack had been a leader on every team—in high school, college, and the pros—he played with," says Reese. "Why not Brooklyn?"

Alston saw the team that had been together nearly eight years as an old club. He wanted to move in younger players, one of the classic baseball struggles. Ballplayers do not go gently into that good night—Jackie Robinson, Pee Wee Reese, Babe Ruth, Mickey Mantle, Willie Mays, Ted Williams, or anyone else. The relationship between Robinson and Alston for the next three seasons would be civil. It would not be warm.

By 1954 a second wave of black players, no longer as on guard, no longer as closely scrutinized, no longer solely identified with the Dodgers, began making an impact on baseball. The big-name black players to emerge in 1954 were Ernie Banks and Hank Aaron. Both Hall of Famers and great home-run hitters (Aaron has the career record for home runs with 755), they owed much to Robinson.

BANKS: "I went to Booker T. Washington High School in Dallas. It was a black school, of course. I was fifteen, sixteen years old and a friend of mine on the school baseball team came up to me one day in 1947 and said, 'We can play up there now.' I didn't know what he was talking about. He said Jackie Robinson was in Brooklyn, and now it was going to be open for us, too.

"I just liked to play. I didn't think about the big leagues. Black players still had to earn their way to the big leagues through the Negro leagues. They weren't signing any seventeen-, eigh-teen-year-old black kids and bringing them along. They had to be stars in their own league first. I signed with the Kansas City

Monarchs and everybody told me that was Jackie's team before he went to Brooklyn.

"He came down with the Jackie Robinson All-Stars, and I got to play against him, and I had a good day, and when the game was over he came up to me and said, 'You have a chance to play in the big leagues. I'll recommend you to the Dodgers.' I don't know what happened after that, but I soon got an offer to go to the Chicago Cubs and play at beautiful Wrigley Field, and I took it.

"It was late in 1953 and I was called up in September for a few games, and we played a series against Brooklyn. You remember the Brooklyn Dodgers? Jackie came up to me, he remembered me and said, 'Young man, I told you that you could play up here. Good luck.' I played a couple of years against him. He was a very fine player, very exciting, and he is in the Hall of Fame and all the little kids can come here and read that plaque, 'Jack Roosevelt Robinson,' and they will not forget his name, Jack Roosevelt Robinson.''

For several years Hank Aaron's brother-in-law, Bill Lucas, was baseball's token black executive. Now Aaron is. He is the farm director of the Atlanta Braves, the third or fourth most important job in the organization. His brother-in-law died of a brain hemorrhage several years ago. Ironically, Aaron has the job once held by his brother-in-law. He is fifty-three years old.

AARON: "I was a kid growing up in Mobile, Alabama, when Robinson came through one spring training with the Brooklyn Dodgers. Every kid at Central High, a segregated school, looked at Jackie's signing the way you would look at a declaration ending a long war. Every black kid in Mobile, every black kid who played baseball in this country, became Dodger fans.

"I played hooky from school the day he came to town. Word got around that Robinson would come to our part of town and meet with the kids. We all gathered at a neighborhood drugstore, waited a little while, and sure enough he showed up. He was dressed in a suit and tie and talked to us on the street in front of the drugstore. The kids just gathered around him and listened as he talked. He kept repeating, 'Stay in school, stay in school.' He stressed how important that was, and he said we all couldn't play in the big leagues, but we all could get a better education and make something of ourselves.

"I signed with the Indianapolis Clowns a couple of years later, and one night, before an exhibition game, I was Jackie's roommate. I was eighteen, nineteen years old then, the Korean War was on, and he kidded me about being called in the draft. He said he would tell the draft board about me if I got too many hits against his team.

"When I got to the Braves we would talk once in a while, but that was a pretty hot rivalry and we didn't spend much time socializing with other players in those days. Jackie used to get on us before the game around the batting cage, calling us the Dawn Patrol, because we had so many guys like Eddie Mathews, Johnny Logan, Bob Buhl, Lew Burdette, Warren Spahn, who liked to stay out late. Jackie would come up to the batting cage and really agitate the guys, needle us, call us playboys, really get on us.

"There were still some racial harassment going on in 1954, and when they called me names, nigger and all that, I would get real upset, and Jackie said, 'Don't let a few crazy people bother you. Just play hard.' Spring training through the South was still pretty bad, and the bus trips were awful. The club would stop for lunch, and I would have to go out back in the kitchen to have a sandwich while my teammates were all eating comfortably in the nice dining room. That really hurt.

"I never said much about it. I thought things would get better if we proved we were just as good as everybody else, and I think that we did that. Black kids coming up today have it so much easier. All they have to do is play. I remember when the city of Jacksonville wouldn't let Robinson play there with Brooklyn, and a few years later in 1953 I won a batting title with the Jacksonville club. Then I went to Milwaukee and the club moved to Atlanta and things were always good for me there.

"It was tough for blacks back then, and I hope black kids today can learn what Jackie went through, what I went through when I started, what all of us went through. Now there is a statue of me outside the stadium in Atlanta. When you think about it, that statue is as much a tribute to Jackie as it is to me. You don't hear his name much anymore. I think people have forgotten. Baseball should do something about that. Baseball owes Jackie Robinson something.''

Willie Mays was back from service in 1954, won the batting title with a .345 mark, and led the Giants to the pennant by a five-game margin over Brooklyn. Leo Durocher led his club to a sweep over the Cleveland Indians. The Indians had set an American League record for victories with 111. There was unrest in Brooklyn and rumors that the rookie manager, Walt Alston, might be in trouble. Those stories were quickly squelched when Alston re-signed with the Dodgers, as he would for twenty-three seasons.

Robinson had turned thirty-six in January of 1955. There was talk that this might be his final season. He had slowed down considerably. He weighed nearly 225 pounds. He was hardly intimidating on the bases. He still had that quick bat and was capable of pulling a ball down the line. The Dodgers won their first ten games in a row in 1955. They lost a game and then won eleven of their next twelve for a 21–2 record. The pennant race was over before it began. The Dodgers had a little midseason slump and brought up a thin, tall pitcher by the name of Roger Craig to shore up their staff. He won five games and one more in the World Series. He would later lose twenty-four games in 1962 for the original Mets, but said, ''You have to be pretty good for them to roll you out there that often.''

CRAIG: ''It was July 15, 1955, and I was playing with the Montreal club against the Havana Cubans. We were down there and Tommy Lasorda was a teammate and he told me I was pitching Sunday. I knew that. Then he said, 'Sunday in Brooklyn.' I was put on a plane in Miami out of Havana and flew to New York. I walked in the Dodger clubhouse and was in awe of those great stars.

''I was talking to Tom Griffin, the clubhouse man, and he asked me where my family was. I said they were up in Montreal and I guess I wouldn't see them for a while because Brooklyn was going on a road trip after the weekend series at Ebbets Field. Jackie overheard me talking with Griffin and said, 'Why don't you fly up there and drive them back?' I said that would be great, and I asked Alston if I could, and he said I wasn't pitching until Sunday and as long as I was back by Saturday that would be fine. Jack said, 'I'll drive you to the airport.' Here I was, a kid pitcher, and Jackie Robinson was going out of his way to see that I got to the airport. That was something.

"Jack couldn't run the way he could earlier, but he was still some competitor. They would knock him down, and he would get up and bunt and then intimidate them on the bases until he scored. He played the game with reckless abandon. If he got on first, you knew he would make second; if he got on second, you knew he would make third.

We clinched the pennant early that year and had a wonderful party in one of the Brooklyn hotels to celebrate. I was new to the team, but they all made me feel part of it. Jackie and Rachel were there, and she hugged and kissed my wife, and Jackie was in tears and he said, 'We won. What am I crying for?' I guess there was just so much emotion built up. Jack should have been the first black manager. He had so much fire and leadership qualities.

"I got along real well with Jackie but I got along well with everybody. I may have been closer to Campy because he was a catcher and we had more in common. Campy also handled the racial thing better. Jackie was kind of a loner on the road, and Campy was always around with us. Jackie was on edge about racial insults and sometimes looked for slights where there were none. Like I said, it was a privilege to know him and play with him. When I think of Jackie now, I think of him as a great player and a great man, but also as somebody who was so competitive, so intense. Jackie was like a great fighter getting ready for the heavyweight championship of the world before every game."

In the last two or three years of his Dodger career, Robinson became more argumentative, more difficult for teammates and opponents, and sometimes more difficult with umpires. Tom Gorman, a former pitcher, became a big-league umpire in 1950. He discussed Robinson shortly before his death last year.

GORMAN: "He was a little crotchety at the end. If you called a pitch he didn't like, he'd make a face or say something. I think he had the feeling that every strike you called on him was because he was black.

"He didn't have to worry about strikes because he was the best two-strike hitter I ever saw. He was a great player, and when I first saw him he was in his early thirties. I kept thinking if he broke in at twenty-one he might have been the best player in the history of the game. He could do so many things. He was also superstitious. I used to play a game with him. He wanted to get to the plate by walking behind the umpire. "Sometimes I'd dust the plate and back up and he had to go around me, and when I kept moving he would say, 'Let's go, Tom,' and I would say, 'Let's go, Jackie.' He would finally get in there, we'd have a disagreement on a couple of pitches, and then he would hit a double."

Billy Cox had been traded away to Baltimore, and Robinson played eighty-four games at third base in 1955. He played ten in the outfield, one at second, and one at first. He batted his career low of .256. The Dodgers won by thirteen and a half games and the World Series against the Yankees—Brooklyn had never played anybody else in Robinson's time—opened at the Stadium with the Yankees winning the first two games. The Dodgers won the next three at Brooklyn but lost the sixth game at Yankee Stadium. Robinson had gone hitless in four at bats. In the seventh game Robinson, suffering with aching legs, was benched. Don Zimmer started at second, Jim Gilliam started in left field, and Don Hoak started at third base. After George Shuba hit for Zimmer in the sixth inning, Gilliam came in to play second and Sandy Amoros, not Robinson, was sent to left field. Amoros, a speedy black Cuban, was able to catch Yogi Berra's slicing fly to the left field corner with two Yankees on in the bottom of the sixth inning. It saved the game for left-hander Johnny Podres. He pitched a 2–0 shutout for the victory. Brooklyn and Robinson—even though he was not part of the last game—finally had a Series win over the Yankees. The final out was a ground-ball hit by the black rookie Yankee, Elston Howard, to Pee Wee Reese. The Dodger captain and shortstop threw on to Gil Hodges for the last out. The throw was low, but Hodges handled it.

"Years later," Reese says, "I was in a bar with Don Hoak, and we began talking about the last play of that game. He began kidding me about the low throw. It was two or three o'clock in the morning, and we had a few drinks by then. Hoak said the throw bounced and I insisted it didn't. 'Let's call Gil.' He was the manager of the Mets then, and his team was in San Francisco. We called and woke him up. I said, 'Gil, I'm here with Hoak, and we're arguing about that last throw. . . . Gil just said, 'It bounced,' and hung up. It didn't bounce, but Gil was a good needler."

The Dodgers did an awful lot of needling that night of October 4, 1955, when it finally happened. The Dodgers were World Champions.

"I never knew how important that was to the people of Brooklyn until I got back to my hotel that night," says Johnny Podres, "and they were gathered out there, thousands of them to welcome me back. They carried on all night, and there was just no sleeping. It was wonderful."

The Dodgers won another bitter pennant race in 1956. They beat the Milwaukee Braves by a single game. Don Newcombe won twenty-seven games to capture the Cy Young Award and the league MVP, and Duke Snider hit forty-three home runs. Rumors of Robinson's retirement rumbled through the league again. More significantly, as the Dodgers played some games in Roosevelt Stadium in Jersey City, the same ballpark where Robinson broke in ten years earlier, rumors of a move out of Brooklyn gained more steam. The Dodgers wanted a new ballpark to replace aged, outdated, small Ebbets Field. A site in Brooklyn over the railroad lines at Atlantic Avenue was discussed. It never gained much support from Dodger executives for a simple reason: it was located in an area then going predominantly black. Walter O'Malley would have Jackie Robinson and Roy Campanella and Don Newcombe and Jim Gilliam on his team. He would not have a ballpark in a black ghetto. He dreamed of the glory, the sun, the trees, the scenery, and the whiteness of Los Angeles.

Bill White broke in with the Giants in 1956.

WHITE: "I remember one game the Giants played against the

Dodgers at Jersey City. I was a young first baseman, and Robinson hit a slow roller to the mound. He had a chance to beat the play at first, and he tried to run me over. I just did get out of his way. I don't know what it was like earlier, but in 1956 Jackie played with hate. He played mad. That was his style. I didn't like him very much. He wasn't particularly friendly. He didn't seem to have the time of day for anybody in a different uniform. That was all right. That is the way it was in those days.

"A year or so later, after Robinson retired, Howard Cosell, who was very close to Jackie, invited me for lunch with him. I got to know him a little. I was becoming involved in the integrating of team hotels in spring training. He said he would support us. I was with the Cardinals then, and they had a breakfast at the St. Petersburg Yacht Club. The black players didn't get invited. I screamed about that. Another time, some cigarette company called the club for a couple of players to do an ad. They recommended Ken Boyer, who smoked, and he got $2,000. I went up to Jim Toomey, the traveling secretary, who handled it and said "Curt Flood smokes.' He just looked at me in a funny way.

"A year or so later Toomey took me to breakfast at the Yacht Club. I told him a lot of things were going to have to change before the black players on the Cardinals—Bob Gibson, Flood, myself, Lou Brock—would feel satisfied. George Crowe was with the Cardinals then, and he was very active in trying to integrate spring training. Then he was released, and you haven't heard his name since. The baseball bosses don't like guys who stir up a fuss.

"This was ten or twelve years after Jackie Robinson broke in, and things still were tough for black players. People talked about me as a potential manager. I never wanted it. It was going to be a headache. I didn't need that kind of headache. I didn't want to go through what Jackie Robinson went through."

It was quite some time after Robinson left the game that baseball was completely integrated in spring training hotels. As late as 1962, when the New York Mets were organized, they could not stay together as a team downtown in a St. Petersburg hotel because they had several black players.

"That's why we went out to the beach in the Colonial Inn," says retired Mets traveling secretary Lou Niss. "They told us we could bring the black players into the hotel, but they also told us they wanted the black players eating in the back of the dining room. They didn't want their regular customers offended. So our few black players, Alvin Jackson, Charley Neal, Choo Choo Coleman, all agreed. Later on that spring I wanted to room Jay Hook, a white pitcher, and Jackson, a black pitcher, together. They were friends. Each agreed, but it never happened because there was always an odd number of blacks left if we did that. Somebody would have to room alone. Nobody wanted that."

Frank Robinson, who would become the first black manager in baseball in 1975, broke in with the Reds in 1956. A Hall of Famer, Robinson (no relation to Jackie) was twelve years old when Jackie broke in with Brooklyn.

ROBINSON: "I remember when he signed with the Dodgers. It was a big thing in Oakland, but I had always played with whites so it didn't seem all that dramatic.

"Jackie was cordial to me when I came to the Reds, but he didn't go out of his way to help me. He was a competitor and I wore a different uniform. Things were still difficult for black players. I had to stay in private homes through spring training and eat in fleabag restaurants. There were still some hotels around the league that wouldn't take us. That always angered me.

"When I became the manager of the Indians in 1975, the commissioner of baseball, Bowie Kuhn, saw to it that Mrs. Jackie Robinson was on hand for the event. I thought that was a nice touch. I don't remember much about it or even talking to her. All I remember is that I hit a home run and we won."

The Dodgers seemed to make a habit of close pennant races, and 1956 was no exception. They managed to win by a game, and of course met the Yankees again. It was another thrilling seven-game series marked by baseball's only World Series perfect game, a fifth game 2–0 masterpiece by Don Larsen who bested new Dodger pitcher Sal (The Barber) Maglie. Robinson hit a dribbler to the mound in his final at bat against "the imperfect man who pitched a perfect game," as News sportswriter Joe Trimble described the hard-living Larsen.

In the sixth game of the Series, Robinson got his final career hit. He made it a dramatic one, naturally. Clem Labine and Bob Turley engaged in a brilliant, scoreless pitching battle until the Dodgers batted in the tenth. Jim Gilliam walked with one out, and Pee Wee Reese sacrificed. Duke Snider was walked intentionally to bring up Robinson. Casey Stengel, who disliked Robinson and did what he could to embarrass him, was playing percentages. He also thought Robinson would be distracted as he screamed at him from the dugout. Robinson lined Turley's 1–0 pitch sharply to left. Enos Slaughter, now with the Yankees in another of those baseball ironies, misplayed the ball. He charged in instead of back, the ball sailed over his head, slammed into the base of the wall for a game-winning hit, and scored Gilliam with the winning run.

For his last time as a Dodger—though only Jackie knew it—he was the hero.

"Jack's knees were bothering him a great deal by then," says Rachel Robinson. "He was also losing interest in baseball. He no longer felt it was a challenge. He wanted to move on to other pursuits. He wanted to get involved in things that were now more important to him than baseball."

In the middle of December, several factors came together to end Jackie Robinson's baseball career, not the least of which was a job offer from William Black, president of the Chock Full O' Nuts chain of restaurants. Chock Full O' Nuts was an outfit specializing in coffee, sandwiches, doughnuts, and juice. Their menu was not extensive but their style was unique. More than seventy percent of their restaurant employees were black. Many were single parents in an era before women with children and without husbands were so identified. Their brand of coffee was expensive and excellent, and service throughout the chain was uniform. A cup of coffee was always offered with a spoon placed gently across the cup and a napkin settled on the right. Waitresses wore hairnets. Service was quick. No tipping was allowed. Robinson was soon offered a job as personnel director for $40,000 a year.

While it was common knowledge in the press that Robinson was contemplating retirement, no one knew for sure it would come so soon. During his playing days, Robinson had been profiled often and excellently by *Look* magazine. He had a close relationship with editor Dan Misch and sports editor Tim Cohane. He had mentioned to Misch that he was close to retirement. Misch decided to make an offer for his retirement announcement. He said he would pay $50,000 for the exclusive story, not an insignificant sum in 1956. *Look* had always flattered Jackie in its profiles and supported him on the race issue. On January 6, 1948, Cohane authored the article "Jackie Robinson's First Year with the Dodgers." Nearly two years earlier, Cohane had written a highly flattering account of Branch Rickey and his controversial move to integrate baseball. The article was called "A Branch Grows in Brooklyn." On September 27, 1949, Cohane wrote a piece on Jackie calling him "Ball Player of the Year." It began with an anecdote about a Cincinnati clubhouse meeting with coach Tony Cuccinello suggesting rightfully that the only way to beat Brooklyn "is to keep Jackie Robinson off the bases."

"Yeah," said manager Bucky Walters, "but how are you going to do it, Tony? Kidnap him before the game?"

Tim Cohane, retired now, lives in Derry, New Hampshire. He teaches communication part-time to corporate executives.

COHANE: "We had a real close relationship with Jackie. It began way back when Jackie first came to the Dodgers. One of Branch Rickey's assistants, Arthur Mann, did an article on the Dodgers and Rickey and Robinson for us. They all liked it and it was a strong seller. We had a paid circulation then of about eight million with about forty million readers. We came out every two weeks and had to keep this Robinson article secret. I met with Jackie privately a couple of times in a Manhattan hotel room. I had done several articles of this type. We announced Wilt Chamberlain's retirement from Kansas to turn pro in the same way. These articles would only be effective if they were kept secret and not leaked until the magazine was on the newsstand. With Jackie you didn't have to worry about him keeping his word."

The contract for two years with Chock Full O' Nuts was signed. The *Look* deal was finished. Robinson knew he was retired. No one else outside the family did. Then came a Dodger bombshell.

One night, Buzzie Bavasi, the Dodgers young, energetic general manager, called Robinson at home. He wanted to meet with him. Jackie said he was too busy with other appointments. He asked Buzzie if he could just tell him what was so important over the phone.

"Well," Bavasi said, "what I wanted to tell you, Jack, is that you are a New York Giant."

The hated New York Giants? Robinson knew he was retired, but the Dodgers didn't. How could they trade him after all he had meant to the team, to baseball, and to the borough? Easy. That's baseball. Before modern baseball's player union gained strength and put no-trade clauses in contracts, and the five and ten rule (no player with ten years in baseball and five with the same team can be traded without permission), almost everybody was traded, especially toward the end of their careers. Babe Ruth was released by the Yankees to sign with the Boston Braves. Ty Cobb was traded. Christy Mathewson was traded. Robin Roberts was traded. Casey Stengel was traded no less than four times. It happens.

"I was stunned," Robinson said later. "I had heard rumors for months that I might be traded to the Giants—and to a lot of other clubs—but I never put much stock in those rumors. I just didn't believe it could happen. So much of me was wrapped up in the Dodgers that I suppose I wanted to believe—foolishly— that a lot of the Dodger organization was wrapped up in me."

The jolt was universal.

"There was such an aura around Jackie Robinson," says Peter Bavasi, the son of the Dodger general manager and now the president of the Cleveland Indians. "When I was a kid in Vero Beach we used to go out near the sliding pits after practice and fly our kites. Campy and Newcombe would come over and fool around with us kids. One time they gave us chewing tobacco for a joke. Jackie happened to walk by and he saw that. 'You shouldn't do that. It will rot their teeth.' He was concerned about us. He was an exceptional man, a presence."

The presence had now been dispatched by Peter's father and

owner Walter O'Malley, they thought, to the Giants. Buzzie Bavasi is now retired after a brilliant baseball executive career with Brooklyn, Los Angeles, California, and San Diego.

BAVASI: "Jackie had a special relationship with Branch Rickey. If Rickey had stayed he would never have been traded. I think Jackie resented Walter O'Malley. They never got along, and O'Malley talked often of trading him. Jim Gilliam was coming along strong as our second baseman, and Jackie soon wouldn't have a place to play. The Giants gave us a left-handed pitcher we needed, Dick Littlefield, and $50,000. The money was important to the Brooklyn club. We operated on a tight budget.

"We were terribly disappointed when Robinson retired. We expected to make a lot of money in Brooklyn and in the Polo Grounds with Jackie playing for the Giants. Don't you think we would have filled Ebbets Field for a few games with Jackie in the uniform of the Giants?

"That was a tough deal for me to make. I had started with the Dodgers as an office boy in 1939. We had followed Jackie a long time. I can't swear about this, but I think Clyde Sukeforth actually saw Jackie play way back in Pasadena with some amateur team. He didn't suddenly appear on the Dodger scouting list in 1945 when he signed his Montreal contract. Rickey was too thorough for that.

"I had a cordial relationship with Jackie. I respected him as a man and as a player. I didn't trade him out of dislike. I just thought he was aging as a player. We had younger players to move in, and we could use a left-handed pitcher and a little money. It was a business deal."

The deal was announced December 13. Robinson had already signed with Chock Full O' Nuts and with *Look*. The press wanted further details about the trade. They called Robinson. He hedged. Robinson called the Giants general manager, Chub Feeney. Feeney gave him no assurances.

One of the most concerned men was Bill Rigney, the manager of the Giants. He had played against Robinson for years, had been named the Giants manager in 1956, and wanted Robinson for his 1957 team. Rigney is now an executive with the Oakland A's.

RIGNEY: "I really wanted Jackie for our ball club. Bill White was our young first baseman, and he had gone off to the Army. I was going to play Jackie at first base. I thought he could still play 130, 140 games for us. He would be an inspirational leader, and I certainly looked forward to those games in Brooklyn.

"When Jackie hit his first homer of his career in the Polo Grounds in April of 1947, I hit two home runs off Hank Behrman. Hardly got a mention in the papers. Things really heated up between the Dodgers and Giants the next year when Leo [Durocher] came over. Leo and Jackie really got on each other. Leo went crazy one time when Jackie walked on the field making a sniffing noise with his nose. 'I smell Laraine's perfume. Do you smell Laraine's perfume?' He kept saying that, and Leo called him every vile name you can think of. Those two were something together.

"He really showed me something after we beat them in the '51 play-off. He came into our clubhouse and boy, did that take a lot of guts. He came over to me and said, 'We didn't lose it, you guys won it.' That was a nice thing to say.

"I remember that first Series against the Dodgers in 1947. We heard that stuff about Dixie being unhappy all spring. I had grown up in California and played against black players, but this was different in the big leagues. I don't think we were prejudiced on the Giants. I think we were damn curious. It didn't take long to know he could play. I spent a lot of time on the Giants bench, and I must admit I enjoyed watching him play. He was older when he broke in, and you knew he wouldn't last very long, not at the pace he played. I think young players today, black and white, can look at films of Jackie playing and gain from them. What intensity, what concentration. He was some competitor. We finished sixth in 1957. We might have finished first with Jackie Robinson. Who knows? Anyway, it sure would have been interesting to see Jackie in a Giants uniform.''

There was not to be a picture of Jackie Robinson in a Giants uniform. It would have been too hard to take for a lot of kids in Brooklyn.

Robinson left the game as he entered it, deeply embroiled in controversy. The daily newspaper reporters were stung by the retirement announcement in *Look* magazine. They resented Robinson for "retiring" to a magazine and not with the ritualistic press conference before the beat reporters he had been associated with for so many years. Reporters were simply jealous of the attention the *Look* article received. Any of them, if the truth be known, would have taken a good paycheck to have written the article for their own papers. They had been scooped badly on a big story by a magazine. It hurt. They answered back as they could. They offered slurs at Robinson's character. Some would exact vengeance for this slight for several years to come.

In his later, often controversial, life in business, in politics, in the civil rights movement, in so many areas of American life, Robinson would be attacked. No man with a typewriter could ever ignore Jackie Robinson. He had come into big-league baseball as the first black. He was leaving as the most significant black. Forty years later it would still be so.

CHAPTER

Thirteen

THE LEGACY
OF NUMBER 42

*H*E WOULD PUT ON A CLEAN
white shirt each day, drive from his Stamford, Connecticut, home
to Manhattan, work most of the morning in his Lexington Avenue office, spend much time on the telephone with company
officials, and visit various Chock Full O' Nuts restaurants.

"He loved that job," says Rachel Robinson. "He wanted an
active position and that job was certainly active. He had access to
the employees, and he would visit several of the stores each day.
He would get involved in their personal lives. He would talk to
them about everything: about budgeting their salaries or saving
their money or dealing with their kids. He talked to the women
who were raising large families on their own, and he would talk
to the men who had just gotten out of jail to their first job. He
seemed to be everywhere with those people. He even started a
company summer camp for the children of employees. Some of
them were leery of that. They didn't want to leave their homes for
fear of what might happen while they were away. These were
urban people, and they had to be taught to enjoy the country. He
had responsibility and authority and the job was a happy experience for Jack."

There are some ballplayers—Willie Mays, Mickey Mantle,
Joe DiMaggio, Ted Williams, Stan Musial—who can never escape their fame. Jackie Robinson was in that class. He was con-

stantly being interviewed on the growing civil rights question, on baseball matters, on housing practices, on international events. Like it or not, Jackie Robinson was a spokesman for black people even though he had no formal training in the area or no legitimate credentials. He had learned from life.

Through 1957 and 1958 he spoke out on many matters. He was often, as he had been as a ballplayer, controversial. He rarely took the easy or obvious way out. He would stir up a hornet's nest with a comment on the fact that some clubs still did not have a black player (Pumpsie Green would not join Boston until 1959 as the player to integrate baseball's last all-white team); he would raise some hackles with comments about Roy Campanella after Campanella's injury in an auto accident and subsequent book; he would agitate leaders of the NAACP; he would criticize his own people on their public conduct; and he would attack the slow process of school integration.

While he was still a vice president of Chock Full O' Nuts, Robinson agreed to do a radio show and also agreed to write a column three times a week for the *New York Post*. His *Post* columns were very popular. His first column appeared on April 28, 1959.

Hi. Since this is the first time I've done a column, I'm naturally very thrilled. But I deeply appreciate this new opportunity also. It's going to be both a pleasure and a privilege to be in this spot three times a week. All during my baseball days, and after I left the game, there were times when my opinions were sought on all sorts of matters. I can assure you I intend to speak out as I always have.

He explained in the column that he would examine the upcoming 1960 presidential campaign and that he would discuss politics, baseball, and international affairs.

"And, too, as a Negro," he wrote, "I could hardly ignore this rare opportunity for one of us to speak to so wide an audience concerning just what we feel and think. That this person happened to be me isn't important. The fact that it is happening is the thing. And let me say right here I don't pretend to speak for all other Negroes, any more than other columnists speak for all those in whatever their racial, religious or nationality group. But I do hope to touch on some things that many of us commonly share and feel.''

On April 30, 1959, he wrote of the lynching of Mack Charles Parker in Mississippi.

Well, they said it couldn't happen any more. We're making tremendous progress, they said, so go slow on "forcing" the issue. Go slow on civil rights legislation, school integration and law enforcement against violence by Southern bigots.

Yet last Friday night a quiet, hooded well-drilled group of men entered an unguarded jailhouse in Mississippi. And when they left they took with them a screaming, beaten, bloodied human being.

It has happened here in our own America, and in 1959.

I can't really express my deep outrage about this terrible incident. I can only point out that the handwriting has been on the wall for all to see for quite a while. The lynching of Mack Parker is but the end result of all the shouts of defiance by Southern legislatures, all the open incitement to disobey the law by Southern governors, and all the weak-kneed gradualism of those entrusted with enforcing and protecting civil rights.

On May 5, 1959, in a prophetic column that would express feelings about his own children, one of whom, Jackie junior, would be in trouble with the law, Robinson wrote, "I read the other day that one out of every five youngsters in the country between the ages of ten and seventeen has some brush with the law. Certainly this is very shocking. Our juvenile delinquency rate is high, and growing higher every year. It is frightening to think that sooner or later one of your own children, or one of the neighbor's, or one of your relative's youngsters, will wind up in a police station charged with some offense against the public good.''

Jackie Robinson, Jr., would have serious problems with the law on drug charges after serving in Vietnam. After straightening himself out, he was killed in an automobile accident in 1971.

In June of 1959, Robinson took on the housing issue. ''Congratulations are in order today for the growing list of New Yorkers who have placed themselves squarely on record as opposing the ill-disguised bigotry of the all-white communities of Glendale and Ridgewood. There, you recall, the local residents are waging a bitter battle to keep 400 Negro school children from overcrowded, sub-standard schools in nearby Brooklyn from utilizing 66 empty classrooms in the Glendale-Ridgewood area.''

Robinson's public stand, as always, made a fuss. Mail poured in to his Chock Full O' Nuts office and at the liberal *Post*.

''My proudest moment of all came,'' Robinson wrote, ''when I received the following letter from William Black, president of Chock Full O' Nuts. Wrote Mr. Black: 'I cannot speak for all stockholders because I now own only one-third of the company. Speaking for my third, if anyone wants to boycott Chock because I hired Jackie Robinson, I recommend Martinson's Coffee. It's just as good. As for our restaurants, there are Nedick's, Bickford's and Horn and Hardart in our price range. Try them. You may even like them better than ours.' ''

Robinson wrote about a near-riot in Harlem, about the elevation of Pumpsie Green to the Red Sox, about a Harlem meeting with liberal senator Hubert Humphrey, and about his general philosophy on race relations.

The column was well read, controversial, brought heavy reader mail, and was well written and timely. It ended, finally, in 1960 when Robinson decided to take a more active role in politics. In the heated 1960 campaign between Republican Richard Nixon and Democrat John F. Kennedy, Robinson chose to support Nixon. It surprised many of his friends. It even surprised his wife.

''Jack thought blacks should have a say in both parties. That was his main reason for supporting Nixon. I disagreed. I remained a Democrat, and we argued often about that," Rachel Robinson says.

Early in 1960, Robinson had separate meetings with both political candidates. He wanted to see what their stands were regarding the civil rights movement and the racial tensions building in the country. He sensed that Kennedy would not be aggressive in addressing racial inequality. He thought Nixon would be more sensitive to this issue—the issue most sensitive to his own heart. After visiting with both candidates Robinson issued a statement supporting Nixon and explaining why he could no longer be an impartial observer.

"I saw Nixon and Kennedy," he said, "and Kennedy said, 'Mr. Robinson, I don't know much about the problems of the colored people since I come from New England.' I figured the hell with that. Any man in Congress for fifteen years ought to make it his business to know colored people."

It was one of the twists of history that although Robinson supported Nixon, it was Kennedy who moved ahead in civil rights matters as president. The most sweeping civil rights laws in American history would be framed during Kennedy's administration and enacted by the Johnson administration not long after President Kennedy was assassinated in Dallas on November 22, 1963.

While the civil rights movement was gaining momentum, Robinson was involved and offered opinions to the press on other matters from the 1960 election to the growing struggles over school desegregation.

New York baseball fans may or may not have had opinions on these weighty matters. What they certainly did have an opinion about was a man named Walter O'Malley. He had done the dastardly deed after the 1957 season. He had moved his Brooklyn team to Los Angeles, and he had convinced Giants owner Horace Stoneham to move with him. The Yankees won in 1958 under Casey Stengel, had an off year in 1959, and won again in 1960. Robinson's writings and interviews grew further and further away from baseball and more toward worldly matters.

His personal life was comfortable and orderly. Rachel

Robinson had gone back to school to complete her education and was working in the nursing field. Jackie enjoyed the job with Chock Full O' Nuts. He came home to practice his golf putting on the living room carpet and spent much time on weekends playing golf with friends.

"He released much of his tensions physically," says Rachel Robinson. "Even in his days as a Dodger we would stop off on the way home at a driving range and he would hit buckets of balls. By the time he got home all the tensions were gone and he could relax, eat dinner, and read the papers."

Robinson never attended a Yankee game for fun during the years away from the game. He returned to the Stadium only once, at a 1959 Old-Timers Day, and enjoyed cavorting with old teammates, including recently retired Pee Wee Reese and Eddie Stanky. He popped up in that old-timers' game but still had that fluid swing.

His contract had expired with Chock Full O' Nuts, and he went to work full-time for the Nixon campaign. When Nixon was defeated by Kennedy in a close 1960 election, Jackie Robinson was out of work.

"A friend of ours knew Governor Nelson Rockefeller of New York," Rachel Robinson says. "He called him and said, 'Do you know Jackie Robinson doesn't have a job?' Rockefeller gave him a position on the New York State Athletic Commission. I think he was paid a hundred dollars a day when he worked. Later on, Rockefeller hired him full-time to work on his campaign and then for the Rockefeller Foundation. He paid Jack $25,000 a year in that job. He had been making $40,000 for Mr. Black. He really worked hard with minority groups for Rockefeller, and Rockefeller did him in. He just wasn't treated fairly."

During his time with the athletic commission, Robinson got to meet and grow friendly with heavyweight champion Floyd Patterson. The first man to ever regain his heavyweight crown, Patterson was the titleholder from 1956 through 1959 and again in 1960 when he upset Ingemar Johannson. Patterson later served on the same athletic commission Robinson had served on.

PATTERSON: "I had lost to Johannson in 1959, and I was fighting him again in 1960. Jackie came to my training camp several times to watch me work out. He said to me just before the fight, 'We'll have a big victory party and I'll be there.' I told him I couldn't think about that, I had to think about winning the fight. He said, 'You'll win. I know it.' That gave me a lot of confidence.

"I did win, and then we had that big party, and it was a wonderful evening. A lot of celebrities were there and I enjoyed meeting them. We both had a lot of fun talking to Gabby Hayes, the old Western star. Jackie told me he always liked cowboy movies. I did, too.

"I grew up in Brooklyn and attended Alexander Hamilton High School. When I was a small kid Joe Louis was my hero because I always liked boxing. Then Jackie came to Brooklyn and I had two heroes, Joe Louis and Jackie Robinson. He made us very proud when he came to the Dodgers, and I think he was an inspiration to a lot of kids in my neighborhood. It showed people what we could do.

"Now when I talk to kids and tell them about my life and remind them you can be a champion if you work hard and really give it your best efforts, I also say that it is a good thing to have heroes. I tell them stories about my heroes, Joe Louis and Jackie Robinson, and I think it is very important that young black kids and white kids, too, know about these great men and understand the suffering they went through to achieve success in their fields.

"I think Jackie Robinson was a very great person. He showed us we were as good as white people, and he showed us how much we could achieve, and he showed us we could do it with pride and dignity. I think Jackie was one of the most important men in America, and I hope people will study his life and profit from what he did. I know I learned a lot from him. I wish he were here now. I still miss him."

Robinson's influence on other black athletes was always significant. So many of their achievements were recorded in terms such as "the Jackie Robinson of . . ." Arthur Ashe was the Jackie Robinson of tennis—the first significant black American tennis player, a U.S. Open and Wimbledon champion. Ashe's playing career was cut short by heart trouble, but he is still a popular tennis announcer, a leader in the antiapartheid movement, and an articulate spokesperson for blacks in many fields.

ASHE: "It was late in the 1960s when I first met Jackie Robinson. It was at some sports function in New York. He was aging and moving slowly and his hair was completely white. Somebody introduced us, and he congratulated me for winning the U.S. Open. I was amazed at how much he knew about my career. He had known Althea Gibson and was very proud of what she had done in tennis, but he said he was very happy a black man had won. It would mean so much more. He seemed so tired that night, but he wanted to talk of our mutual interests, and we spent quite a lot of time together.

"I was born in 1943 so I didn't become aware of Jackie Robinson as a baseball player until late in his career in the middle 1950s. I grew up in Richmond, Virginia, and went to a segregated school, Maggie Walker High, and I played a little baseball, but when I got into tennis I gave it up. My father had been an Army officer and a policeman and we were reasonably comfortable. I got a chance to play a lot of tennis. Some wealthy people supported me as I traveled, and I was able to become successful in the game.

"The reason blacks today don't know a great deal about Jackie Robinson and what he went through is because they don't read about him. The way you learn is by reading biographies, and that doesn't seem to be stressed in school. I read biographies of Jackie when I was young and of Joe Louis and Jack Johnson and of Lou Gehrig, who was one of my earliest heroes.

"When I started playing I ran into a lot of racism. I was called names, but I just blocked it out. I once played a match against Tom Okker of Holland. He is half-Jewish and apparently the people at this club knew it and they said anti-Semitic things about him, and somebody else yelled out, 'Why are they letting that nigger play on this court?' and it was ugly and uncomfortable for a while.

"I played a match against Ilie Nastase, and he called me a nigger on the court. I think it was during a Davis Cup match, and I was representing my country in tennis, and everybody just sat there. Like Jackie, there was always the hate mail and the notes scribbled in crayon calling me every name you could imagine. I don't think a black athlete today has to go through that anymore, but occasionally somebody will pass a remark. Racism never completely ends. My racist mail seems to pick up when I get interviewed on South Africa and say something some people don't like about the conditions down there.

"I think Jackie was subject to some unfair criticism during the 1960s by the young black militants. They didn't understand his position. He was supportive of the movement but wanted to do it through the system. Some of the younger people were impatient, and they painted him with some derogatory brushes.

"There's no question in my mind that Jackie Robinson had the broadest impact on American society of any black athlete. I think there was a survey by *Ebony* magazine only recently about the most significant blacks in American history, and Jackie was in the top ten. It is also important to understand that much of what Jackie accomplished and stood for occurred after his playing days were over. He may well be the most significant former athlete in American history when it comes to his influence after his playing days. In my mind he is up there with Whizzer White, the Supreme Court justice, as a person whose postathletic career influenced so many other lives.

"I know I had a lot more pressures on me in tennis than a white player of equal talent would have had when I was first starting out. I think a lot of what I did and a lot of what I went through was made easier by Jackie Robinson. If people want to say I was the Jackie Robinson of tennis, that's fine with me. It's an honor to be linked with Jackie Robinson's name in anything."

Through the early 1960s, as he worked diligently for Rockefeller, Robinson's health began declining. His hair turned completely white. His weight increased. His face became fleshy and jowly. On those rare occasions when he would show up at an old-timers' game and put on a baseball uniform, he seemed awkward and out of synch with the scene around him. He seemed to be growing further away from the game that had offered him fame. He grew more sarcastic when asked about baseball, was cynical about the chances of any black ever managing a baseball team, and lost touch with the changes in the game. When an old adversary would surface, the old fire would return.

After the Dodgers and Giants left New York for the West Coast in the 1958 season, Mayor Robert F. Wagner put together a committee to bring another National League franchise to New York. When that idea was quickly rebuffed by the baseball establishment, Wagner threw his support behind a new league. National League president Warren Giles, asked shortly after the Dodgers and Giants left if the league would miss having a team in New York, replied, "Who needs New York?" The committee, led by a sharp, hustling young attorney from the powerfully connected firm of Shea, Gould by the name of William Shea, set out to entice an existing franchise to New York. They went after Giles's old team, the Cincinnati Reds. The Reds were interested but soon decided against a move. No other team seemed inclined to take over the New York franchise, especially without a suitable stadium.

Wagner, Shea, and the powerful committee decided the route to take was a new stadium and a team to follow. Wealthy men in other cities also wanted a piece of the action. They got together to form a new league. The league was called the Continental League and Branch Rickey was enticed out of retirement to help it get started. As president of the Continental League, with proposed franchises in New York, Buffalo, Houston, Denver, Toronto, Minneapolis-St. Paul, Atlanta, and Dallas-Fort Worth, Rickey was back in action. Would Jackie Robinson be involved in this new venture? Evidence suggests his name never came up in any of Rickey's meetings. Robinson had moved forcefully into politics by 1960. Not even Rickey, apparently, thought of him as a potential manager or general manager. There were, one must note, no significant blacks in Rickey's Continental League operation.

As Shea's proposed stadium and the Continental League moved forward, the baseball establishment moved quickly to kill it. The American League expanded at the end of 1960 to include two teams to play in 1961: Los Angeles and Minneapolis-St. Paul. The National League added Houston and, of course, New York, for the 1962 season.

The new stadium would be named Shea Stadium. The new team in New York, destined to become the darlings of the city, was called the New York Mets. The manager, an old Robinson foe, was Casey Stengel.

Stengel was a funny man with more than fifty years in the game when he was hired in October of 1961. He was seventy-one years old. When asked about his health and age, Stengel replied, "My health is good enough above the shoulders, and I didn't say I'd stay fifty years or five."

The Mets lost 120 games under Stengel that first season. They lost 111 the next year and 109 the third year. By 1964 there were suggestions the 74-year-old Stengel had outlived his usefulness. One of the people who suggested this often was broadcaster Howard Cosell. Stengel and Cosell always had an uncomfortable relationship. Stengel always found Cosell pompous and a bore. Cosell always found Stengel bigoted and phony. Stengel had thrown Cosell out of the Mets locker room early in the first season when he and Ralph Branca had a pregame show. Stengel had thrown Cosell out of a Yankee locker room years earlier.

Cosell was a neighbor and close friend of Jackie Robinson. Robinson never attended a Mets game but was kept abreast of the Stengel doings by Cosell. Robinson was happy to hear negative things about Casey sleeping on the bench or maligning black players or drinking heavily. The animosity went back as far as 1949 when Stengel joined the Yankees, and Robinson was with Brooklyn. Stengel often used the term "nigger" for black players in those days and went even further calling blacks "coons or jungle bunnies," terms of derision often used only by the worst of bigots. Stengel was born in Kansas City in 1890. Few people born in Kansas City in 1890 did not use those terms, and, unfortunately, it was not until too many years later that Stengel decided to stop using them.

Elston Howard, the first black player on the Yankees, always spoke highly of Stengel. "He always bragged about me, called me his three-way platoon [Howard caught, played the outfield, and could play first base], and treated me with kindness and respect," Howard said. "I never saw any signs of bigotry."

Alvin Jackson, a black Mets pitcher, was very fond of Stengel. "He gave me a chance when the Pittsburgh Pirates didn't," he said. "When I beat Bob Gibson and the Cards 1–0 on the last weekend of the tight 1964 pennant race, Casey bragged about it for a long, long time."

It is probably fair to say that Stengel's attitudes on race were no better, no worse, than most people of his time. He probably was bigoted to some degree. So was the country he lived in.

Robinson spoke at a midwestern college, and when his remarks were reported by the wire services, another fire storm began. Robinson had attacked Stengel in a question-and-answer session with students. He said Stengel was too old to manage and should retire. He did not suggest publicly at that college session that the former Yankee manager was a bigot. Sportswriters, familiar with the thinking of both men, knew the background. They also understood the animosity. When Robinson's quotes were read to Stengel he replied, "What do I care about Rob-i-son," deliberately mispronouncing his name. "Besides, I remember when he popped up and my little bantam [Billy Martin] climbed over the mound to catch it."

I wrote a column in the sports section of the *New York Post* about the Robinson speech and the Stengel reaction. I quoted several Mets players on Stengel. They all said his age was no factor in his abilities, and he was more alert than most of them. Players quoted included pitchers Larry Bearnarth and Tracy Stallard, catcher Chris Cannizzaro, and outfielder Jim Hickman.

Robinson fired off a letter to me from the Rockefeller National Campaign Committee headquarters. ("Jack loved to write letters," says Rachel Robinson. "He would read something in the paper he liked or disliked, agreed with or disagreed with, and write a letter. He wrote to people he knew and he wrote to strangers. He just enjoyed getting things off his chest by letter.") Robinson wrote:

It would have been just as appropriate to ask Casey Stengel if he thought he should retire as it was asking the ballplayers. You would have gotten the same answer. On the other hand I do not have to play under Casey's man-

*agement so I can offer my opinion whether you like it or
not.*

*When age catches up to Charles DeGaulle [One of
the things Bearnarth said in my* Post *article defending
Stengel was a reference to French leader Charles
DeGaulle, still in power at the same age as Stengel—
seventy-four years old that spring of 1964.], he will have
to resign. When age catches up with the Pope, he too
will resign. Or should. It caught up with me as far as
ball playing goes at 37. I resigned. It may take 74 years
for it to catch up with Stengel, but it certainly has caught
up.*

*I suppose you will say it isn't age that causes Casey
to fall asleep on the bench [a constant Cosell charge]
during the game. Honest reporters who know what the
story is and who are not earning their livelihood from
the tremendous public relations job that Casey is doing
for the Mets will admit what I am saying.*

In his defense of Stengel, pitcher Tracy Stallard had suggested
that the energetic old man was probably in better shape than
either he, or Jackie Robinson. Robinson, subtly admitting the
pressure of his advanced years and declining health, said, "Tell
Tracy Stallard for me that he is absolutely right—Casey may be
in better shape than I am. That's why I retired."

We exchanged letters again a few weeks later. I suggested
that if Stengel did retire, maybe Robinson himself would be
interested in returning to the game and managing the Mets.

"Personally, I couldn't be less interested in managing. Not
only isn't baseball ready for a Negro with guts enough to call
things as he sees them but it is obvious some narrow-minded
reporters aren't either."

Was the denial of managerial ambitions a ploy? Did Jackie
Robinson want to manage a baseball team after all? A year or so
later I wrote a magazine article suggesting it was time for a black
manager. I named several black players I thought would be qualified. My favorite for the job was Bill White, the leader and star
of the Cardinals. I called Robinson for comment on the possibil-

ity. He did not change the position he had stated earlier in the letter to me.

"There won't be a black manager in my lifetime," he said. "The powers that be in baseball just don't want it to happen."

Of course, Jackie Robinson was proven correct again. It was more than two years after his death that Frank Robinson was named the manager of the Cleveland Indians.

Jackie Robinson continued to work for Rockefeller through the turbulant 1960s. He was deeply involved in school desegregation and traveled extensively through the South. He appeared at many fund-raisers for the NAACP and for the Southern Christian Leadership organization of Dr. Martin Luther King, Jr. He entertained Dr. King at his Connecticut home. He supported the 1963 March on Washington strongly. He saw, early, the linkage between racism and the Vietnam War. His own son came back a victim of that war, addicted to drugs. Some militant civil rights extremists attacked him by name, suggesting he was of another time, demeaning what he had done, finally attacking him for working for a white man within the white establishment. On several speaking engagements he was booed and called an Uncle Tom. Jackie Robinson an Uncle Tom? How crazy were the 1960s?

"He understood their youth, their impulsiveness," says Rachel Robinson. "They wanted blacks to be separate and strong. They wanted to stress that link to Africa, to our heritage. Our own children changed hairstyles and dress. Jack was upset but he understood. Finally, even I took to wearing African dresses."

His public appearances decreased. With his declining health, he was anxious to cut down his travel schedule.

"He was a sober man," says Rachel Robinson. "He would come home from the office, relax, hit golf balls on the carpet, play cards with friends, work on crossword puzzles. He wasn't much for television or big parties. We did have one nice party when he turned fifty years old in 1969. It was in January, and it had just snowed. We had a wonderful dinner with friends and family, and then we went outside to walk in the snow. There was an old washbasin sitting outside in the snow. Jack always enjoyed challenges. He just got in this thing, pulled his feet in and slid down our hill onto the frozen lake. Then he went flying across the ice. He was laughing so much. It was a wonderful moment.''

The Mets won the pennant in 1969. Gil Hodges was the manager. Jackie and Rachel felt very happy about that.

"In all our years with the Dodgers, the Hodgeses were probably the only couple we ever really socialized with,'' Rachel Robinson says.

The Mets victory was exciting. But it was not as momentous for baseball history as a trade made later in St. Louis. Outfielder Curt Flood had been traded to the Phillies. He refused to report. It would begin the most revolutionary moves in baseball history. A complete restructuring of the rules of the game regarding trades and releases and free agency would result.

Flood sued baseball with a challenge to the reserve clause. With Marvin Miller and attorney Richard Moss handling the preliminary case, it moved through the legal system. The attorney hired by the Players Association was Arthur Goldberg, the former Supreme Court justice. Curt Flood remembers the most emotional day of the case.

FLOOD: "The courtroom was packed. This was Superior Court in New York, an imposing building. Somebody was testifying and suddenly the courtroom doors open. This large black man comes through the doors. I could see that he was ailing. He had obviously had a stroke or a heart attack because he walked so slowly and with so much effort. He came down the aisle and nobody stopped him, and he walked forward to where I was sitting. I turned to look at him, and I realized it was Jackie Robinson. I couldn't believe my eyes.

"The last time I had seen him was in 1956 when I was breaking in with the Cincinnati Reds. He was with the Brooklyn Dodgers, and he was a magnificent, athletic specimen. I had never spoken to him personally. I didn't know the man. All I knew was his name, the legend.

"I grew up in the segregated part of Oakland, California, West Oakland, with Vada Pinson and Frank Robinson and Bill Russell. We all went to Herbert Hoover Junior High and McClymond's High. I was always crazy about baseball as a kid.

My father had three jobs to support the family: a job as a porter, as a male nurse, and as a laborer in a foundry. I was nine or ten years old, before Jackie made it to Brooklyn, and my parents would say, 'Why are you doing this? Why don't you go out and get a paper route like the other boys?' Instead I played ball after school, and they couldn't understand it.

"Then Jackie came along and he made it and we all figured we could make it. 'There's no future in sports, it's a waste of time, you can't make a living at it,' my father would say. Then we heard more and more about Jackie, and suddenly our parents thought maybe, just maybe, there would be room in baseball, big-league baseball, for a few more of us. I never heard any more about the paper route. My father didn't insist on me getting a real job like he had in the foundry. He figured if Jackie Robinson made it to the big leagues, his son could make it.

"I got to the big leagues with the Reds and then went over to the Cardinals and had a good career there. They traded me to the Phillies, and I didn't want to be traded. I wanted to stay in St. Louis. I decided to fight it.

"I was in that courtroom that day, and Jackie Robinson walked in, and I got a lump in my throat. I never called him. I wouldn't dare. He just volunteered, showed up on his own, and told us he wanted to take the stand and describe what it was like for a ballplayer. He got up there and just talked about his signing and the conditions and the unfairness of things for players, and he did it without any prompting from Marvin Miller or Arthur Goldberg or anybody. Then he was finished and left the stand and walked out of that room and every eye was on him.

"Ballplayers have it pretty easy today. The salaries are terrific, the conditions are great, and everybody is doing just fine. I don't know if young players pause to think about Jackie Robinson or think about Curt Flood and how times were different back then. I guess they don't have to. That's the way things are. People don't pause to think how their grandparents struggled to make things better in their own families.

"All I know is that I will never forget that day Jackie came to that courtroom, and I will always owe a debt to his memory. He didn't have to do that. Nobody called him to do it. He just showed up, just volunteered his story because he wanted to do it, because he simply thought it was right."

In June of 1971, Jackie Robinson, Jr., was killed in a single-car crash on Connecticut's Merritt Parkway. He was apparently speeding when he lost control of his brother David's sports car and rammed into a concrete barrier. Only twenty-four years old, he had begun to straighten out his life after service in Vietnam— a shrapnel wound, drug addiction, arrest and, finally, rehabilitation. He was working in a drug rehabilitation clinic at the time of his death. The loss shattered the family. When young Jackie was first arrested, Robinson had said, "I thought my family was secure, so I went running around every place else."

When the boy was killed, Robinson did not hide. As always during his career, he was available to the press. "You don't know what it's like to lose a son, find him, and lose him again," Robinson told the assembled press. The photograph taken that day of the former ballplayer shows a very tired, very sad, very quickly aging man.

His friend Gil Hodges died the following April. Robinson would make his final Dodger appearance that June in Los Angeles. His number was being retired along with Roy Campanella's and Sandy Koufax's. No Dodger would ever wear number 42. He seemed very happy.

"I think I saw him play for the last time," says Detroit coach Dick Tracewski, a former Dodger. "It was the year before, at the 1971 old-timers' game. He was in uniform and the old Dodgers were kidding him about being fat. He said he wouldn't play and then the old-timer's game started and he was on the bench and a couple of guys were swinging bats and he walked to the end of the bench and he took a swing and said, 'Let me try it.' Then he was at the plate, and the pitcher threw one up there, and he swung that bat out there the way he always had and lined a ball to left. He could only jog to first, and he stood there with a big grin. God, that was exciting. I don't like to think about sad things. When I think of Jackie Robinson I'll just remember him swinging a bat and lining a hit to left field."

And getting ready to steal second base.

CHAPTER

Fourteen

LOOK BACK
NOT WITH ANGER

$\mathcal{J}$HE AMERICAN REVOLUTION OF
the 1960s was filled with far more trauma than the American
Revolution of the 1770s. Americans began dying in increasing
numbers in Vietnam. Blacks sat-in at schools, stores, and offices.
Women marched in street demonstrations and burned their bras-
sieres to emphasize their fight for freedom. The gentlemanly
sport of politics turned ugly and violent. Colleges became bastions of unrest. Students shifted emphasis from the harmless acts
of stuffing themselves into telephone booths and swallowing
goldfish to the burning and looting of the offices of school officials. Martin Luther King, Jr. was murdered. Bobby Kennedy
was murdered. Malcolm X was murdered. Draft-age males fled
to Canada. Young women made love in public parks. John Lennon
said the Beatles had more impact on the world than Jesus Christ.

On a glorious summer Sunday in July of 1962, Jackie
Robinson was inducted into baseball's Hall of Fame in his first
year of eligibility. Standing alongside Bob Feller, Edd Roush,
and Bill McKechnie, Robinson was all smiles as he held his
plaque and posed for pictures on the steps of the Hall of Fame
Library and Museum in Cooperstown, New York. It may have
well been the final pleasant moment Robinson had as a retired
ballplayer in a baseball setting.

The rest of his years seemed filled with frustration. He withdrew from any serious connection with baseball except for the occasional appearance at a Shea Stadium, Yankee Stadium, or Dodger Stadium old-timers' event. He harped constantly on the treatment of blacks in baseball, especially the lack of a black manager. Aligned with Rockefeller and the conservative spectrum of American politics, he seemed pulled away from mainstream black thinking. Jackie Robinson, the man who battled bravely and alone, was shunted aside as his dark-skinned brothers, no longer accepting the slave term of Negro or colored, espoused "Black is beautiful." The public awareness of Jackie Robinson faded in the late 1960s.

It was, however, a happy and peaceful time for Robinson. He traveled extensively. He worked for the Rockefeller Foundation. He became involved later in other private business ventures in housing and banking. He was still called upon by the NAACP for speaking engagements. He addressed college groups. He enjoyed the serenity of his beautiful home in Connecticut. He played golf with business partners and friends. No matter where he was, he always managed to line up a golf game.

"I was just a kid when I played for the Dodgers in the middle 1950s, and Jackie was the team's great star," says Don Zimmer, now a coach and former big-league manager. "We were not terribly close. I think the guys who had been together for so many years in Brooklyn had their own group: Jackie, Pee Wee, Duke, Gil. I was comfortable with them on the field but not socially friendly with them off the field. Jack had retired after the 1956 season, and I was finished about ten years later. I made my home in Tampa and one winter, around 1968 or 1969, I was doing some work at home. The phone rang. 'Wanna play golf tomorrow?' I recognized the voice immediately. It was Jackie. We made a date to play the next day. What a thrill that was. Jackie was as warm as could be. He really seemed as if he was a very happy man in retirement."

Player relationships are tricky at best. They can be so terribly aggravated by status and standing, by personality and performance, by age and position. In his last two or three years with Brooklyn, Robinson's body was wearing down. He had played so hard and so long that as he entered his late thirties, he no longer had the resiliency to come back from a long game or a hot summer Sunday or an extra inning encounter. He had been a four-sport athlete in high school, junior college, and at UCLA. He had played with much intensity at Montreal and in his early days of Brooklyn. He was slowing down noticeably in 1954, 1955, and 1956. He was playing fewer games and had fewer at bats. He spent more time in the dugout.

While his body was creaking, his mind was alert. He never stopped thinking of ways to win.

"I was just a kid pitcher in 1956 as a rookie with the Brooklyn Dodgers, just nineteen years old," says Don Drysdale, the Hall of Fame right-hander and popular sportscaster. "I was completely in awe of the famous Brooklyn Dodgers when I joined the club out of school in California. They were all very kind to me—Pee Wee, Duke, Jackie, and the rest. Jackie always seemed a figure larger than life. He had gone through so much, and he had so much hurt put on him. I remember that spring of 1956 we barnstormed North, and Jackie was unhappy about the housing situation down South, the segregated hotels and the segregated restaurants. We would take the field and there would always be some loudmouth there to scream at him from behind a dozen other fans. It was a long time after he had broken in, he was a great star, and he still had to take that abuse. What could he do, run in the stands and fight all of them who called him a name?"

Drysdale threw hard and was mean on the mound, unafraid to challenge a better inside or high and tight if necessary.

"Jackie would offer little tidbits of advice on the bench when he wasn't playing or come up to me on the mound when he was playing and say, 'Throw hard, don't let up, challenge the hitters.' He instilled a lot of competitive fire in my soul. I was an impressionable kid. I admired him so much, hero-worshiped him, I guess, just wanted to prove to him and all the veteran Dodgers that I really belonged up there with them."

No Dodger on the 1956 team remembers Jackie talking of retirement. None can recall him ever discussing a career in baseball after his playing days ended.

"I can't say Jack wanted to manage a big-league ball club,"

says Pee Wee Reese. "Let's put it this way. Most everybody who has played the game likes to be asked. It flatters your ego that they think enough of you to consider you for a leadership position. In that respect I don't think Jack was much different from the rest of us."

"He knew an awful lot about baseball," says Don Zimmer. "Jack could see things on the ball field that other guys didn't see. I played a lot of second base that last year he was there, and I remember him more than once telling me to look for a batter to hit a certain pitch a certain place. He was uncanny that way."

"Jack played so hard, with such intensity, that he made you try that much harder," says Carl Erskine. "You simply couldn't let up if you were on the same ball club as Jackie Robinson. I know that I became a better pitcher, a tougher competitor, because I played with Jackie. I think he could have made the same kind of contributions to a ball club as a manager. I'm certain a ball club managed by Jackie Robinson would be in every game until the last batter was out. I would have liked to have seen that. I think Jack would have liked to manage. I really do."

Robinson still retained some significance as a baseball name in the early 1960s. His Hall of Fame election forced people to reevaluate his performance on the field and his contributions to the game. Blacks were by now routinely accepted in the game, and no fuss was made any longer of a black player being signed or a black player breaking a cherished baseball record.

In 1962, the year Robinson joined the game's immortals at Cooperstown, a wispy Dodger shortstop named Maurice Morning Wills exploded on the baseball scene with 104 stolen bases. Ty Cobb had stolen 96 bases back in 1915. Jackie Robinson, with a career high of 37 in 1949, had often been described in the press as "the black Ty Cobb," a description that probably infuriated the bigoted Cobb. Robinson's style of play, the use of the bunt as a major offensive weapon, the stolen base, the dashing extra base, the intimidation of pitchers, catchers, and fielders with his brazen speed, was probably as close to Cobb's style as baseball has seen. When Maury Wills, playing for the *Los Angeles* Dodgers, actually broke Cobb's mark for stolen bases, Wills became the new "black Ty Cobb."

A dozen years later, Lou Brock of the St. Louis Cardinals stole 118 bases to set a new mark. Brock, a Hall of Famer, considered himself a direct baseball descendent of Robinson.

BROCK: "Where I grew up in Collinston, Louisiana, blacks were sharecroppers, dirt farmers, not baseball players. We picked cotton and corn and talked about the reality of our lives.

"Then Jackie Robinson came along in 1947. I was eight years old then, and my thoughts about professional baseball were changed forever. Baseball had been a white, society, country-club game. There was no room in it for blacks. Everybody knew that. Then there were pictures of Robinson, that black face, in the newspapers, and it hit us with the impact of an H-bomb. He touched our world. We could have a fantasy, too, just like the white kids; we could dream of playing that great American pastime in huge stadiums before big crowds. It meant more than just baseball to us. It meant we didn't have to be dirt farmers anymore. It meant we could have our dreams and go out and make something of ourselves. We could look at the farm master and tell him we were leaving. We would live our own dreams. We could play baseball in that fantasy world if we wanted, and if we were good enough.

"Jackie Robinson put blacks in the mainstream. He was the pioneer, the symbol, that paved the way, the hero to millions of small black children who had these private dreams and never could express them before Jackie. Not just dreams of baseball and sports but dreams of being a successful man. I played sports in school, but I really wanted to be a schoolteacher, and I went to college because I saw other opportunities opening for me. Jackie Robinson had flung open so many doors.

"I thought of Jackie often in the early days of my career. I had read books about him, and I knew what he did on the ball field, and mostly I knew about his competitive spirit—his desire, his willingness to pay the price. He was a pioneer of course, but he was a pioneer with a lot of arrows in his back.

"I made it to the big leagues with the Chicago Cubs in 1961 and went on to the Cardinals, and a lot of sportswriters said I ran bases the way Jackie did: aggressive, hard, with no fear.

"There are times now I mention his name and I get a blank

stare from young people. They have to read the history. They have to know what went before. They have to learn that Jackie Robinson was responsible in some ways for a lot of what we all have today. It is important to pause and study the past. The life of Jackie Robinson should be a part of every young person's education.''

As the turbulent decade of the 1960s ebbed, Jackie Robinson's name appeared less frequently in newspapers. There are always new names in sports, new heroes, new controversies. There would be an occasional public appearance, an occasional speech, a rare interview. It was not that Robinson became reclusive. It was more that there were new men and women articulating the black revolution. It was shocking to many to see Robinson on television when his son was killed in the 1971 car crash. Diabetes had been chipping at him for years. He was a monument that needed resurfacing. It could not be done with human beings.

Finally, in 1972, there was the death of Gil Hodges and the labored appearance of Jackie Robinson at the Brooklyn funeral. There was that too-late symbolic appearance in October at a World Series game. The last days were so difficult for this proud man. The end came on an October morning.

Many cared. Some hardly noticed. His passing did not evoke national trauma. No one called for a Jackie Robinson holiday. Flags were not lowered at public buildings. His former teammates were touched and kind in these sad hours. His funeral captured most of the drama of the event. A young minister by the name of Reverend Jesse Jackson delivered a ringing eulogy.

JACKSON: "I was a small boy growing up in Greenville, South Carolina. The Brooklyn Dodgers flew into Greenville to play an exhibition baseball game, and we all rushed to the airport to welcome them. These were the famous Brooklyn Dodgers of Jackie Robinson and Roy Campanella and Don Newcombe, and we had to see them, hopefully touch them, reach out to them. It was raining very hard but we didn't care if the game was canceled as long as we could see our heroes.

"The players came off the plane and came into the small

lounge in the airport to use the bathroom facilities, and we waited and waited for our heroes. Jackie Robinson did not get off the plane. I waited for many minutes and soon the white players were walking back to the plane and the plane was taking off again and we were terribly distraught that we had not seen Jackie. 'Why can't we see him, why can't we see him?' One of our leaders, Reverend James Hall, came over to us and told us. 'Jackie Robinson can't get off the plane because they won't let him use the bathroom. It was for whites only.' I remember that like it was yesterday.

"Jackie Robinson was our champion, our hero, and this was another way the white man cut us down. Jackie Robinson rose above segregation, rose above discrimination; he was a man of dignity and honor. When he came into baseball and assumed that pioneering role, he knew he was responsible for people, for all the people; he knew he had to be good and force people to respect and honor him.

"In 1947, people were dealing with those old-fashioned pseudopsychological ideas of inferiority. Black people were taught by whites that they were inferior, that they were cursed by God to be lesser humans. It was one of the devices used to justify slavery, to explain the injustices of the time, to keep blacks oppressed in our country.

"Now along comes Jackie Robinson, this proud knight in baseball armor, and he was not inferior. He showed that it was talent and intelligence and skills that could lead a man out of the poverty and persecution of his surroundings. He was a marvelous player—dynamic, exciting, a true Renaissance man with a variety of abilities. It destroyed so many racist concepts about the shiftless, lazy black man. He literally lifted black people out of depression by his success. He was a therapist for the masses by succeeding, by doing it with such style and flair and drama. He helped level baseball off, to make it truly a game for black and white, with excellence the only test of success.

"I truly believe there was a connection between Jackie Robinson's success and the Supreme Court decision in 1954 to break down the segregated school system. Baseball was a team game of nine men, and the Supreme Court was a group of nine men, and all worked together to better the team or the country, and I can clearly see the connection.

"Through the 1960s I got to know Jackie and Rachel Robinson, and they were both very supportive of our work. Then Jackie died and it was very sad and that day I received a call from Rachel Robinson. 'Will you deliver the eulogy at Jack's funeral?' I was honored she had chosen me, and she said it was something Jack had wanted. Rachel felt strongly that I should be given this national platform as a young man. She wanted me to have an opportunity before the world to speak of him. I looked out at all those faces, black and white, and felt so moved that this great man had brought people together in so many ways.

"I was an athlete in school, always interested in sports, and I followed Jackie Robinson's career so closely. I'll never forget the 1951 game when he caught the line drive off Eddie Waitkus's bat to help get the Dodgers into the play-off. He was knocked out, and then he came back to hit a game-winning home run. It was such a marvelous performance under pressure, so much a part of the legacy of Jackie Robinson.

"Jackie's daughter, Sharon, works with us in our Washington office, and she is a dedicated young lady. We are so fortunate to have her, and I talk to Rachel, and I try to remind people about the contributions of Jackie Robinson to the movement."

In 1977, Reggie Jackson joined the New York Yankees. He was a flamboyant figure, a man of enormous talents and larger-than-life ego. He had been wooed and won as a free agent by Yankee owner George Steinbrenner, and now he stood on a platform in the Princess Suite of the Americana Hotel. The Yankees would pay Jackson some three million dollars for five years of service. He nervously posed for pictures holding his new Yankee pinstriped uniform. The number on his uniform was 44.

"I had considered asking for uniform number 42," he explained later. "I had written a letter to Rachel Robinson asking her if that would be all right and if I could wear the uniform number 42 in honor of Jackie Robinson. I wanted so much to do that because he had meant so much to me as I was growing up in Philadelphia. She said I could certainly do that, and she knew that Jackie would be happy if he could have been there to see that. I thought about it a good long while. Then it suddenly dawned on me that this was New York, this was where Jackie Robinson played his baseball career. I didn't think it would be right if I wore that uniform number in this town. I decided to ask the Yankees to give me uniform number 44. I realized that uniform number 42 belonged to only one man, Jackie Robinson, in the city of New York, and I couldn't equal what he had done. I still cherish the kind letter I received from Rachel Robinson. That meant a great deal to me.''

Jackson became an exciting, if controversial, Yankee, and no one wore his uniform number 44 after he left New York.

''I think the thing about Jackie Robinson,'' says Ken Singleton, the former Baltimore outfielder and now sportscaster, ''is that for blacks he was baseball. We were always baseball fans in my house when I was growing up in Mount Vernon [New York]. We had the game on all the time. The only team we ever listened to were the Brooklyn Dodger games, the team Jackie Robinson played for. That's the way the Dodgers were identified to blacks for a long, long time. I think that holds true today. When I was in the American League, fans would tell me they rooted for the Orioles in the American League, but they always rooted for the Dodgers in the National League. For some black fans the Dodgers, even the Los Angeles Dodgers Jackie Robinson never played for, would always be their team.''

The generation gap between those who knew Jackie Robinson personally—knew a lot about him, cared about him—and those who had only the most vague name recognition, widened in the 1980s. Several New York black baseball stars could barely identify the name when questioned.

''Jackie Robinson? I know he played,'' said record-holding base stealer Rickey Henderson, ''but I don't know anything about him. When I was a kid I was a football player. I knew the names of lots of football players, but I didn't know baseball players. I just wasn't that interested in baseball. When I started to play I studied pitchers and opposing players, I didn't study anything about old ballplayers."

"I'm not sure I know who he is," said Dwight Gooden, the incredibly talented and successful pitcher of the New York Mets. Gooden was only nineteen when he joined the New York team in 1984. "I don't want to say anything wrong. Am I supposed to know him?"

Mookie Wilson, an outfielder for the Mets from South Carolina, was fairly typical of many ballplayers when he said, "I just played the game, I didn't read about it. I know his name, but I'm not sure what he did. I was out there playing, so I guess I didn't read as many books about baseball as I should have."

Dave Winfield, baseball's first two-million-dollar-a-year player, said he knew Jackie Robinson was the first black player in baseball. He knew little else about his career.

"There was this play, *The First,* about his life a couple of years ago, and I got a call inviting me to the opening night on Broadway. I didn't know much about Jackie Robinson, and I thought I could find out. I went to the play and I met Rachel Robinson. She was a very nice lady. I sat through the play and enjoyed it a lot. I think I learned a lot of things about Jackie Robinson that night. He didn't have it easy, did he? None of us do." Then Winfield laughed. "And he didn't even work for George Steinbrenner."

Darryl Strawberry, the outfield star of the Mets, grew up in Los Angeles. He is twenty-five years old.

"I was living in Compton then, and I played in the Jackie Robinson League. I didn't know much about him other than he was from California and he was the first black to play in the big leagues. I had heard things were kind of rough for him in those days. There were people, coaches and older people around our league, who mentioned his name once in a while, and I remember them saying how he dealt with the negatives. They admired him for that, and I remember hearing that if I was going to be a ballplayer I had to learn how to take what comes. I guess Jackie Robinson had to do that more than most. I know times were different then. We don't have to put up with that stuff now, thank goodness. All we have to do is hit the ball and we can make a living.''

When older blacks in baseball are asked about Robinson, they talk about hero worship and they talk about a bitter time in their own lives.

PINSON: "I remember once in 1961, when I was with the Cincinnati Reds in the World Series in New York, and I met him at some Series event. We got to talking about the old days and how it was for him,'' says Vada Pinson, now a Detroit coach. "He told me a few stories of the segregation and the racism, and then he looked at me and said, 'Rachel had to rub my legs because the trainers wouldn't touch my black skin.' This was years later, but I could still see how much that hurt.

"I had grown up in Oakland in an integrated neighborhood, and when I first went to spring training in Florida, there were still signs of segregation. We couldn't stay in the team hotel, and I boarded out with an old woman, a Mrs. Elder, and we did the best we could. She told me the only shower in the house was down the hall, and it was humiliating to have to go out in the hall and walk to the shower. Frank Robinson was a star with the Reds by then, and he was staying in the same old boarding house. I ran into him in that hall on the way to the shower, and we both sensed the embarrassment of having to put up with this when we were big-league ballplayers. 'This has got to change,' Frank said. Pretty soon it did.

"I know what I went through, and it was a long time after Jackie. I can't imagine how he survived all that anger, all that animosity he was faced with, and all alone, too. No black player today should ever take the field without thinking of Jackie Robinson and how much he owes to him. For me, even when I broke in to the big leagues in 1958, baseball *was* Jackie Robinson.''

"Kids are always looking for heroes, role models, and that is as good a reason as any to keep Jackie Robinson's name alive,'' says Reverend Jackson.

In business, in the professions, in the arts, in politics, in all human endeavor, there are men who set the pace for others to follow. Jackie Robinson was a baseball player. His influence was first felt there. It carried over to almost every area of American life for young blacks. Whites understood that.

"I was just a small girl in nursery school in St. Alban's in Queens," says Kate Wigderson Harris, a media relations executive in the office of Georgia senator Julian Bond. "I went to school with Sharon, Jackie's daughter. Even at that age I had some understanding he was an important man. I remember one day Sharon and I were swimming in this little pool at the school and we spotted a spider. We panicked. Jackie Robinson just took care of it and soothed us. Knowing Jackie Robinson, going to school with his daughter, was a point of pride in my life. Later on my family was driving past Ebbets Field, and my father pointed out that that was where Jackie Robinson played. I used to listen to the games on the radio after that. I was pleased to be a friend of Sharon's. I remember saying once, 'Your daddy plays baseball on the radio.' We came from a liberal white family. I was influenced knowing Jackie Robinson. How much? Who's to say. Every person we meet probably has some influence on our lives. I don't doubt that I would not be working for Julian Bond if I hadn't some vague connection with Jackie Robinson."

The measure of any man is probably a combination of his life, his deeds, and the messages he leaves behind to family, to friends, to history. Don Newcombe understands that.

"We cannot ever let the memory of Jackie Robinson be forgotten," says the former Dodger pitcher. "What do they say: if we do not understand the past we are doomed to repeat it. I want young blacks and whites to know what it was like forty years ago. I don't want those times ever to return."

CHAPTER

Fifteen

RACHEL'S REMEMBRANCE

*H*IGH ABOVE EIGHTH AVENUE AND Fourteenth Street in New York City in an old distinguished building are the offices of the Jackie Robinson Development Corporation.

There is a school in Brooklyn called the Jackie Robinson Intermediate School, on the site of what once was Ebbets Field. There are the community building and playground buildings in Pasadena. There is a park in the small town of Little Rock, California. And there was a United States postage stamp issued two years ago with the first-day cover offered only at the post office in Cooperstown, New York, site of the Baseball Hall of Fame. It showed the flashing feet of Jackie Robinson. Jackie Robinson's name remains alive in all these places, and with old-time ballplayers—if not with the youngsters of the 1980s.

The true keeper of the flame sits behind a desk at the Jackie Robinson Development Corporation, a minority owned and operated company devoted to the development of low and moderate income housing. The company is run by Rachel Robinson.

Gray haired and still lovely, Rachel Robinson is a grandmother of six and great-grandmother of one. She rides the subways from her midtown Manhattan apartment to the offices on Eighth Avenue.

RACHEL ROBINSON: "There was a lot of mail after Jack died in 1972. Then it slackened off. There wasn't much for years. Now that the fortieth anniversary is close, we are receiving more mail asking about Jack, asking about what it was like in 1947.

"I have a ten-year-old niece in Arizona. She wrote me a letter the other day. She knew she was the niece of Jackie Robinson, the baseball player, but she didn't know much else. She ran across Jack's name in some book. She decided to pursue it. She asked me for more information about him. She was supposed to write a piece for school on a hero. She discovered a hero in her own family. I hope many other youngsters will discover Jack that way.

"I try to tell young people about Jack. The Jackie Robinson Foundation holds bi-annual meetings where they can talk about their triumphs and obstacles in gaining an education, the societal forces impinging on them, and most importantly how they are coping. I tell them about those days, and I remind them about discrimination and what a rocky course it was. Sometimes we gain significant things through athletics. I also remind them what you are forced to give up when you stand up.

"There is still discrimination. There are still problems now, forty years later. Things are far from perfect. I try to emphasize the progress with these kids. I try to talk about the triumphs. I want them to leave here inspired and hopeful. I want Jack's life to be a motivating force for them.

"Jack and I came from different backgrounds. His family was sharecropping in Georgia. Then his mother Nellie moved with the five children to Pepper Street in Pasadena, California, where through her extraordinary strength and religious conviction she was able to build and maintain a warm and loving family. My father was born in Chico, California and my mother in Houston, Texas. He was a bookbinder with the *Los Angeles Times*, and she had her own catering business. There was a great deal of prejudice in those days. We couldn't sit in a movie theater except in the balcony, and we couldn't be served in certain restaurants.

"Too often in those days, black people were made ashamed of their appearance. Jack was never ashamed of being black. In fact, he did something few blacks ever did. He always wore a white shirt. It showed off his dark skin. Many blacks wore dark shirts or colored shirts so that their skin color would not be so noticeable.

"I went to UCLA and studied prenursing. I met Jack at Kerkhoff Hall where the black students gathered. It was through Ray Bartlett. I knew him, and he was a friend of Jack's. Jack was very shy with girls, and he always thought a girl who talked to him at school was only being friendly because he was a big athlete. I didn't know anything about sports then. I just knew he was a nice young man and very handsome.

"Things were very difficult in the early years of baseball. The days were filled with indignities. What sustained Jack was his religion. For the first five or six years of our marriage, I can hardly remember a night when Jack didn't get down on his hands and knees and pray to God. That was something he considered very important, something he got from his mother. It was deep within him.

"Even after he became a star with the Dodgers, there were some terrible times. Little things could be so difficult. In the first year at Vero Beach, 1949 I think, I wanted to get my hair straightened. That's the way I wore it in those days. I asked the black help and they said there was a lady in town who did it. There was a bus that came to the Dodger camp a few times a day bringing the black help back and forth. They could not ride the regular city bus. Because the local taxis would not pick up black passengers, my son and I had to take that bus, and I was so embarrassed I hid my head as we passed the barracks. Jackie, Jr., then a child of only three, saw some of the kids of the other players in a swimming pool, and he stuck his head out the bus window and greeted them. When we were coming back to camp I decided not to take the bus, as a protest. We would walk in. We went a mile or so, but Jackie, Jr. was getting tired, and I didn't want to punish *him*, so when the bus came, we boarded it. Jack was so determined to see things like that change.

"In 1955 he began thinking of retiring, and by 1956 it was time. He was hurting, and he just couldn't play anymore the way he had. He didn't want to hang on. The trade to the Giants and the *Look* article made it appear that he had quit because of those things. He just didn't have the heart anymore for the game. He wanted to move on. Jack made a superb adjustment. He never looked back. He had that job with Chock Full O' Nuts, and he was very happy there. Mr. Black was very kind to him.

"He did his share in helping to raise the children. He was a very good father. Things were changing in the relationship between men and women in the 1960s, and I remember one time my daughter, Sharon, asked, 'What does Daddy do for you?' Jack was an old-fashioned man in a lot of ways. He didn't do much around the house to help out. After I got my degree in nursing and wanted to work, he was very upset, very much against it. He was the kind of man who believed the woman stayed home with her husband and family. Since his father had abandoned his family, he felt very strongly about that. It was something we had conflict over. However, by working very hard we were able to to resolve that difficulty. He enjoyed his home.

"There were some incidents with young blacks in the 1960s that made him uncomfortable, but he understood the generational struggle. We had it with our own children. He listened and he learned from them. He changed in a lot of ways as he became more aware of their anger.

"We still keep in contact with the Dodgers. We are close to Peter O'Malley. He calls every so often and I have been invited to some events out there. We were invited to Vero Beach to celebrate the thirtieth anniversary of the 1955 Brooklyn Dodger championship team. That was a wonderful event, and we got to see so many old friends.

"Now that the fortieth anniversary is almost here, I am sure there will be more interest in Jack and his career and what he stood for and the battles he fought. I am proud of all that interest. I am very proud of Jack's accomplishments. Jack had a great sense of humility. He was more interested in reminding kids to stay in school and to work hard than he was in describing his own career.

"Some people thought I made him into a saint. I don't know about that. I do know he was a remarkable man."

The humidity was high and the temperature was in the nineties. Small black children, maybe a half dozen or so, were playing ball against a wall of a store across from the building housing the Jackie Robinson Development Corporation. They howled with glee when one of them caught the edge of the storefront and bounced a ball far into the street. The ball rolled down the street, and one youngster took off after it. He had a funny stride as he ran, maybe a little pigeon-toed, I thought, and he seemed so determined to get that rubber ball before it disappeared under some passing cars. He caught it before it reached the intersection and hustled back to his friends. He held the ball high in his left hand and gave his playmate a vigorous, slapping, high five with his other hand. Then they all exchanged high fives before the game could resume. I could hear the laughter as I stepped down into the subway station.

Maybe one of them would grow up to be another Jackie Robinson. Forty years later, the path that youngster might take would be so much easier.

INDEX

Ruth, Babe, 47–48, 91, 112,
208

Sain, Johnny, 112, 113,
118
St. Louis Cardinals, 69–70,
110, 204, 229–30
strike against Jackie
Robinson, 135–37,
138, 141, 142–44
Scully, Vince, 170–71
Shotton, Burt, 110, 156, 163,
165
Shuba, George, 78–80
Singleton, Ken, 243
Slaughter, Enos, 135,
139–41, 142, 155, 206
Smith, Hilton, 42
Snider, Duke, 115–18, 181,
187, 190, 191, 196, 197,
203, 206
Spahn, Warren, 111–12, 121,
130, 150–52, 199
Sportswriters, 128–29, 170
Stanky, Ed, 100, 110, 121,
130, 132
Stearns, Turkey, 49, 50
Stengel, Casey, 28, 107, 130,
178, 179, 206, 208,
225–27
Strawberry, Darryl, 244–45

Sukeforth, Clyde, 44, 49, 57,
69, 72–76, 110, 185, 209

Tatum, Tom, 83
Thompson, Hank, 162
Thomson, Bobby, 177, 183,
184, 185, 186
Tracewski, Dick, 231

Veeck, Bill, 61, 161

Wade, Ben, 188, 189
Waitkus, Eddie, 182, 183
Walker, Dixie, 91, 93, 95,
96, 97, 100–1, 110, 121,
132–33, 166
Walker, Harry, 133–34
Walker, Rube, 182, 185
Walker, Willa Mae Robinson,
17, 18, 19, 20–22, 25–28,
29–30, 39, 127
Washington Senators, 62
White, Bill, 6, 195, 203–4,
227
Wilkinson, J. L., 42, 43
Wills, Maury, 61, 103, 133,
238
Wilson, Mookie, 244
Winfield, Dave, 244

Zimmer, Don, 236, 238